Tales

from

a

Bygone

Era

SIMON & SCHUSTER

NEW YORK   LONDON   TORONTO   SYDNEY   TOKYO   SINGAPORE

BASEBALL
in the
Afternoon

ROBERT SMITH

SIMON & SCHUSTER
SIMON & SCHUSTER BUILDING
ROCKEFELLER CENTER
1230 AVENUE OF THE AMERICAS
NEW YORK, NEW YORK 10020

DESIGNED BY SONGHEE KIM
MANUFACTURED IN THE UNITED STATES OF AMERICA

1   3   5   7   9   10   8   6   4   2

LIBRARY OF CONGRESS CATALOGING-IN-PUBLICATION DATA

SMITH, ROBERT, 1905–
BASEBALL IN THE AFTERNOON : TALES FROM A BYGONE ERA
/ ROBERT SMITH.
P.   CM.
INCLUDES INDEX.
1. BASEBALL—UNITED STATES—HISTORY.   I. TITLE.
GV863.A1S683 1993
796.357′0973—DC20   92-35934
                                      CIP

ISBN: 0-671-73930-1

PHOTO CREDITS
AP/WIDE WORLD PHOTOS, 26; COURTESY OF THE BOSTON
PUBLIC LIBRARY, PRINT DEPARTMENT, 17, 18, 19, 20, 30;
BROWN BROTHERS, 10; COURTESY OF FRANK CROSETTI, 28;
CULVER PICTURES, 2; NATIONAL BASEBALL LIBRARY,
COOPERSTOWN, N.Y., 1, 3, 5, 6, 7, 8, 9, 11, 12, 13, 14,
15, 16, 21, 22, 23, 25, 27; COURTESY OF THE OBERLIN
COLLEGE LIBRARY, 4; UPI/BETTMANN, 24, 29.

To Emlen, a writer in the making.

Chapter 1

HAPPY DAYS

The first baseball bat I ever owned was a Stuffy McInnis–
model Louisville Slugger, which weighed about two and
a half pounds and had a split in the handle. It was
given to me by Ed Barrow, manager of the Boston Red Sox, when
I was (I think) still in first grade. My brother mended the split
with friction tape, but I don't believe I was ever able to heft the
bat nimbly enough to swing it at a baseball. Still, it stayed by
me for two years or more to remind me of that mystic afternoon
when my brother and I, goggled-eyed and nearly dumb from
excitement, sat, by invitation, on the Red Sox players' bench
before a game began. We were surrounded by hulking men in
clean baseball suits, every one of whom carried a name that all
by itself, when said out loud, could cause strangers all over town
to stop and listen. There was Stuffy McInnis in the flesh, the
chunky first baseman who never made an error; Harry Hooper,
the only man left of the "Giant-killer" outfield that had done in
the New York Giants in the 1912 World Series; Everett Scott,
who never missed a game and hardly ever let a ground ball get
by; Wally Schang, the catcher, whose name I could not pro-
nounce; and an exceptionally happy looking young man, as tall
and as solidly built as a blacksmith, whom everyone called Jidge.

His *real* name (if I had only known it then!) was Babe Ruth.

There were many things I did not know, and would not have believed had I been told, about those Red Sox, whose very team title was dearer to me than my nation's flag. For there was a great deal of rowdiness in professional baseball then, when run-of-the-mill ball players earned less than streetcar conductors and were often alert for some way to turn an extra dollar. Stuffy McInnis, my hero, who played almost errorless ball (his fielding average was .992), nourished his batting average and thus increased his value to the club by "trading hits." A great many ball players in that era, when the season had begun to wane and their teams were clearly out of the money (before 1918, only the pennant winners shared in the Series loot), would repair their batting averages with help from their opponents. But Stuffy, one of his teammates told me years later, was the most adept of all at shifting his position sufficiently or moving with something less than his wonted quickness so that a ball he could easily have fielded would look like a clean hit. And of course when Stuffy came to bat, he would expect his generosity to be rewarded—as it invariably was. As a matter of fact, if the truth could be computed, some of those balls that sped swiftly and untrammeled through his position might have proved impossible for him to field and might have injected a dozen more errors into his league-leading fielding record.

But most of the rowdiness of that day was of a far less sophisticated sort. The Boston Red Sox locker room was often less orderly than an overcrowded monkey cage, with Babe Ruth, who was probably the biggest and the strongest of the crew, roughhousing amid the wild laughter and angry curses and screams of anger. In that era, before zippers had been dreamed of, it was considered one of the cleverest of tricks to rip open a fellow player's fly with a quick flick of the hand, leaving him with his shame exposed—preferably in mixed company. Big Babe would call an innocent teammate over and, pointing to his own left shoulder, say, "Look where the horse bit me." The man would move in closer to peer at the spot, and Babe would quickly half undress him by undoing all of his fly buttons with one swipe of his free hand. The victim did not always find this prank funny. But it was a fact that no one on the Boston team ever stayed mad at Babe Ruth. He was simply too openhearted, too full of fun, and too quick to lend a man a dollar—or twenty dollars—for anyone to nurse a permanent grudge against him. A few of his practical jokes, however, could keep a man snarling for half a day. One of his favorites was to slip a piece of cardboard, scorecard, or new bandage into a man's pregame sandwich and urge everyone to watch as the man tried to get his teeth through it. Or he might drop a lighted cigar inside a teammate's uniform pants as the man was pulling them on. Pants in that time being full at the knee, bloomer-style, a man could walk as far as the dugout before realizing that his clothes were on fire.

Antics of this sort would have made my brother and me laugh aloud and, like Babe's teammates, we also might have been inspired to invent methods of evening the score. Larry Gardner, the Red Sox third baseman, discovered early on that Babe was scared of snakes or anything that wriggled and he could send the big man screaming across the outfield by threatening him with a caterpillar. And Bullet Joe Bush, when he joined the Red Sox, could set Babe to growling by reciting a jingle he had invented: "Big Babe Ruth was picking his tooth/With the limb of a coconut tree!"

There were off-the-field doings in some of the bush league clubs, however, that brought fierce blushes to the cheeks of the teenage rookies, as when young Waite Hoyt, not quite seventeen years old, found himself in a hotel room with most of the Lynn club of the Eastern League, and those bold laddies, who had loaded their bathtub with ice and bottles of beer, undertook to remove the underdrawers of the proprietor's wife so they could administer what they had decided was a deserved spanking. Waite suddenly wished he were home—just as my brother and I might have, we being many years younger.

In our minds, however, no such naughtiness was ever connected with baseball, the game that every boy in the land—and

even some girls—seemed saturated in almost from birth. While
our visits to big league parks were less frequent than trips to the
circus, we all knew the names of every man on the Red Sox
roster and of the stars everywhere else throughout the league.
There were two teams in Boston, but in our neighborhood there
was only the Red Sox. Although men still talked of George
Stallings and his "Miracle Team" of 1914, the Braves might as
well have played in Burlington, Vermont, as far as we were
concerned. Probably because the Braves, back when they were
called the Beaneaters, long nourished in their ranks an anti-
Catholic cabal—heirs to the pre-Revolutionary antipopery fever
that infected the Bay Colony—the local Irish had made the Red
Sox their own as soon as they began to offer their wares to the
old South End grounds. And devil a bad word or a salacious
rumor did a man dare offer out loud about the Boston Americans.
(They had first been called the Pilgrims and the Puritans and
were finally named the Red Sox to suggest to old-time fans a
connection with the original Red Stockings of Cincinnati, the
nation's first professional ball club, which had been transplanted
to Boston in 1871.)

In most cities in the country, and especially in Boston, it was
accepted as truth that leaders and heroes of every sort must be
presented to the young in the purest of light, lest some suspect
that fame and preference still might be won even if there were
dark blots on your copybook. So we knew McInnis as the soul
of honesty and courage and Babe Ruth as an upright young man
who never fudged his Easter duty or said a big *D* out loud. We
thirstily sought the outcomes of games from the sports page of
the *Boston Traveler,* or learned them from the shrill newsboy who
hailed everyone who passed his corner with the cry "Yay! Red
Sox win!" And we never doubted that our boys had come out
ahead at least partly because their hearts were pure.

It can't be said that we tried to imitate our heroes on the
diamond, however, for our games were but crude misrepresen-
tations of what occurred in big league ballparks. We called our
game scrub and it resembled two games that were the forerunners, .

although not the true parents, of baseball: rounders and One-Hole Cat.

My brother and I counted ourselves singularly blessed at that time, for we moved every year, when school had closed, to a "summer apartment" near the beach—really a shabby little place, one of a long row of identical flats sharing a long, somewhat ramshackle porch. But our quarters, being at the end of the line, looked onto the vacant lot that we had made, by a sort of juvenile eminent domain, into a baseball field. Our bedroom window, turning on a pivot, opened directly onto the field, so that we could slip out, ready to play, without disturbing our mother—who would certainly have impeded our flight with breakfast or other rituals such as clean underwear, shoes, and clean socks. We needed no socks nor shoes to play our game. For nightclothes, we wore our bathing suit tops (back then, not even children dared walk topless on the beach), so we needed simply to pull on our khaki pants, buckle our belts, and gather up whatever gear we owned and needed, such as the bat and a puffy glove known as a "Tenney," after Fred Tenney, star first baseman for Brown University and the Boston Beaneaters, who had first used a cut-down form of a catcher's glove to ease the pounding his hand would take from fearsome infield throws.

The special advantage of reaching the ball field first was that one could then cry out, on the first sight of an approaching playmate or two, "Let's have a game of scrub—*One!*" Number One in this game became the batter and others followed in the order in which they were able to shout out the next number. The boy who then first shouted "Two" became the catcher; "Three," the pitcher; and "Four," the baseman. The others became random fielders, for there was only one base in our game. When Mickey Mantle first played this version of the game on the alkali flats outside Commerce, Oklahoma, it was called work-up, because that was its peculiar feature: As the batter made out—either by swinging at and missing three pitches, by having a batted ball caught on the fly, by having the batted ball retrieved and transported to the base ahead of him, or by being tagged with the ball before he reached the base—he was demoted to the outfield and all the others moved up one place: Two becoming the batter, Three becoming the catcher, and so on. But what appealed to us most about scrub—and what often became the despair of neighboring mothers—was that there was no end to it. No score was kept, no innings were counted, and the game could go on and on and on, until sometimes a tight-lipped mother, grim as an umpire, might move in and extract her young for feeding and watering. (Mickey Mantle in a much later day sometimes played until well past dinnertime with only a few drinks of water for nourishment.)

There were people, although none in our limited orbit, who called this game One 'Ole Cat and imagined that it had some connection with the wearing out of a tired feline. But "One 'Ole Cat" was the name of a wholly different game, derived from cricket, that was played throughout the nation since before the Revolution. In that game, there was the one "hole" where the bat was grounded, and some sort of goal that the batter had to race to, carrying the bat, then race back and get the bat in the hole before the ball was recovered and returned. This game was born in England as "catapult ball"—hence the "cat"—for the ball was sometimes popped into the air from the end of a board laid seesaw fashion across a rock. (An even simpler version of this game, which kids could turn to when there was no ball to play with, was "kick the bar," in which a short stick or bar was laid against a tree and kicked by the child who was "up"—to be retrieved and put in place before the kicker could get to the base and back.)

Of course, even real baseball closely resembles these sports, for the object still is to cover as much ground as possible before the token, be it ball or stick, can be retrieved and returned to put the player out. It was American aggressiveness, impatience, ingenuity, and devotion to victory at almost any cost that turned it into a game of infinite complexity that could involve the hearts and minds of entire communities to a degree that only a shooting war could match.

Not much older than seven when I began playing scrub, I made an immediate fool of myself by standing face-on to the pitcher, when the style then was to stand sideways, left foot toward the pitcher (if you were right-handed), peering at him over your left shoulder. Too late to mitigate my shame, I discovered that Heinie Groh, squat third baseman for the Cincinnati Reds and the New York Giants, besides using a "bottle" bat that looked like a war club, also stood face-on to the pitcher until the ball was on its way. Of course, knowing nothing of Heinie Groh and not much more about the New York Giants, I corrected my stance at once and joyfully ridiculed any newcomers who repeated my own mistake. In that day, with no Little League to make sure we kids performed in a professional manner and consequently no red-faced parent to scream his dismay at your stupidity, we were permitted to avoid dumb stunts by doing them and being corrected—no less raucously—by our peers, just as we perforce cleared our own diamond, marked out our own base paths, and found a rock or a plank or even a sheet of cardboard to serve as home plate.

There were no Little League bats then either and, scorning the few toy bats that were sometimes given to very small kids at Christmas, we used bats of big league length and heft, shortening our grips sufficiently to enable us to keep the bat from drooping like a banana stalk. Occasionally, one or two of the older boys might join us and wield even a thirty-six-ounce bat with some authority. But their batting was inhibited by a rule that obtained nearly everywhere baseball or one of its derivatives was played in thickly settled environs—that is, over the fence was out! No Babe Ruths or Cactus Cravaths in our league. A long hit too often brought only a sudden horrified intake of breath from the entire assembly as we all tensed ourselves to await the distant crash and tinkle that meant a broken window in the house across the lot.

It was the big boys who were most likely to commit this offense and they intruded themselves into our games only when there was no immediate action elsewhere, or because the opportunity to flaunt their prowess in public proved irresistible. But even they sometimes had difficulty hitting a ball beyond the fence, for our baseball was usually so laden with black friction tape that it weighed a quarter pound more than it should have. Once or twice, when someone had brought in a real "dollar-and-a-quarter" baseball, the official implement, perhaps recovered outside a fence somewhere or given to one of the crowd by an older brother or an uncle, one of the big boys might send it flying off into an adjoining yard and we might never see it again. We would not see it if it broke a window in the house of Mrs. Barrett—known as old lady Barrett to us because she was gray and somewhat wizened and at odds with everyone in the area. If a baseball fell into her garden, she would seldom notice it until the boy who had committed the deed climbed the fence to find it. Then she would pop out, like a trap-door spider, and rail at the boy until he scrambled, ball in hand, back over the fence. After that she might call on one or two of the neighboring mothers and urge them to apply a solid whacking to all the boys in the lot—which she always called "her" lot even though everyone in town knew she had no title to it.

But if the baseball actually burst its way in a shower of splintered glass into her living room, as two or three times it did, she would capture it and hold it for keeps—then visit every mother whose home was visible, or perhaps leave labored notes decorated by small symbolic drawings that only she could have decoded. But no one paid her any mind and no one was so lost to reason as to try to talk her into returning the ball. As it happened, the few times such a ball was lost, it belonged to one of the older boys who was bent on showing off anyway and, bitterly as we begrudged the loss of a baseball, we felt no lasting regret at watching the big boys bike off somewhere to play the grown-up game.

The grown-up game was played with "sides" that were usually selected on the field by the toss of a bat to decide first choice. One of the two "captains," who were often self-appointed, would toss the bat for the other captain to catch in one hand. Then the two would grip the bat alternately, one boy's hand over the other's, until there was no more room for a hand to fit. After that, the boy not holding the bat would try to take the knob of the bat in his fingers and fling it. If he could do so, he could choose the first player, and he almost always selected the only lad in the neighborhood who could throw a curve. As for us, when we had developed sense enough to be allowed to wander afar, we could sometimes find a place still open in the outfield in the big boys' game and we began to learn about baserunning, about called strikes, and, of course, about umpires, who were usually recruited among the spectators and sometimes were grown men who had no more fruitful way to invest a warm afternoon.

There always seemed some idle man to serve as umpire, as well as fans enough to crowd the stands at Fenway Park whenever the Red Sox were home, even though the bulk of the male population ought to have been gainfully employed somewhere else. Women at the park were seldom indeed in that age, although there was always a coterie of "dead-game sports" to civilize the grandstand slightly. The bleachers, however, were no place for pretty shirt-waists and clean skirts, for nearly every third man in the seats there would be chewing tobacco or smoking a cigar so rank that he frequently had to spit the taste out of his mouth. More than once, when I had grown old enough to go to big league ball games with no one to watch over me but my brother, I came home with my blouse stained by splattered tobacco juice, or my new tan shoes made tanner still by the contributions of the man on the bench beside me.

The fanaticism the Fenway Park fans displayed for the Red Sox may well have been matched throughout the land, for all we knew, but in our area there was nothing to equal it. There was a self-constituted association of more than two hundred "Royal Rooters" that attended every game and at World Series time put on a parade around the diamond before hostilities began. They carried signs inquiring "Are ye there?" or flaunting the name of some current hero. There were parasols to distinguish the faithful and even a theme song, "Tessie" (which had nothing to do with baseball). One favorite banner declared "Third base! Nuf Ced!" This, as it happened, was a pet cry of a South End tavern owner named McGreevey, who became known as Nuf Ced McGreevey because of his habit of forestalling argument with that catchphrase. When he would lift one hand and declare "Third base! 'Nough said!" he meant that there was no disputing the fact that Manager Jimmy Collins, the third baseman of the Bostons, and the man who invented the bare-handed grab and throw of a bunted ball, was without a peer at that position in the whole land. And Jimmy proved this assessment again and again in the first World Series ever played, in 1903, when the "bush league" Boston Americans subdued the mighty Pittsburgh Pirates, who themselves were wont to brag of owning the greatest shortstop in the universe—Honus Wagner.

But by the time baseball first entered my consciousness, that day was but a faint memory and the mighty Bill Dinneen, who had thwarted the Pirate sluggers with his sizzling curves, had turned into an umpire, and so was fair game for fans and players alike. And when people did talk of the 1903 Series in my day, they were as likely to recall that skinflints Hank Killelea and Joe Smart, who owned the Boston club, had actually made the Pittsburgh owner, Barney Dreyfuss, pay his way into the games. Or that someone (God knows who) had offered Boston catcher Lou Criger $12,000 to throw the Series—and Criger (depending on which man you were talking to) either spit in the guy's face, or punched him in the nose, or threw the money in his face, or just ignored him.

What men and women were still talking about when my memory began was the World Series of 1912, when Jake "The Giant-Killer" Stahl led the Red Sox to victory over the supposedly invincible New York Giants of John McGraw. Until the day she died, my mother could recite the 1912 roster of the Red Sox, or at least name all the pitchers, with emphasis on her own favorite, twenty-two-year-old Hugh Bedient. And she told us again and again, with diminishing accuracy, the story of the famed Snodgrass muff—the dropping by the Giant center fielder, Fred Snodgrass, of an easy fly ball in the tenth inning of the final game.

But our own immediate heroes were of a lesser caliber, for we had to worship the Red Sox from a distance, except when some kindly uncle came to town or when our own estranged father showed up to ease his conscience by taking us to a big league ball game. The men we watched most were the stars of the local town team, notably a very tall young man named Queen, who pitched every game. As the team played only two or three times a week, this was no strain on the lad's arm. The team played in a partially fenced-in park where it was impossible to limit the attendance to those with tickets, so the "gate" was really the hat that was passed all through the crowd at about the sixth or seventh inning. The club wore uniforms, shoes with spikes, and caps of varying hues, inasmuch as each man had to supply his own head-gear and some had long clung to caps that had been awarded them in high school or carried the insignia of the town that had previously owned their allegiance.

There were always, at these games, incidents to betray the bucolic nature of the proceedings—the children dashing out on the baseline to be bowled over and left, prostrate and howling, in the runner's wake; a horse shaking himself loose from his careless hitch to pull an empty buggy, all unconcerned, out where he could crop the outfield grass; or the town drunk, invariably greeted with friendly shouts and howls of laughter, stumbling out to expostulate to the umpire's face at a strike call.

There was one sometime player on the town team whom we would never have been allowed to call a hero but whose deeds all the same set us to yelling his praises and seeking afterward to slap his sweaty back or even touch his hand. The only name of his that I will ever recall was Pete, for he was Uncle Pete to everyone, even though I seem to remember now that his given name was not Peter at all, but something completely unlike. Still, our friend Tommy, who often trotted up from the steamy center of town in his worn-out britches to join our games, called him his uncle, so he became uncle to all of us. Pete, it was generally acknowledged, was a burglar. My mother even insisted that he was the very man who had tried one day, when he thought our apartment was empty, to climb in the side window. She had risen from a nap and sent him scuttling off but had seen enough of him, she declared, to know exactly who he was.

"What a fool stunt!" she exclaimed afterward. "What could he possibly steal from *us*?"

It was no secret that Pete had served a term or at least part of a term at Deer Island Penitentiary and it was believed on the streets that he had actually escaped from the place and had been in hiding until the local coal dealer, who, it was said, owned a part of the Lynn baseball club and also sponsored our town team, arranged with the local police to allow him freedom to play ball. It was earnestly believed by the small boys of the town that Pete's freedom was contingent on his performing satisfactorily on the diamond, so in our hearts there was a really excruciating suspense whenever Pete stepped to the plate. Would he hit safely and retain his freedom? Would he strike out and be hauled away in handcuffs?

Pete never did strike out in my memory, but he did strike some mighty blows for our cause. Visiting outfielders, all having heard stories of Pete's ability to muscle baseballs out of mortal reach, nearly always backed up to the board fence when Pete came to the plate. And even then they frequently became mere spectators as the ball took flight for the adjoining bay. Over the fence was not out in this game except in the sense that the ball could never be recovered. The loss of a baseball, which probably cost the management almost a dollar, was not to be made light of in that day, when ball players in the minor leagues were sometimes required to hop into the stands and wrest baseballs away from the spectators. So even Pete made no protest when the manager of the town club barred him from batting practice. One day, it was said, Pete lost all the balls before the game even began and play was delayed nearly an hour while someone scouted through the town for enough "official" baseballs in clean condition to last through nine innings. Six were always sufficient and sometimes two baseballs would complete the course.

(Come to think of it, this particular niggardliness in what had always been a pinch-penny sport may explain why pitchers in the early days could work so many dazzling illusions on batters. A scraped baseball, as even today's pitchers understand, can be made to behave with notable eccentricity.)

But Pete, even if he had been paying for the baseballs himself, would never have swung at one with less than his entire strength. He was what was known in that day as a "country fair" hitter, a term used to ridicule big farm boys who acted as if each pitch was the last one they would have a chance to swing at until haying season was done. Pete, however, was no country boy and when he swung at a pitch, the very least he ever seemed to do was drive it foul or pop it half a mile into the air. Pete owned the sort of inbred devotion to baseball that has always seemed to mark young men who were destined to achieve some greatness in the game. (Mickey Mantle says his father put a baseball into his crib.) Men in town told of seeing Pete, when he was a little boy, sound asleep at home with his baseball cap on. But poor Pete, as far as I knew, never made more than tobacco money out of the game, what with his penchant for borrowing other men's goods without permission and his incurable predisposition to violence. The clearest memory I have of Pete is not of any great hit he made but of the day when he—with due cause, we all agreed—set out to dismember the hapless umpire, who was himself a fairly case-hardened man, nearing middle age, who had some sort of job at a local dock where boats were mended. Exactly what the decision was that unseated Pete's reason I cannot recall. It was most likely an "out" call at home plate, for Pete would have confined himself to curses had it been merely a called strike. As it was, I can still see Pete as he seemed to mount right into the air. He was a man who never combed his hair, so when he yanked his cap off and hurled it from him, his black hair seemed to stand erect from rage and his face took fire.

In our day, wicked epithets such as "bastard" and "son of a bitch" very seldom assailed the ears of youngsters. But compared to the names Pete found use for that day, they would have been no more caustic than a nickname. It was years before I even understood the true meaning of some of them. And many of them were lost in the uproar from the gathering fans. The umpire, trying to affect a big league pose, stood his ground at first, gripping his borrowed chest protector, from which the buckles had fallen off, and may even have returned a small portion of the fire. But then Pete all of a sudden grabbed the man's chest protector, tore it free from the umpire's neck, and sent it sailing. With this the umpire, white as a flounder, lifted both hands in a sort of gesture of appeasement, then turned and headed for safety. But there was no safety. Men had been hustling out of the stands for a minute or two and, while those nearest the umpire at first made way, a few of the later arrivals on the field tried to lay hold of the man. His eyes enlarged with terror, and his little blue cap already knocked off, the man dodged and pulled away bare-headed, one sleeve already in tatters. Scooting like a terrified dog, he headed for the street beyond the park. Instantly a whole mob of angry men was at his heels, like tomahawk-wielding Indians in a motion picture. The roar that rose up from a hundred mouths or more must have sounded clear across the water. My friends and I stood frozen. A little girl with a big ribbon in her hair began to cry. We watched as the umpire fled to the sidewalk, across the wide street, past storefronts where men stood wondering, leapt in one quick vault over the rail fence that bounded the railroad cut, then staggered down to the tracks. When we saw him last he appeared well down the narrow-gauge railroad, mouth open in a silent scream, with the yelling mob, now dwindled to Pete, a few teammates, and half a dozen fans, pounding along the cinders two or three yards behind. And there they still hang in my memory, as if they had been painted there.

As for Pete, he moved out of our lives sometime soon afterward, having been offered a chance, it was said, to wallop baseballs for money with the Lynn club a few miles east. After that, I remember only that he "got into trouble" again somewhere far off, this time for swatting a man with a baseball bat. But that may have been just a story kids invented to keep his legend alive.

Most boys my age, once they had moved up from the primary

grades into grammar school, had a chance to try out for the school baseball club, of which there were some half dozen in the town where we lived from fall to spring. Some of my immediate playmates, but not I, were soon wearing the school uniform and playing two or three times a week in well-tended playgrounds, under professional rules—ninety-foot baselines and sixty-foot pitching distance. Some boys who had not yet got their full growth were too severely handicapped to compete. But each school, almost in a body, did attend the games, where excitement often climbed as high as it ever did at Fenway Park. Baseball was the major sport in all our lives, throughout the spring while the schools were open, and all summer long in vacant lots and on beaches.

It also seemed to be the major sport in the lives of most American males, whatever their surroundings. When we moved into the countryside to try (in vain) to make a modest living on a farm, there was not a young man within five miles who did not consider himself a baseball player, even though opportunities to play the game were scarce indeed, particularly in the summertime, when most men were "haying it" on days when it did not rain. I can remember walking five miles or more on dusty gravel roads to attend Old Home Days at towns all around, where there would always be, in addition to ox-drawing contests and attempts to capture and hold a greased pig, a long-touted ball game between one town team and another, the team always recruited a week or two in advance and the games invariably replete with mishaps that often provided much of the fun—missing bases, missing equipment, or even a missing right fielder, who would have to be filled in for by some incompetent volunteer whose very appearance on the diamond would set all his friends to howling mock encouragement: "Bring your bucket with you, Ernie!" "Hold her, Ernie! She's a-rearing!" I recall one such game when the right fielder (right field was always the spot where it was reckoned that incompetents could do the least harm) had no cap and, finding none that would fit him, had to borrow from his girlfriend a straw hat with a feather in it, giving the game from time to time the air of a comic opera.

Playing fields at these affairs were untended and unfenced, so that often the "outfield" was two or three fields deep, with a running stream at the far edge or a sky-pond where cattle might gather. If there was a downhill slope, a long hit might roll halfway to the next county before anyone could catch up with it. (A young man who became a famous slugger in the big leagues told me once that he had shifted from outfield to shortstop on his hometown club because he grew weary of shagging fly balls that might bounce a quarter mile beyond him across the boundless prairie.) Often the adjoining field might still wear a crop of unharvested hay where a baseball could lose itself in an instant. And there being often only one unblemished ball to begin with, its disappearance would prompt an immediate recess while both teams, the umpire, and many of the spectators joined in a search through the tall grass. Now and then some little scoundrel would find the ball and pocket it without being seen, so the game would be suspended until one of the beaten-up practice balls could be agreed on.

Umpiring was elementary in the extreme, for no one gave much thought to choosing an umpire until the game was about to begin. Then some watcher too old to take part or some local eminence who was reputed to "know his baseball" would be coaxed into taking up the standard post behind the pitcher's mound, where he was positioned so he could call balls and strikes as well as plays at every base. Why anyone should accept this role, except out of an urge for self-chastisement, always bewildered me, for it was a certainty that at some point even his neighbors would find bitter fault with his decision. It is not possible for one man alone to call the outcome of every play, for while he watches to see if a fly ball is fairly caught, all sorts of mischief may be going on behind him. In one game, the aging gentleman who had taken on the task of deciding all the yeses and noes, ran close to watch as a runner slid into second base, just as the mighty throw from the catcher arrived. He stood for twenty or thirty seconds without making a sign and finally, when nearly everyone on the field was shouting for the call, he turned and said to the surrounding players, "Durned if I know. That's too close for *me* to call!"

The howls of indignation that greeted these words certainly doubled in volume what might have ensued had he called the runner either safe or out. Now *both* sides were outraged and there was no one this side of the county seat who would have taken his part. After much vain and profane urging to say *something*— to call it, for Christ's sake, one way or the other—the old gentleman was relieved of his duties. He accepted his dethronement without emotion and walked off with his dignity unimpaired while both captains strove to recruit, among the followers of both clubs, a man whose impartiality would not be *thoroughly* suspect. The old man, of course, had probably given the only honest call that could have been supplied, without a confession from one of the players involved. But the runner would not name himself "out," nor would the baseman ever concede that the tag had come too late. That was simply not *baseball*, even though it might have been cricket.

It is a fact that deception and even dishonesty have been features of baseball since long before Mike Kelly, of the Chicago White Stockings, omitted third base from his itinerary while the lone umpire's attention was drawn elsewhere. The great A. G. Spalding himself, the man who first provided a proper structure for professional baseball, bragged in his autobiography of performing an illegal "cap catch" and other dodges behind the umpire's back. And, in the same spirit, he resorted to falsehood and concealment of every sort in his struggle with the striking Brotherhood of Professional Baseball Players.

The emery ball, the shine ball, the insertion of a phonograph needle under the skin of a baseball, the substitution of a "pounded" ball for one that had been knocked over the fence, the banking of baselines to keep bunts from rolling foul, the storing of baseballs in the ice box, the use of hand mirrors in the stands to temporarily blind a batter or fielder, the tripping, bumping, and even holding of base runners were all honored devices of early professional baseball, just as the application of petroleum jelly or other slippery substance to a baseball by the pitcher is studiously practiced and laughed at today.

It is hardly a matter to marvel at, then, that umpires too, toiling as they did for the standard fee of five dollars a game, should be susceptible to corruption. While the history of baseball lists only one professional umpire, Richard Higham, who was ever found guilty of overt wickedness (he used to send coded telegrams to gamblers, telling them which teams were going to win the games he had been assigned to), there were surely many more, in the long history of the disorganized and organized game, who succumbed to bribes or threats, or merely to a lively understanding of who was spreading the butter on their bread. Some of the great traveling teams would carry along their own umpires, men who surely were disposed to avoid offending too deeply the men they worked for. And in other instances a man might yield quickly to the looming presence of some angry ball player who took instant issue with a call. The great Cap Anson, dour and combative leader of the Chicago White Stockings, once thrust his mighty chest into the face of an umpire during a game with the St. Louis Browns and explained that the official had been dead wrong in calling a runner out. The umpire immediately discerned where his mistake had been and called the man safe.

Even after baseball had been organized and the umpires were assigned and ostensibly sanctified by the league authorities, the pay was just as miserly, the quality of umpiring just as indifferent, and the men themselves just as responsive to bullying. John McGraw, after he had grown up to be manager of the mighty New York Giants, once barred from the ballpark an umpire named Johnstone whose decisions had offended him and assigned a substitute infielder named Sammy Strang (real name Nicklin) to call the next game.

But umpires had been fair game for decades before that day and the true marvel is probably that there were still so many of them who would face down threats of and even perpetration of violence rather than alter a call. A good many of those who sought work as professional umpires were just used-up ball players who could find no other way of turning a dollar and a few were semiprofessional drunks. Still, there must have been many a sturdy citizen among them.

All the same, in the 1880s, some years after professional baseball had been organized into the National League, the *Chicago Tribune* had this to say about umpires' social standing: "The average league umpire is a worthless loafer." And fans at the ballparks, as well as players on the benches, offered more fragrant assessment. About the same time, some Cicero in Cincinnati declaimed, via the *Cincinnati Enquirer,* "How long will the public put up with Bradley's umpiring?" while the *Boston Herald,* to sustain its charges that league umpires were largely cheats and liars, reported a game in which the umpire called a ball fair, then foul, then fair again, with two runs hanging in the balance. A decade later a Philadelphia newspaper thus described umpiring in the league park: "Umpires have ranged from indifferent to rotten. . . . We have had a belly full of O'Rourke and Stage. O'Rourke is a living illustration of the fallacy of the theory which makes the staff of umpires a refuge for decaying ball players."

In the parks, umpires were often given shorter shrift. One umpire, after frequent threats against his life, took to packing a gun under his umpiring regalia. In Baltimore, when McGraw was running the show there, a crowd of slavering fans—"hissed on," a sportswriter said, by McGraw himself—waited outside the club-house for more than an hour holding a length of rope with which to string up umpire Connolly.

It may well have been McGraw, and his imitators throughout the bushes, who taught us all when we were young to think of league umpires as the born enemies of our heroes. We used to laugh at the fact that McGraw always identified Bob Emslie, the National League umpire, as Blind Bob. And the Boston players long kept alive the merry moment when some angry catcher had suddenly backed up and set his spikes on umpire Earnest Quigley's toe with a resultant yelp of anguish from Quigley

Yet in our sandlot games, where the selection of an umpire was always an afterthought, the worst we ever offered an umpire was a wild scream of protest and perhaps a dirty name. I remember a high school game, however, when darker doings seemed afoot.

Our school club, our darlings, who seemed on the way to a championship in the suburban league, were done in one day by a succesion of what seemed to our side outrageous decisions— not merely a strike call that sent our mighty hitter back to the bench but two baserunning calls for the other side that bred among us a nearly unanimous conviction that the umpire was deliberately weighing the scales against us and in favor of the home school, which, we privately assured each other, must have been the school the umpire himself had attended. The umpire, who wore the unforgettable name of Magloire Labelle, was ob- viously a Frenchman, and there were, by gosh, a *lot* of French in that town.

Then we discovered that, two weeks later, we were to meet the same team on our own grounds—and that the umpire again would be . . . who? Well, naturally, Magloire Labelle, who, we all declared, had most certainly wangled the assignment so he could see to it that "his" boys cleaned up again. In preparation for his appearance we invented and practiced a cheer: "Union Label [that was our version of his name]! Union Label! Dumbbell! Dumbbell! Rah! Rah! Rah!" And just in case this affront failed to dent his hide, many of us carried along to the park, concealed in pockets or lunch bags, about a half bushel of gone-by citrus fruit, retrieved from the garbage pail or solicited from the fruit store in town—mushy lemons and soggy grapefruit and oranges that would splatter at a blow. We all sat, or rather crouched, on sidelines and stands awaiting the first excuse that Labelle might offer us to shower him with our favors. The trouble was that we had little fault to find with any of his first ball-and-strike calls. Our patent cheer, much repeated, brought not even a flush to the man's cheeks. Then there came a strike call that *might* have been a little on the doubtful side. One lad high in the stands, his patience suddenly petering out, sent a grapefruit flying in a wobbly arc to land some six feet from the umpire's feet, where it plopped like a bag full of mud. There was laughter and a few cheers. Then other missiles came flying, not in the roaring barrage we had imagined but in a random and badly aimed bombardment that was as embarrassing to us as it was to the target. Labelle himself paid not the slightest heed, nor did he need to, for not a single one of the missiles came close enough even to soil his shoes. The whole affair dwindled to some spasmodic booing. And the enemy won the game without any obvious assistance from the umpire. All the same, our hulking right fielder, a teenager who had already got his full growth, confronted Labelle in the locker room and offered, in recognition of the umpire's earlier misdeeds, to punch the small man's nose for him. But Labelle looked him very coolly in the eye and advised him, "Don't be silly, son." We all had to admit to ourselves after that, that Labelle, dumbbell or not, had all the better of the set-to and we never so much as heckled him again.

This fervor to come in first, which is at the root of all these deceptions, threats, catcalling, and organized villainy, was not always a feature of baseball. The game, which began as the "New York Game" among a group of well-to-do young bachelors in New York City, had in the beginning strict rules of behavior which did not countenance so much as a bad word on the playing field, encouraged no spectators beyond the members of the club that first played the game, and relied on an umpire who held himself somewhat aloof from the play, equipped with cane, stool, and top hat, and offered decisions only when the players could not agree among themselves.

But all young bachelors in that day, alas, were given to gaming, i.e., laying wagers on the outcome of all sorts of contests. And baseball proved such a fine vehicle for wagering that it very early became necessary to promulgate a rule declaring invalid any game on which the *umpire* had a dollar riding. Still, it was acknowledged a deadly bore to keep losing bets on the game, so little by little the gentlemen's clubs began to initiate to membership a few of the "greasy mechanics" whom they had been wont to bar from the field. Eventually, all of the gentlemen's clubs in the city, which had long held a monopoly on the game—but which could not prevent lesser beings from imitating it on the West Side dumps—soon fielded baseball teams that carried men on the rosters who accepted club membership and other emoluments, such as "clerkships" without duties, in order to render the club mighty in battle. Ordinary members then who still played the game for fun were consigned to the "muffin" nine—"muffin" (derived from "muff") being the name for baseball duffers. And it was among these folk that love of the game for its own sake flourished.

By the time my friends and I had grown long-legged enough to run from base to base, the muffin spirit still endured on every playground, vacant lot, level pasture, and hard-baked beach in the nation and it was impossible for anyone, boy or girl, to grow to adulthood without absorbing at least some of the language of baseball. Of course we played the game to win, for without that urge it is impossible for a player to involve himself utterly, and without utter involvement there is very little joy. But we did not think of the game as a battle, for from one day to the next, friends became foes, then friends again, or at least teammates, who for the two or three hours the game might last were dearer than our brothers. And scores, though sedulously recorded, were soon forgotten. We naturally lost our tempers betimes—usually at the umpire. But we never felt any urge to lynch the fellow, who was often a playmate or a parent, nor did we indulge in such bloodthirsty tactics as spiking a baseman or aiming a pitched baseball at an opponent's ear.

We were amateurs then, in the true sense, for we loved the game, winning or losing, more dearly than many who played the game for cash. (John McGraw once declared that unless he was "out front and winning" the game meant no more to him than a bag of peanuts.) And nowadays, when I inhale the full and mellow fragrance of a new baseball glove or pick up a new baseball, gleaming like a jewel, I find it easy to summon the light of other years around me, with the moist caress of young grass, dainty as a christening, blessing my naked feet, the dawn chill just beginning to dissolve in the sun, the faint cries of long-vanished playmates ringing somewhere beyond the edge of sound, and the prospect of a whole day full of baseball beginning to warm my ribs like an embrace.

●

I never played baseball for money, or not for real money—I do not count the scanty few dollars taken up in a hat and spent on ice-cream sodas, Necco wafers, hot coffee, and lunch-counter pie. But, along with a clutch of other young soreheads who failed to make the high school team, I did play it all through my schoolday afternoons and in the long summers, too, until I was deemed too old not to be working. The favorite on our club was a long-legged boy named Quirk who had mastered a curve that would have been a joke to a professional ball player but that baffled nearly every young batter who ever faced him. Nowadays it would be merely a curve or a "breaking ball." We called it an out-drop, for it faded quickly down and away from a right-handed batter; ball players of an earlier day would have named it a cunny-thumb curve. Ordinarily it was thrown by bending the thumb at the first knuckle to eliminate the friction usually imparted by the pressure of the thumb, and letting the first two fingers provide all the spin. But Quirk threw it by holding his thumb up and away from his fingers as he threw the ball. Consequently, when he let the ball go, there was his thumb sticking up like a small semaphore to betray what was coming. Still, even after they caught on to this signal, boys who could hit that curve safely were few indeed.

But there was more than Quirk's out-drop to commend him to us. He was a young man on whose face a frown would have looked like a contortion and I never in all the days I knew him—including the afternoon many years after these days were done, when he appeared before me all ablaze in the dress uniform of the United States Marines—met him without a smile either already shining on his face or faintly foreshadowed there. Yet Quirk took his pitching seriously enough. He hardly seemed to see the batters facing him, so intent would he become on the target—the big glove the catcher was holding up. We did, it is true, have one substitute catcher who did not much care for standing up to Quirk's or anyone's pitches; he would always jump aside as the pitch came in and merely hold his glove out to catch the ball at arm's length—this despite profane pleas from us, his teammates, and ridicule from the scattered spectators. But this upset Quirk not at all; nor did he ever exhibit any irritation, or even concern, when one of us let a ground ball trickle through or heaved a ball far over a baseman's head. Quirk would simply offer a faint smile and turn back to the job of getting the next batter out.

In later years when I began to associate with men who pitched baseballs for a living, I learned that this ability to shut out all distraction was a talent almost as valuable to a pitcher as an ability to make a pitched ball deviate sharply from its course. The few professionals who owned that talent for utter concentration seemed able to hold their jobs until their sight began to dim.

But Quirk never became a professional, nor did any of the rest of us, although we were sometimes able to finance, from our collection, trips to distant small towns to cope with the local heroes—often farm boys who were invariably stirred by a countryman's natural scorn for city folk with "an easy way of making a living." We traveled once clear to New Hampshire to meet a team like our own in a small town where one of our teammates had distant relatives. Our appearance here prompted jeers and catcalls and raucous laughter at some of the gear two of our dandies sported: checkered knickers that might have frightened a buggy horse and pullover sweaters with zigzag patterns that, according to the local hearties, only a girl or a "fairy" would be seen alive in.

But soon after the game began the locals on the sidelines began to take delight in Quirk's ability to send the neighborhood strongmen fishing vainly after his sweeping out-drop. Again and again, as one of their "country fair" sluggers, holding a heavy bat by the utmost inch of the handle, spun himself around like a drunken dancer in vain effort to whale the insides out of the baseball, the crowd would howl in delight. "Go git it, Bill! You're gitting closer!"

The crowd named Quirk "Smiley" and before the fourth inning was complete he had become the favorite of everyone except the young men on the enemy team, one or two of whom at first ridiculed Quirk's curve as a "roundhouse" that they would knock into the distant pond. When the game was over, nearly everyone, even the guys he had humiliated, wanted to make friends with Smiley, who was the easiest man to make friends with that God ever created. Quirk showed small boys and a few grown-ups how he held his magic curve, nestled deep in his hand, with three fingers providing the spin and his thumb waving free. And before the sun was low, we all of us had been urged to stay over in the town and join in "the celebration." This being July 3, the celebration was going to consist of organized deviltry throughout the village and surrounding countryside, it still being traditional then, in our parts at least, to celebrate the night before the Fourth as we had always "celebrated" Halloween.

The old folks who had arranged the game allowed, out of old-fashioned country hospitality—and I am sure with some reluctance, if not dismay—that all ten of us could bed down in their hayloft and could make out a sort of supper from what could be found in the pantry. But most of us had already stuffed ourselves with "tonic" and whatever else of ready-to-eat comestibles the two general stores could provide, so we accepted only a few small platefuls of the cold ham and pickles that our second baseman's kin found for us. By sunset we had all hiked down to the village square, where there was a large decorative basin set up for horses to drink from, but dry now and stained green inside. Most of the ball players were there, including the enemy pitcher, who greeted us all as if we had come to a school reunion. We were waiting, it appeared, for a contingent of muscular young men from the nearby granite quarry who had promised to bring along dynamite and blasting caps enough to blow the night wide open.

Meanwhile, there were some who had a supply of cannon crackers—"two-inch salutes"—that they would light and toss into the air from time to time, or flip to the ground behind some passing young lady, so there was an almost constant bombardment keeping the birds awake. At dusk a mustached fellow in stained overalls appeared out of somewhere whom everyone greeted with the sort of mock heartiness usually applied to the town half-wit.

This fellow was no half-wit. Perhaps a three-quarter. He was certainly a foolish old fellow who was constantly suggesting some complicated prank that no one had any taste for. But he had brought along a whole pocket full of double-O shotgun shells that a man could use to kill a horse with, and after he had offered two or three wild suggestions for setting them off where they would do the most harm, the local pitcher, who was Asa somebody-or-other, calmly picked up the shells when the old fellow was not looking and painstakingly cut the shot out of them with his pocketknife.

The old man (perhaps fifteen years older than most of us) was called Dip by everyone, but whether that was short for "dippy" or really an abbreviation of his own name I never knew. He did ultimately come up with one suggestion that was happily seized on.

The local hotel—a two-story boardinghouse where commercial travelers stayed—was just across the street. On its second floor one window stood open, with the room dark behind it. Dip conceived the idea of tossing some explosive into that room and while everyone rejoiced at the notion there was enough common sense in the crowd to realize that some innocent sleeper might be blinded by the stunt. So Asa modified it to holding a lighted two-inch salute, hitched to a pole, right outside the window. Someone soon came up with a ten-foot pole such as was used to fish for pickerel. Asa held the pole, another young man, after binding the cannon cracker to the far end, touched a match to the fuse, and Asa promptly hoisted it window-high and let it bang.

The result was as satisfying as a three-base hit. There was a cry of dismay from the dark and a tousled dark head soon appeared to bellow at us, "What the hell's going on?"

"Happy Fourth of July!" Asa cried.

"Son of a bitch!" said the man, and closed the window. It had grown dark by now and, with the quarry boys still belated, the crowd decided to get on with the normal activities, which were concerned mainly with hunting out wheeled vehicles and hustling them down to the square, where they could be sent headlong into the base of the horse trough. There was a buggy or a wagon in almost every barn, so that there was business enough to keep the whole crowd—now numbering some thirty or forty young hellions—occupied in racing down the converging roadways, hell-a-hooping, as the locals phrased it, to send one farm cart or buggy after another careering into the horse trough with a smash like a shed collapsing. After most of the nearby vehicles had been commandeered, someone made note of the heavy baggage carts that slumbered on the dark railroad platform. A dozen young men, including me, pounced on them and set out to start them rolling. But all three were firmly fixed to the pillars by heavy chains that no human hand could sever. But we tried nonetheless, with much grunting and shouting, until suddenly a plump dark figure appeared and fixed us in the faint light of a small flashlight, one of those little pocket jobs with a lens the size of a button. It was, one of the locals told us, the village constable, huddled into a coat, although the night was warm indeed.

One of the village crowd, a hatchet-faced young man with a small mustache, dropped to one knee and aimed an imaginary rifle. "Which hand has he got the light in?" he cried. "Right or left?"

"Look out, Lloyd!" someone called to the constable. "He'll put a slug in you!" Everyone laughed except the cop. He stood in his place, a good ten yards away, and urged us in an uncertain tone, "Don't break anything, now."

"Hell, no!" one lad shouted and we all assured him happily that nothing could be farther from our thoughts. So we gave up on the baggage trucks and move farther afield to bring in contributions from outlying stables. The first one we approached, however, was our last. Two or three of us had just begun to tiptoe down the slope to the double doors of the carriage barn when a disembodied voice out of the dark roared, "Get the hell out of here!" And at that instant a shotgun blast, almost in our faces, sent us scattering. We did not know but what one of us had been flattened by the shot and each of us was intent on getting his own tender behind well out of range. But as we fled up the roadway, there came a quick and steady pattering, like an unexpected shower of rain, that told us all the pellets had been fired into the air. We laughed then. But we kept on running. No telling where the next blast might be directed.

By this time the quarry boys had found us and we gathered to learn what new atrocities they might have cooked up. The leader of this gang was a squarely built young man, six feet tall, arrayed in heavy wool pants, long-john underwear, and clodhopper shoes, his head shaved convict-style, revealing a knobby skull. He carried a small satchel with him which he assured us held explosive enough to flatten an icehouse. But we had no such fearful project in view. We were bent merely on mischief. Still, we welcomed the idea of filling the now pitch-black night with hideous noises, so we urged him to set out a blasting cap or two to reawaken that part of the village that had been able to sleep through our earlier ceremonies. There was one light in the village that served to make the near storefront visible and faintly illumined a few of the clustered houses. Dip, hailing us all as "my gang," invited us down to the area where the light enabled us to know each other's faces. But Joe, the dynamite man, would have none of that. And neither would we, so poor Dip marched off with not a soul behind him.

Joe selected a small cement hitching post, deep in the shadow, to place the first charge. When we had all backed yards off, some even seeking the shelter of the piled-up buggies in the square, Joe lit the fuse with his cigarette and then sprinted for cover. The cap exploded like a dozen cannon crackers, actually causing the light to flicker and fade, and the distant store window to shiver as if it might crack wide open. Lights came on in two or three houses and, one by one, a dozen windows opened and pale faces popped out like weasels in a woodpile. "My God!" someone screamed. And we all knew a sudden deep delight at having earned such a thrilling response. We moved along to a new hitching post and repeated the deed, and then sought better response by hiking a few rods along to a cluster of summer cottages above the pond. Here again we won a terrified reaction from every sleeping household so that the whole neighborhood seemed to be leaping to arms.

By this time the supply of caps had dwindled to one and Joe was insistent on using the last one to set off a small charge of dynamite that he had lugged down from the quarry for no other purpose but raising some hell. We argued him at last into moving out into the farm country, where there was no chance of our blowing some innocent clean through his roof. So we marched together, unable to make out more of each other except the few near forms and recognizing each other only by voices. It was a wondrous spooky feeling, with all those young feet stirring the dust of the road with a determined and ominous tread, the cool dust rising gently to dry our nostrils, and the crickets keeping up a tuneless fiddling on every side. There was never an automobile on those roads at night and what houses there may have been had long been dark. We marched more than a mile before Joe was satisfied with the look and feel of a rail fence, barely discernible in the rank grass along the road. He felt his way to a post and vowed he would place the dynamite on the top there and set it off.

"Jesus, no!" one voice beseeched him. "What if it hits the house?"

"No house there," said a deeper voice. "Just Jack Higgins's old cow barn. Ain't been used in a hell of a while. And, Christ, that's pretty near a quarter mile inside the fence."

"But the goddamn dynamite will blow a hole in the road!"

"Ah, no," said Joe. "She'll just blow off in the air. Now get the hell back."

So we got the hell back, stumbling into each other, but watching to see the splutter of the fuse. The cigarette glowed bright as Joe put it to his lips and part of his face appeared, vignetted in the dark. Then the fuse began to hiss and spit and we all went pelting down the road. The explosion was almost instantaneous and I felt the force of it ripple up the back of my shirt. The noise was indescribable. It seemed to burst the sky into shards and dump it down upon us. The echoes raced like a hurricane wind across the fields and were thrown back again and again before the invisible hills absorbed them.

"Holy Jesus Christ!" I breathed, feeling as if I had dodged a thunderbolt. Then we all heard, in the near distance, an ominous and seemingly endless smashing of glass, undoubtedly falling windows striking the ground. The cry of "Let's get the hell out of here!" brought unanimous compliance. We must have run half a mile or more before we dared slow down and speak to each other.

"It was only Jack's old barn," someone assured us. "No real harm done!" But it sounded like real harm to most of us and we decided to keep going toward safety. We slowed down at last and marched once more in a body, although there seemed fewer of us than there had been.

When we had put a good mile between us and the site of the explosion our courage had returned sufficiently to allow us to sing, not in unison exactly, but at least all at the same time, that traditional old chant that all New England young men seemed to have learned in their early boyhood:

> The night before the Fourth! The night before the Fourth!
> Oh, they put me in a dark hole
> And covered me over with charcoal!
> The flames came out me arse-hole!
> The night before the Fourth!

Now we began to recall that we had been baseball teams to begin with and as we straggled back into the pale light of the village lamp, we sorted ourselves out into teams again and said our individual farewells. Asa shook every hand, with special concern for "Smiley" Quirk.

"Let's have another game sometime soon!" he cried. "You can learn me that curve. Come back before school is in!"

"Oh, we will for sure!" we told him. "We will! We will!"

But of course we never did.

Chapter 2

GROWING PAINS, UMPIRES, AND OTHER AFFLICTIONS

/. *When I was still too young* to go to professional baseball games, there was a pink-cheeked and broad-shouldered young man, still in his teens, who was recruited by the Red Sox.

This was Waite Hoyt. And all I knew about him was that he was called Schoolboy because he looked it and because he probably still should have been one. And he became, therefore, my private hero and remained so for the two seasons he put in with the Red Sox. What I could never have foreseen, could never even have dared dream, was that, in a far-off day, Waite Hoyt and I would become best friends and stay that way until he died. "More than friends," he wrote me once. But "friends" was good enough for me. And between the time his name first entered my half-baked consciousness and the day I had to say good-bye for good, a lot of water flowed down the aqueduct, not all of it fit to drink, or even to swim in.

Waite, a star pitcher with Erasmus Hall High School on Flat-bush Avenue in Brooklyn, had his first try-out with professional baseball when he appeared, at age fifteen, to show off his skills to the secondary brass of the Brooklyn team at Ebbets Field. He accomplished nothing memorable there, although he did receive (and reject) an offer to pitch batting practice. One spectator, who had cast a skeptical eye on the event—an ex-dental student named Stengel and called K.C. because he was born there—was able to recall years later that Hoyt had appeared "in his mother's bloomers." Actually, he was wearing "baseball pants," probably run up on the sewing machine by a favorite aunt who, like every kindly lady in that day, believed that all boys' clothes should be made a little larger than normal so a kid could "grow into them."

This may well have been the same aunt who, when Waite was indeed making ready to leave home to join a professional baseball club, presented him with two man-style pongee shirts, with tails so long they rustled about Waite's knees as he walked. Waite was on his way to take a train for Lebanon, Pennsylvania, where he had been consigned after he and his father—Waite still being but fifteen when it happened—had signed with John McGraw of the New York Giants. Carrying his first suitcase (called a "dress suit–case" in that day) and wearing his first long-pants suit, Waite walked to the trolley stop along an avenue where there were friends on every porch to wave him good-bye. Flatbush in that time was as snug as a small town, where neighbors shared the intimacies of each other's lives, so that everyone within five minutes' walk of Waite's home knew that the Hoyt boy—tall, square-shouldered, and handsome—was off to play ball for money. And Lebanon, a full day's journey away, seemed as far off as London.

I don't suppose there are more than a few roomfuls of men still alive in Brooklyn who can recall the gut-deep thrill of first putting on long pants. It was a thrill deeper than the one that went with winning a ball game and more lasting than the excitement of one's first Communion or Bar Mitzvah. It told the whole watching world that you were a man, able at last to discard the baby clothes that marked you as still of little account. A boy in that day did not wear a shirt but a blouse that ended at the waist, knee-length britches with elastic at the knee, and, when he was in his best clothes, a panty-waist that supported the garters that held his knee-length stockings up. A *man's* shirt, however, had tails that tucked under the trousers, collar buttons to hitch the starched collar, and links to keep the cuffs from flapping. His stockings were short socks that reached the calf and they were supported by garters of wide elastic that snapped on just above the calf. And a true man of the world could wear, instead of a boy's ankle-length shoes with metal hooks to catch the upper ends of the laces, low-cut "oxfords" that left his ankles in the breeze.

When Waite found a seat in the day coach of the train that was carrying him to Lebanon, he took care to hitch his new long trousers up with thumb and forefinger, as he had seen men folks do, so as not to spoil the crease when he sat down. All the same, the conductor, accepting his ticket, winked and smiled at him, bringing the ready blush to Waite's cheeks and ears.

At the hotel in Lebanon, where Waite was careful to deepen his voice as he asked, "How much are your rooms?" he earned a sharp squint from the room clerk, who took him for a runaway. "We get a lot of runaways here," the clerk explained after Waite had identified himself as a ball player. But Waite, in keeping with his promise to his mother, very soon found room and board with "a nice family," where the kindly housewife sent regular reports to the Hoyt home and where Waite had a room where he could hide the homesickness that overtook him. But when Waite wrote home he told only of the six-inch raisin pie, almost as good as he got at home, that could be had at the local bakery for five cents. (He had left home with twenty-five dollars in his pocket.)

Homesickness has been the daily fare of many a small-town boy who has left home to play baseball miles away. Decades later, young Mickey Mantle, sitting in the train that began to carry him out of Commerce, Oklahoma, to the Yankee training camp, felt hot tears running down his cheeks. Of course Flatbush was no small town and had not been since the bridge first hitched it, along with the rest of Brooklyn, to the wicked city across the river. But it felt no larger than Lebanon did to the families who dwelt there.

In that era, the ferocity of the rivalry between one city and another—invariably brought to a boil in the baseball games—would have shocked a sadist. While, among solid citizens, it might linger as a mild contempt such as a southerner would feel for a Yankee, among the young and the less refined it would fester into a rancor that could prompt instant physical violence. When the Cleveland ball club visited Baltimore in 1895, in the Temple Cup series that matched the first- and second-place finishers to determine the National League champion, it was less welcome than a troop of thieves. The players were pelted with dirty names and pre-owned vegetables on the way to the ballpark, and even after Baltimore had beaten them on the diamond, the home fans were not appeased. As the horse-drawn omnibus carrying the Cleveland Spiders to the train station moved through the streets, wild-eyed folk on every side bombarded it with missiles meant to do mortal damage. While most of the Spiders had sense enough to lie flat on the floor, their bold second baseman, "Cupid" Childs, who scorned to lie low, took a rock on the side of the head that laid him willy-nilly down beside his fellows. A decade or so later, the deep hostility of the denizens of Mount Carmel, Pennsylvania, toward their like in nearby Shamokin, was as bitter as that of the Irish toward the Dutch. (One Irishman on a crutch, my devoted uncle taught me, could lick a thousand dirty Dutch!) Of course, the ball players who represented the two clubs were probably none of them from either town. There were rowdies from New York, schoolboys like Hoyt from Brooklyn, farmers from New Jersey, and mill hands from almost anywhere. So the warlike spirit was all bottled inside the seething hearts of the fans from the opposing towns.

The "diamond" at Mount Carmel, where the "pitcher's mound" was a hole in the ground, was cluttered with rocks from base to base, and no effort was made to clear them. When one ball player, new to the area, asked a fan why no effort was made to make the third-base line playable by raking off the rocks, the fan laughed darkly.

"Don't you worry none about them rocks," he said. "Before

the game is over, we'll have them out of there. Any Shamokin bastard gets this far'll git a dozen of them behind the ear. They's better'n five hundred bucks riding on this game!"

Indeed, it was a Mount Carmel brag that in an earlier game, Harry Coveleski (that goddamn Polack who had the gall to have been *born* in Shamokin) had been knocked clear of his senses by a carefully aimed rock when he was trying to complete a home run that would have put his club ahead. The game then was abruptly canceled and there were no payoffs. (Harry Coveleski, the gods be thanked, lived to pitch for Philadelphia and for Detroit, where he won twenty-two games one season, and never hit another home run.)

In the smaller towns, where there was not patronage enough to keep a professional club in eating tobacco, the rivalry usually centered on the high school teams, where the enmity was nourished just as sedulously among the players as among the fans. I can vividly remember my own dismay (shared by all my fellows) when we loyal Brookline boys heard that a former star of our own school had actually *married* a girl from *Newton*! And, in a great many middle-sized cities and large-sized towns when the century was in its teens and twenties, there were "town teams," usually collected into a league of sorts, and "city leagues," with teams named after local merchants who footed the bills. The players in such organizations usually played largely for fun, although often admission was charged or a hat passed about to provide "coffee and cake" money for the players, or even an extra ten-dollar bill or two for a pitcher.

Boys who played for their school or college teams could count on offers of every sort to come play baseball—perhaps for a summer resort out among the New England hills and beaches or the western prairies. In Boston for several seasons before night baseball was more than dreamed about, there was a "Twilight League" where college players could find a comfortable summer payday, provided they took care to disguise their identity sufficiently so as not to bruise their "amateur" standing. (One young infielder from Brown, in the 1920s, whose real name was Trumbauer, found he needed to do no more than call himself "Trum-blower" to escape damage to his virtue.) Eddie Collins, who Connie Mack always contended was the greatest base-stealer who ever played for money, was still going to college when he signed with Connie Mack, and he had used the name Sullivan in order to remain an amateur while he played summer ball in Plattsburgh, New York, and other towns. When he came to Philadelphia to sign with Connie Mack's Athletics, Connie was dismayed to have him walk in when there was a visitor in Connie's office who might blow Eddie's cover, for Eddie still wanted to play ball for Columbia. So Connie raised his hand and called out, "Oh, hello, *Sullivan!* Go down to the clubhouse and I'll see you later." So Eddie Collins played six games for the Athletics under the name of Sullivan. Lou Gehrig, years later, and also enrolled at Colum-bia, disguised himself with the name of Lewis while he played ball for Hartford in the summertime.

But you could play ball for money in many places and not change your name at all. More than one preparatory school in New England was ready to offer "scholarships" that included comfortable living expenses to athletes who would come and add glory to the sacred name. A noted New England preparatory school, one of the few schools that accepted both sexes, kept one young man on the payroll until he was nearly twenty-eight, when a nearby university outbid it. Its own baseball team traveled New England over, sometimes filling the summer months under the name of an industrial plant or merchant and adding a few outright pros to the roster. The coach was a notorious character who, it was said, never changed his underwear. The libel held that he took off only jacket, hat, and shoes when he went to bed. On arising, he would put on his shoes and jacket, spit on his hands to flatten his hair, plunk his hat on his head, and walk out to meet the world. He was not, some players reported, a man you wanted sitting next to you on the bench.

In these circuits, of course, there was seldom the sizzling enmity of team for team—or fans for fans—that marked so many of the rivalries in the minors or even in the majors. (A Brooklyn priest, when he was old and the century was young, once confessed to a sportswriter, "I *hate* the Giants!") But in one town at least, a young man who had managed his high school club to many victories over their natural rivals held the team together after graduation, added a few outsiders, called the club the Colonials, and almost instantly found a name-calling enemy. For there was another club in that city that dared call itself the champion of New Haven. That was the Humphrey Athletic Club, whose "manager" took issue in the local press with the efforts of the Colonials' manager to rate his club number one. But George Weiss, a slight, apple-cheeked grocery clerk (in his father's grocery), who managed the Colonials, had long before (as a would-be and could-be journalist) learned to score a rival's hide with sarcasm. So after an exchange of haughty challenges and wholesale belittlement, with fans all over town trying to edge into the row, the Colonials did meet the Humphreys and the Colonials won. From that time forth young George Weiss's club, on which he sometimes played right field and once actually pitched a game, roamed the whole county seeking whom it might devour—and even ranged the entire state to meet anyone who dared pick up the challenge. They beat the Highwood Outlaws, the Branford Hustlers, the Woodmen of the World, and even the Asylum (the employees, not the inmates). Eventually they began to play openly for "expenses." (It was a memorable day when the rival team offered to pay not only their carfare out to West Rock but even their fare back home.) Finally, they began to draw in semipros such as the "Yale Ineligibles," who had been bounced from the college team because they had been found playing for money at Quogue. They even lured the great Charley Brickley, a high school classmate of George's, back home from Harvard, where he was a famous dropkicker and a baseball star.

With no better transportation to start with than their bicycles or the horse-drawn grocery cart, they soon graduated to the trolley—and then to the steam cars—and, drawing as many fans as they did, soon earned the snarling rivalry of the local professional ball club, which played in the Eastern League. (George even borrowed their pitcher for an occasional Sunday game, Sunday baseball being forbidden in the Eastern League.) And out of that enmity grew a long story we can listen to later.

Adding heat to such rivalries, of course, was the wholesale betting that backers indulged in to demonstrate their loyalty. After every game there were suddenly swollen wallets in New Haven and a host of empty pockets to match them. It had *always* been this way since the game began. The players themselves did not hesitate to wager on their own success and when there was a big game pending, every cigar store in New Haven became a betting parlor.

In discussing his own early addiction to baseball, Al Spink, who organized the first "St. Louis Browns" and founded the *Sporting News,* made this confession: "I was the very devil of a lad, willing to play on any Sunday and to bet my last dollar on the result of a game." Such bettors were not usually moved by any conviction that their heroes were invincible but by a sort of aggressive instinct, often aroused by a challenge to "put your money where your mouth is," and, of course, to bet *against* your team, whatever the counselings of common sense, was an act of outright treachery. If they *were* going to lose, you did not want to be happy about it.

Professional baseball players, naturally, were not often quite so naive and had been known to arrange matters so that, if they did suffer the inevitable, it would not be entirely wormwood and gall. Ty Cobb and Tris Speaker, rival managers in 1926 and, of course, future Hall of Famers, were strongly (and, their employers decided, correctly) suspected of arranging the outcome of certain games between their clubs, to their mutual enrichment. Both were promptly "let go," but innocent ears were never offended by any such public scandal as had fallen upon the "Black Sox." Both men wound up their careers in Philadelphia under the tender care of Connie Mack, who, twenty-two years later, wrote me that he had always deemed Tris Speaker "the greatest outfielder in all baseball." (All I know about his opinion of Ty Cobb was that he constantly warned his catchers, "Don't make Mr. Cobb angry!")

At least until the reign of Commissioner Kenesaw Mountain Landis, the notion of laying a bet on a ball game never raised the hair on anyone's head. Throughout the whole history of the game, players had made bets with their rivals, or the game was played for a "winner-take-all" pot, as in the first great championship series between St. Louis and Chicago in 1885. In a Giants game one distant day, Christy Mathewson gave all of his teammates the chills when he filled the bases with enemy players enough to win the ballgame, then in the ninth inning. One infielder after another hurried in to remind Christy that every man on the club had fifty dollars riding on the outcome, and that he *had* to get somebody out. Christy, who always worked well within himself, bade all be at peace, as he was going to finish off the opponents on the instant. Whereupon he wiped out the enemy in order and joined the general rejoicing in the locker room.

In earlier days, there was talk of crooked doings in almost every league city. And in the days of the big traveling ball clubs the gamblers seemed to have come close to owning the game. There was frequent talk of a "big" club's throwing a game to a weaker rival to build up the odds for a future game. And newspapers spoke freely of the crooked work obviously being done on the diamond. In 1878, *Spirit of the Times,* the leading sports periodical, said this about baseball in St. Louis: "Baseball, as a professional pastime, has seen its best days in St. Louis, and the people have had so bitter a dose that they will not want to repeat it. The amount of crooked work that has been done of late is indeed startling."

In 1882, the *Buffalo Express* suggested that the local team should "fold up if it cannot play a square game."

And this was after the National League had been formed and the league authorities (in 1877) had expelled four Louisville players for deliberately throwing a game to Hartford.

But even after Commissioner Landis had come to drive the money changers out of baseball's temple, there were baseball people of every stripe who had bets to settle after every game was done. In the game outside the official organizations, particularly among the black clubs, where pay often varied with the size of the crowd, profitability sometimes depended on wagers between the club owners. And sometimes the spectators—all with cash riding on the game—would suddenly swell the take by tossing coins on the field.

Spectators in the beginning had often tossed (or slipped) money to ball players—occasionally with the understanding that something might be done to bring the game out right. And in those days, all the betting was done openly, with pool-sellers passing among the spectators, like the beer-sellers of a later day, or even setting up stands like bookies in Britain, with the odds posted. Naturally, ball players, even umpires, were tempted to lay a dollar or two on the outcome. Eventually, the ultimate arbiter of the game (a gentle old fellow named Henry Chadwick, whom everyone in that day thought of as "The Father of Base-ball") allowed that a wager on a game on which the umpire had placed a bet was "not fairly won."

Some of the violence on the diamond in that day must have been prompted by the thought of a fat wager disappearing down the drain, and it is true that there was often man-to-man violence done upon umpires when the ball players and spectators in general were watching in quietness and calm.

In Kansas City one summer afternoon, a local fan who very likely, as my Irish grandfather would have expressed it, had a drop taken, walked out on the diamond in the midst of a game and fetched umpire Bob Stewart a crack on the jaw. And in Chicago, in 1908, after the Boston Puritans had beaten the Chicago White Sox, a lawyer named Robert Cantwell, who must have decided that Boston had got the better of too many close decisions, strode out upon the field and broke umpire Jack Kerin's nose for him.

And in one instance, in more civilized times, umpire George Magerkurth, working in Ebbets Field, was suddenly set upon by a husky young man who leapt out of a nearby grandstand seat and undertook to beat poor George to the ground. George, having wriggled free from his protective equipment, was soon giving back as good as he got and the two rolled together in the dirt while spectators gaped in awe, not sure which side to cheer for. It turned out, however, that there was no real dispute at all. The attacker was the accomplice of a pickpocket who, while his friend kept the spectators entranced, was busily extracting contributions from unwitting customers. Magerkurth's attacker was soon subdued by the cops, but his friend must surely have collected enough in the meantime to pay the man's fine and leave a little over.

While John McGraw had many differences with umpires, they never had their roots in wagering—even though John was a famous gambler. His rows with umpires were over points of judgment and he often made his point violently. Once he hurled a baseball, with all his force, at umpire Bob Emslie (and missed him), but what the dispute was about no one alive can recall. McGraw did not confine his vituperation to umpires, for he maintained a lifelong bitter feud with Barney Dreyfuss, owner of the Pittsburgh Pirates.

One afternoon, as the Giants made ready to take on the Pittsburgh club, McGraw appeared on the balcony of the Polo Grounds clubhouse, high above center field, and yelled, "Hey, Barney!" When McGraw was sure he had Barney's attention he began to recite, at the very loudest reach of his voice and to the stunned attention of the gathering fans and the players of both clubs, a list of Barney's delinquencies, which included (according to McGraw) welshing on race-track wagers, failure to pay his personal debts, and a few smaller sins. To enliven the show, McGraw garnished his recital with most of the obscene adjectives at his command. Then, to put a resounding period to the list, he offered to bet Barney $10,000 that his Giants would beat the Pittsburgh club in the game at hand. Barney, who apparently lacked both the lung power and the venom that boiled in McGraw, did his best to scream his defiances, so that he and McGraw seemed like two angry children on opposite fire escapes. But Barney did not take the bet.

●

When the game was newborn, and called the Knickerbocker Game or the New York Game, and participation was limited to the members of a few "gentlemen's clubs," the use of strong language on the playing field could earn the transgressor a twenty-five-cent fine. And after Kenesaw Landis had taken up the task of brightening baseball's countenance before the world, he decreed that filthy language and vulgar gestures would soil the baseball scene no longer. He even docked umpire Bill Klem (the man who vowed that he had never in his career called a play wrong "in my heart") a day's pay for using a naughty word out loud, not on the playing field but in a hotel elevator, during the 1933 World Series.

In between those hallowed times, however, foul language and vulgar gestures at ballparks won only passing notice unless there were "ladies present" or when they were accompanied by threats or actual deliverance of bodily harm. Umpires in the nineteenth century would have settled for nasty names and vulgar gestures, for there were fans throughout baseball who felt that each game was just a battle in a never-ending war, with the umpires sometimes enlisting with the enemy. Philadelphia (perhaps in an effort to shed the "brotherly love" slogan that struck some as effeminate) produced some of the most violence-prone fans in the league. The Boston Beaneaters, after a game with the brotherly lovers, were once forced to flee for their lives from a mob who even chased their streetcar up the street, hurling missiles at it. And once, in the final days of the century, Philadelphia fans did set upon umpire Ormsby and clobbered him nearly senseless, perhaps because he had given the decision that left them on the wrong end of every wager. In 1886, when the Detroit club was playing Philadelphia and a decision by umpire Ellick gave the game to the visitors, outraged Philadelphia fans would have dismembered the umpire had not police with drawn revolvers come to his rescue. Ellick escaped with contusions and abrasions and promptly sent in his resignation to league president Nicholas Young.

It was only two years later that umpire Phil Powers had to draw his own revolver to hold off the Philadelphia fans who sought to dispute, with club, fist, and foot, one of his calls. And other umpires of that day took to packing guns when they came to Philadelphia.

There was one umpire, however, who scorned to carry a pistol. Tim Hurst depended on his own two fists and he saw no sense in fining ball players to keep them nice.

"It learns them nawthing," said Tim, "and a good sock on the jaw is cheaper."

Still, despite all these wars and rumors of wars, umpires in the old days could sometimes have fun at their jobs. Joe Cantillon, before he became manager of the Washington club, put in a spell of umpiring and earned a lifelong enemy when he was just trying to enjoy himself. Duff Cooley, of the Boston Beaneaters, who called himself Dick and was known throughout the league as a dedicated umpire-baiter, once, in a game against Chicago, drove a ball to deep center field and took off at top speed. As he rounded first base, he saw that the ball was sailing well over the head of center fielder Bill Lange and he felt sure he had himself a home run. Head down, he fled for third base, where Joe Cantillon stood, obviously waiting to make a call. As Dick came close, Cantillon shouted, "Touch the base or I'll call you out!" Dick dutifully hit the bag with one foot as he wheeled past and noticed, when he sped for home, that Cantillon had started after him. There being just one umpire per game in that day, Dick knew that Cantillon was expecting a play at the plate. Running almost at Dick's ear, Cantillon cried out, "Slide!" Never questioning Cantillon's right to advise him this way, or perhaps thinking that it was the third-base coach following him down, Dick slid hard across the plate past the feet of the wondering catcher.

"You're out!" Cantillon yelled.

Cooley came to his feet in a jump.

"What the hell do you mean 'out'!" he screamed. "Where the hell is the ball?"

Cantillon offered a fiendish grin.

"Lange caught it," he said. Obviously that must have happened before Cooley had passed second base. And Dick never spoke to Joe again.

Bill Lange, who had taken Cooley's fly with a tremendous leap and a one-handed catch, was one of the fastest men who ever played the game—known as Twinkle-Toes or Little Eva not just for the speed of his feet but for his light-footedness on the dance floor. Connie Mack recalled, in a letter to a friend more than a half century after the event, one of Big Bill's most startling feats— scoring all the way from first on an overthrow by the pitcher. Bill, having reached first base on a solid hit, promptly took a long lead, as base runners often did in the days before pitchers became thoroughly practiced in holding runners close. This time, Connie recalled, the pitcher did make a quick throw to catch Bill, but the throw escaped Jake Beckley, the first baseman. Jake had a notoriously weak throwing arm, so Bones Ely, the right fielder, dashed in to retrieve the ball. He had seen Bill sprinting past second base, so he heaved the ball to third. But Bill Lange had already left that base behind. And Connie Mack, who was catching, stood goggle-eyed behind the plate with only an empty glove to tag Bill with. All those years later, Connie recalled the play vividly. "Never could understand why Bill did not use his speed to steal bases," he wrote.

Bill perhaps was saving his agility for the dance floor, to which he was addicted. When he was seventy-seven, he allowed, "I still go dancing. But not every night." George Kelly, the famous "High Pockets" of the New York Giants, was Bill's nephew and he had a clear recollection of Uncle Bill on the dance floor "making up his own steps," dipping and sliding and twirling his partner. "No matter how big the crowd," George reported, "he was never called out for interference."

Another lighthearted umpire who never took himself too seriously was Jocko Conlan, of a later era, who may have been the shortest man ever to hold the job—shorter than most second basemen. Jocko, who was not often the target of bad words, was not a man to be bulldozed. Once a very large pitcher, headed for the bench between innings, took a short detour to inquire of Conlan, "How many lousy calls are you guys allowed in one game?"

Jocko looked back into the glowering face and never blinked. "Oh, about a dozen," he replied mildly.

The pitcher had to swallow twice to find a response. "Well, you've gone over your quota," he growled and kept his face shut thereafter.

Perhaps the last umpire to earn a short brush with actual mayhem was Jack Powers, who had the misfortune to umpire a game between the original New York Giants (organized by one Jim Mutrie in post–Civil War days) and the Cleveland Spiders, who were perhaps the roughest crew ever assembled in one ball club, rougher by far than Ned Hanlon's ungentlemanly Orioles, with a bandit at every base to stay a stranger's passage. They included a first baseman named Jake Virtue, who seemed bent on living down his name; a second baseman named John "Cub" Streaker, who spelled his name "Stricker" so it could be pronounced right, and who was always ready for a fight or a frolic; a shortstop called Big Ed McKean, who was not big at all but seemed big when he set out to knock a runner off stride; and at third base, the hairiest Spider of them all, Patsy Tebeau, who ran the show. At one point in the game, umpire Jack Powers made the grievous error of calling Cleveland outfielder Jimmy McAleer safe at second base, bringing the New York catcher raging out on the diamond with obscenities fouling the air before him, to explain to Powers how very wrong he had been. After considering the matter for the better part of a minute, Powers realized Jimmy had been out all along. But when he raised his thumb in the "out" sign, it was as if he had opened a tiger cage—or spilled a bucket full of tarantulas. Headed by Cub Stricker, the whole Spider team set upon poor Jack Powers, joining McAleer in casting opprobrium upon him, along with loose gravel and other foreign objects. They shoved Powers back and forth among them and finally sent him to the sod, screaming for help. But there was no immediate help at hand, for no one in the tiny crowd of four hundred felt moved to come to Jack's aid. So Jack crawled to his feet and sprinted for the clubhouse with fear lending him wings. He reached his goal just in time to get the door locked behind him and he continued to yell for help, while Tebeau's huskies battered at the door with shoulder, foot, and fist. At length, the uproar brought a squadron of police, who persuaded Powers that he would be safe in their charge. Out he came, tousled and trembling, to march back to his post with cops all around him, while Spiders and spectators howled imprecations. Cops guarded the foul lines as the game proceeded and huddled around Powers when the teams changed sides. And Powers lived to tell his friends about it.

Not all the violence was visited upon umpires, however. Oftentimes, even after the game had become relatively civilized and visiting ball clubs could travel practically unmolested from park to hotel, even in Philadelphia, nasty words from the seats might bring swift retribution from the field. Or the shoe might be on the other foot altogether, and the umpires would visit discomfort upon the spectators in response to some dark motive of their own.

In Washington one day, the start of a game between Washington and Baltimore was held up until half past four, to suit some petty government officials who could not leave their desks to make the regular starting time. Naturally, in those pre-daylight-savings days, dark began to gather before the game was half done. But umpire Jack Kerin seemed impelled to complete at least four and a half innings of the game, lest the fans earn the right to come to the next game free. After much vain pleading with Kerin, catcher Wilbert Robinson (who earned greater fame when he became the frolicsome manager of the Brooklyn club) secured a lemon from somewhere and slipped it to his pitcher, John Clarkson, who kept it hidden in his glove. When Robby was ready, Clarkson hurled the lemon toward the plate. "Strike one!" Kerin announced. Without a word, Robby turned and showed Kerin the lemon in his glove. "Game called on account of darkness," Kerin declared quietly, and the sad little politicians went home unappeased.

Kerin, of course, escaped lynching, and it was not long before A. G. Spalding was moved to proclaim that violence against umpires was "no longer deemed part of the game." (The obvious implication being that it *had* been one of the features the fan sought in return for his quarter.)

Violence, however, did not wholly disappear, and no newspaper would evermore declare, as a western journal once did in the days beyond recall, that the local baseball club was made up of "eighteen of the most respectable young men in town." In Brooklyn one day, when the Giants were engaged with their dearest enemy, the Brooklyn pre-Dodgers (then called the Superbas), the Giants' wiry third baseman, Art Devlin, took violent exception to a dirty name selected for him by a Brooklyn fan and climbed over the rail to straighten out the fan's morals. It turned out that there were a number of fans eager to lay hands on a live New York Giant, so Devlin had far more than he could deal with. Other players promptly piled into the fray, creating such an uproar that Charles Ebbets himself, proud owner of the Brooklyns, hastened to the scene to berate John McGraw for having instigated the row. The Brooklyn cops managed to bring the battle to a close, however, while Ebbets and McGraw were still screaming at each other and had not yet taken to beating each other upside the head.

At another time, Ty Cobb, too, jumped into the stands to have it out with a crippled fan who had imputed doubtful ancestry to him with annoying frequency. (It is hard to believe that Ty did not notice that the man was missing one hand and part of the other.) Ty was suspended for this and the entire Detroit club went out on strike, prompting the recruitment of a team of has-beens and never-would-bes from the coaching staff and nearby colleges, to provide a nine for the next game and thus protect the franchise. The strike ended promptly. What became of the guilty fan, history does not record.

New York's great underhand pitcher, Carl Mays, whose temper was never too securely seated, once threatened to lay a fastball right on the skull of a fan who had kept taunting with uncomely names. The fan stood and dared Mays to try. Whereupon Carl let fly. He missed the fan, else he would certainly have killed him, as he did poor Ray Chapman, Cleveland shortstop, who could not get out of the way of Mays's sizzling underhand pitch.

Waite Hoyt, who seldom let a man call him out of his name, would never have killed anyone, but once he was taunted by the New York Giants until his temper broke loose. Waite had been featured in an ad for some soap that was supposed to help maintain a "schoolgirl or schoolboy complexion" and Waite did indeed have the rosy cheeks of a healthy youngster. But when some Giant player tossed out to him, as he walked by the Giant bench, a cake of the same soap all done up in ribbons and urged him to take it home and repair his complexion, Waite had reached his blow-off point. He picked up the soap and slammed it with all his strength straight at the Giant bench, where grim John McGraw sat leading the chorus. John ducked and the soap hit the back wall of the dugout with an echoing whack. If it had hit John, it might well have put out McGraw's lights for good.

Men and women who knew George Wiess when he was the top baseball executive in the country, would never have taken him for a man who would yell bad words at umpires, to say nothing of offering to do them down in physical combat. But long before George developed into the good gray genius, the quiet, seemingly emotionless man who drove tough bargains and made shrewd trades, he was a leader of a bush league baseball club whose chief desire was to win a league championship. And he felt that urge with special force when he took over as president of the New Haven club in the Eastern League and led them into their brand-new modern stadium, called, without his willing it, Weiss Park. George then seated himself in the "owner's box," where he could almost look over the umpire's shoulder. Early in the season, George, who had been yelling occasional comments on the umpire's judgment, came right out of his seat when the man called a ball fair that, in George's view, was foul by more than a foot. When the umpire failed to agree with George's anguished complaints, George got hold of a spade and carefully lifted up a large section of turf, showing the foul line and the dent supposedly made by the ball when it dropped—well outside the line. He carried this exhibit with tender care and presented it to the umpire. The umpire may have told George to take it home with him. He was not impressed.

Another time, George, after a series of what he deemed blatantly improper decisions, loudly assailed the umpire's ears with a number of remarks so personal and specific that the umpire called time and walked back to George's box to inform him that if this barrage continued he might very well feel impelled to punch George's nose. George, who had not yet attained the girth that eventually would mark him, rose up to his full five feet eight inches and promised the umpire that he would be most happy to hand back whatever the umpire offered at whatever time the umpire thought suitable. George admitted later that when the umpire, after the game, seemed to have forgotten the challenge, George gave silent thanks and went straight home.

But next season, or the one after, when George was stage-managing a wild celebration after winning the championship, he saw to it that the festivities included the presentation to the umpire of a "gift" of a beat-up ancient Ford touring car rescued from a junk heap.

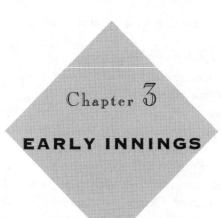

Chapter 3

EARLY INNINGS

Baseball (called base-ball then) did not turn into the national game until the Civil War gathered young men from all over the nation into army camps (and prison camps), where they had to cook up ways to keep themselves agreeably occupied in whatever free time they were granted. There had been base games and ball games of all sorts before that, and even farm boys, in town on town meeting day, had learned about "town ball," which was played with ball and bat, and posts for bases, without "sides" and without innings. Every boy in town would get a chance to come to bat, to hit the ball with a long stick and run like hell to get to a base and back before anyone could hit him with the ball.

The New York Game, contrived by one Alexander Cartwright, and designed to be played originally by those whom A. G. Spalding identified as "gentlemen in the highest social sense," had been adopted in cities throughout the land as the best of the base games, although there were also a Philadelphia game (with a smaller base circle) and a Massachusetts game (with four bases in addition to the "striker's point"). But the New York Game eliminated the element that had made town ball and its derivatives attractive to young roughnecks (in the lowest social sense)—i.e., soaking the runner with the ball while he was in full flight. (Games that featured this move were often called soak ball or burn ball.)

In a very few years after the surviving soldiers had all gone home, the New York Game, with some new features, was played in town and city and countryside.

Had you been a pencil pusher then in somebody's counting house, or a counter-jumper in a retail shop, or even a flatfoot on the local force, you would surely have been recruited—provided you owned the requisite number of arms and legs—to join the base-ball club that represented your calling. And if you were one of that lily-livered crew who simply refused to risk a crocked thumb or a fat lip while playing with that "deuced hard ball" you might well discover, on your desk or fixed to the door of your locker, a white chicken feather, the standard symbol then of rank cowardice. (In a later, less delicate age, you would most likely be simply informed that you had shit in your blood.)

In the post–Civil War era, base-ball, New York style, was truly national, in that it was played in every town large enough for the trains to stop at by upwards of a dozen truly amateur nines, representing the milkmen, the letter carriers, the firemen, the bankers, the schoolteachers, the teamsters, the grocery boys, the police, perhaps even the street cleaners. These were often "morning glory" teams, for they began their games as soon as the sun came up, as early as four in the morning in the summer, so the game would be done before it was time to go to work. Those young men who could afford to would often carry removable shoe spikes that they could put back in their pockets when the clocks called them to the job.

In the game as these clubs played it, there was little danger of nastying up your clothing or ripping your pants. There was no sliding; that was brought into the game later on by a frisky young fellow named Eddie Cuthbert, who played for the Philadelphia Keystones, and for a long time it was deemed a clownish and unsportsmanlike stunt. And a runner was in no danger of being soaked with the ball as he fled for the safety of a base.

The large cities, like Boston, for instance, fielded a dozen or more amateur base-ball teams that played the game for fun and gave not a single damn whether anyone came to watch. Besides the team at Harvard, which lived only to defeat Yale, there were, in the city or on its fringes, the Mystics, the Alerts, the Crescents, the Excelsiors, the Unions, the Oxfords, the Albions, the King Philips (named for the Indian leader who had been the scourge of their ancestors), and the Lynn Live Oaks—all of whom might be found, at different times, playing unfenced on the Common. Then there were the half a hundred high school teams and the haphazard "teams" that rearranged themselves from day to day from the local schoolboys.

Of course, when the great traveling teams came to town, there were crowds to watch, and to pay as much as twenty-five cents for the privilege. (In the very beginning, the Knickerbockers, the first of the clubs to play the New York Game as it was meant to be played, laid a charge of twenty-five cents—not to make money but to limit the crowd.)

Before ever the gate receipts for a game had turned base-ball into a business called by the one-word name "baseball," the game seemed essentially to belong to the fans (called kranks at the time), with the "owner" simply acting as a sort of angel who kept the operation afloat. That was certainly how it was in New York, just after the Civil War, when the great Mutuals ball team was financed by Boss Tweed himself, the political overlord, who let it be known that his "Mutes" were the mightiest base-ball team in the land, who could, if you wanted to know the truth of the matter, stand up even to the mighty Cincinnati Red Stockings and beat the trousers off them—never mind the fact that the Red Stockings had never been beat and were acknowledged the champions of the whole nation.

To understand what happened when the teams did meet—on June 15, 1869—you need to learn what the game looked like. It looked very unlike the game you and I call baseball.

To begin, the dimensions were different in several important respects: The "pitcher's point," marked by a six-foot plank set edgewise in the ground, with just about two inches protruding, was only forty-five feet from the "striker's point," which was also the home base. This was marked by four quoits set in the ground, flat side up and painted white. The "striker," eventually named the batter, stood with one foot *on* this mark. The pitcher was still required to "pitch" (i.e., toss) the ball to him, although by this time the rules permitted him to try to deceive the striker. Earlier, the pitcher had been almost a nonentity, sometimes called the "server," and it was deemed decidedly unsportsmanlike for him to try to keep the striker from getting "his hit," as the game did not really start until the ball had been struck into fair ground (inside the baselines or their extension). If a ball *landed* first inside the baselines, even in the infield, it was still fair, no matter how far off among the spectators it might roll.

Strikers wielded their bats in several different styles. Some would hold the skinny stick at the small end and take a full swing, although the experts in the game advised that they never swing so hard as to lose their balance. Others would hold the bat like an ax, in woodsman's style, with one hand at the lower end and the other several inches higher, ready to slide the upper hand down to complete a swing. A few would choke the bat, with both hands near the middle, and try to *push* the ball into fair ground.

The catcher, first called "behind," stood a few yards behind the batter and received many pitches on the bounce. He, like all the fielders and basemen, caught thrown balls with his hands held in a sort of open-clamshell figuration, the wrists together and the fingers extended toward the throw.

The only full-time infielder was the shortstop, who was indeed a shortstop, for he was charged with protecting all the field inside the baselines, right and left, and behind the pitcher. The three basemen, while they might handle balls hit within their reach, were usually positioned with one foot on the base, ready to lay a gentle tag on any enemy runner who might approach.

The umpire took his stand behind the striker, but well to one side. In the professional games he was usually equipped with a top hat, to honor his position. But alas, one contemporary writer mournfully reported, he could not *always* please *everyone* with his calls.

So that's the way the game was to be played that cloudy afternoon when the Red Stockings came to town, after a nationwide tour in which they had never found the team they couldn't lick. They had, it is true, been *tied* in one game, that being the one against the Lansingburgh Haymakers. But no one with the sense God gave a goose thought that game was anything but a fake. For didn't sly old John Morrissey, as thefty a rascal as ever stole a pig, being the man that had put the Haymakers together, just pull his team off the field once they had managed to tie the score at 17–17? It was all because the umpire tried to cheat, Johnny declared. But nobody believed a word. (The truth of it was, between you and me, that John had laid some $60,000 or the like with some pack of fools that the "Red Stockings would not win." And devil a penny did those damn fools ever lay hold of, for Johnny just told them—and it was the God's truth—that the Red Stockings *didn't* win. Now did they?)

There was cash past counting laid on this game between the Mutes and the Red Stockings, you may be sure, for Boss Tweed (may his shadow never grow less!) had given every working man in his domain the day off to watch the game, and every last one had a spare dollar or two in his pocket. As it turned out, the Boss couldn't make it to the game his own self, but there was no helping it. He had to be on hand, after all, to bid a decent farewell to President Grant, who, after a bit of a visit with the soldier boys at West Point, had slipped into town all unbeknownst and would be off this very day on the S.S. *Providence* of Jim Fisk's Fall River Line. So naturally, who would be the man to lead the lot that would escort the President to the pier but Brigadier General Tweed, no less, for today anyway—him in his bright blue uniform with all the stars. And along with him, showing the President the way to the Chambers Street pier, came all the other generals, Morris and McQuade and the rest, to lead him up the gangplank. And who should be standing at the very tip of the gangplank but Jim Fisk in person, and him in a bright blue uniform of his own with five pounds of gold braid on his cap and three stars on either sleeve, and lavender kid gloves, and a diamond stuck in his shirt as big as the tip of your thumb? And behind him stood all his boys decked out in their own stars and ribbons and whatnot while along behind the President came a whole mob of carpetbaggers, whatever they might be, piling on board to raise an unholy row.

It was really a hell of a day to try to play ball, with the wind whipping the river to froth and the rain clouds scudding over like there was no end to them. When the Red Stockings filed off the ferry in Williamsburg and climbed into the big wagon the Mutuals had sent to fetch them, they were telling each other there would be no game at all. And the kranks must have felt the same way, for there were only two thousand of them gathered at the Union Grounds when the Red Stockings arrived, even though everyone in town had been saying this would be the greatest game ever played anyplace in God's world, with two unbeatable clubs facing each other for the championship of the nation. But when game-time arrived (God be praised), never a drop of rain fell on the field. By then the Irishmen had begun to arrive in droves—in carriages and carts, by ferrys or in skiffs, even in brewery carts with the seats fitted in them so they would hold a dozen men apiece. Most of them, it must be said, were men who, because they parted their hair right, had been given jobs by Boss Tweed himself, the old Americus fire laddie, who had found work for all of them—grubbers and shovelers and car men—to help dig the biggest hole in God's creation, right up in Central Park, to hold what was going to be a reservoir twice the size of the old one.

Of course, there was more than a game of base-ball for a man to cheer about in those days, for even though the news was going around that they did be arresting the poor Fenians by the dozen back in Ireland, Charles Parnell was rallying all the decent folk to the Home Rule Party and there was hope that all might live to see a free Ireland yet. And here at home, it seemed like the cannon still echoed as if they were just after celebrating with a boom! boom!—a hundred times, they said—to mark the hitching together of the two railroads last month so now a man could travel on the steam cars from one coast to the next. What with nearly a million new Irishmen having landed here in the year just gone, along with nearly as many Dutch, the city had spread itself so it was near a half day's walk from top to bottom. And they did say plans were afoot to build a new cathedral, bearing the name of the blessed Saint Patrick himself, far above the city at Fiftieth Street, eight blocks north of the Rutgers College for Women, with spires so high there'd be clouds around them. And at Thirty-fourth Street—would you believe it?—A. T. Stewart, the old moneybags, was building himself a regular palace, that looked as if it would outlast the whole city, so big and solid it was, made from blocks as big as brewery carts. And on Fifth Avenue and Fourteenth Street, what with all the swells parading there of a summer Sunday, the silk hats were gleaming so, they would near blind a man. Why, the way things were going the Brevoort Hotel would be far downtown in less time than it takes to tell. Delmonico's, too, what with all the new hotels, like royal palaces, going up around Madison Square Park. And where you used to be able to wander above the Forty-second Street reservoir and see nothing but the empty lots and the big black boulders all painted over in white letters to tell about Drake's Plantation Bitters or Old Doctor Townsend's Sarsaparilla or the Balm of a Thousand Flowers, whatever in the world that might be, there were now marble mansions a-building with stones brought clear from Ohio.

So the Red Stockings saw a brand-new city when they arrived, except for a few of them, like George Wright, who had been born right up there in the Harlem Flats, and who had played for the Unions of Morrisania for many a season, and Harry himself, who had played cricket around New York for twenty seasons, and Charles Sweazy, the Red Stockings' second baseman, long a standby for the base-ball club in Irvington, New Jersey.

But the Red Stockings had no time to see the sights this day.

Having just beat the Harvard College boys in Boston and missed a chance, because of rain, to do in the boys at Yale, they were a-thirsting for a go at the Mutuals, who were, to a New York Irishman's eyes, the best team that ever knocked daisies if you wanted the truth of it.

When the Red Stockings took the field, there were handshakes all around and both teams gathered to see the toss of the stone, the trick being then to spit on a stone and then call wet or dry at the toss. The Red Stockings won the toss and they chose last innings, which was the way the top ball-tossers did it now. The carriages were still pulling in beyond the outfield when the first striker, Charlie Mills, stout-hearted catcher for the Mutes, took up his bat. By this time the crowd had grown to more than seven thousand and that's not counting the hundred that had climbed on the rooftops to watch, or the kids who were crawling between men's legs to get near the play, or the dozens who had found peepholes in the fences. There was plenty of money showing now and the pool-sellers were having a time of it picking the bets up right and left. The odds were nearly even now: 100 to 75, with the Red Stockings favored, or even 100 to 80.

When Charlie Mills moved up to get his hit, the whole crowd, in the far outfield and up and down the baselines, seemed to yell with one throat: "A daisy-cutter, Charlie!" And Charlie struck with a will at the first ball pitcher Asa Brainard tossed him. The ball bounded down toward third baseman Fred Waterman, who plucked it neatly from the turf and delivered it quickly to lanky Charlie Gould at the first base, saving Mills the trouble of running all the way down there himself.

The game went on from inning to inning with the Mutes seeming to suffer a little from nerves when they were in the field and the Red Stockings unable to produce more than the single run they earned in the first inning, when young Dave Eggler, the eighteen-year-old infielder for the Mutes, let Doug Allison's easy ground ball get away. It might be said that it was an Irishman who was not there who really counted, for tricks cooked up by little Dickey Pearce, including the "fair-foul" hit, made, in a manner of speaking, all the difference. The clouds had come back and there were frequent spatterings of rain. But the crowd kept growing as word spread that the two greatest base-ball teams in the country were fighting it out, with the Mutes having gone *five* full innings without a single score! Five blinds in a row! That had never happened in history! Or had it? Certainly not in anyone's recollection. Most ball games then, even among the clubs that played for pay, ended with scores for both teams in double figures—sometimes in triple. Indeed, when the luckless Chicago team contrived to get through all nine innings without making a run, such a shutout for several years following was known as a "Chicago," thus immortalizing their shame.

But there was no shutout today. The Red Stockings had scored again on George Wright's hit, followed by a slashing daisy-cutter by Waterman that set young Eggler to hopping about once more. In the eighth inning McMahon of the Mutes broke the spell when he bounced a ball toward third base that struck fair ground and then rolled busily off in Dickey Pearce style among the scurrying legs and feet of the spectators who lined the third-base line. Waterman plunged after it and three or four other Red Stockings joined the search, but before they could corner the ball, there stood McMahon on the second base, laughing his head off. It took only one daisy-cutter then to fetch him across the home base, and start the crowd to screaming their joy, while the lady kranks, of whom there were more than one or two on hand, brightened the scene with fluttering white handkerchiefs from rooftop and window.

In the ninth inning, the Mutes set the kranks to screaming again when they tied the score and set their followers to counting up the cash they were going to carry home. There were still two men on base and no hands out when young Eggler, bent on redeeming himself, walked jauntily up with his long bat on his shoulder. Now the entire assembly seemed to hold its breath. Even the whiskey-sellers hugged their baskets tight and ceased to cry their wares. It was a sure thing now that at least *one* Mute would score his run and secure the glory.

But Dickey Pearce's shade was playing no favorites. When young Eggler, swinging full force, could do no more than lift a fly ball toward Waterman, the company of kranks moaned—and prayed a little, too, that Waterman, who had done plenty of damage already, this time might, just *might*, be unable to grab the ball tight. Then there would be only one hand out and some good strikers to come. And then glory be: Waterman, having taken the ball in both hands for a full second, while the runners all held tight to their bases, let the thing *drop!* The crowd screamed. The runners all set out for the next base. But Waterman coolly, in the manner invented by that devilish Dickey Pearce, just scooped the ball off the ground, stepped on third base to capture one runner, and snapped the ball swiftly to the second base to capture another there. *Two* hands out! That was Pearce's "trapped ball" trick that was to bedevil rule-makers for decades before they invented the "infield fly" rule. But to the current spectators, it was a damned bit of trickery! It was illegal!

Some of the baseline kranks hastened to appeal to umpire Charlie Walker, but he gave them no comfort. The runners were *out.* Rinie Wolters was next to bat for the Mutes and he did not swing his bat. After a warning to pitcher Asa Brainard, the umpire awarded Wolters his base on three wides. But that offered little sustenance. What was needed was another daisy-cutter. Just one sharp whack to bring Eggler in. McMahon was next and he seemed bent on waiting for wides. But when he did see a toss he wanted to strike at, the best he could do was raise a short foul to Allison, who easily tucked it away.

Well, there would be another inning. And the way we were knocking those daisies last inning, it was sure . . .

But the Red Stockings rallied as if they meant to end it there and then. Andy Leonard earned his first base with a sharp knock that eluded everyone. But once on base, he was seized by impatience, took far too much ground, and a quick throw by Wolters trapped him on the baselines. The entire Mute team yowled in delight as poor Andy dodged and twisted to avoid being tagged. The Mutes tossed the ball back and forth until it seemed as if every man on the club had handled it. Finally, big Ed Mills chased Andy clear off the baseline and the umpire called him out. Andy walked back to the sidelines with his head down, while his mates growled in disgust. That one run would have been all they needed to take home the win.

But the Mutes still seemed overcome by nervousness. When the next striker, pitcher Asa Brainard, rolled an easy ground ball right into Swandell, the Mutes' second baseman, Swandell, after plucking the ball easily off the turf, threw it high over first baseman Ed Mills's head, and Asa Brainard, whiskers flying, made it all the way to the third base before the ball could be captured. On the very next toss, the catcher, Charlie Mills, who had already let five of Wolters's pitches get by him, missed still another and Brainard trotted in for an easy score. By modern rules, that run would have ended the game, but in 1869 the game was played until all hands were out. So Sweazy got his turn at bat and made the most of it by driving the ball so nearly out of sight that he was standing on the third base before the ball was thrown in. Wolters thereupon tossed his next pitch far over poor Charlie Mills's head so that Mills never put a finger on it. And Sweazy came home to make the score 4–2. And that is how it ended.

It was a dismal defeat for the great Mutuals, who had been rated by many in the know the best team ever put together. But there was *some* glory in it after all. Not a single fly catch missed. Not one! Not even that skyscraper hit by Harry Wright that nobody on the field thought Dick Hunt could hold onto. But hold it he did! Perhaps the greatest catch ever made on the Union Grounds, or any grounds! And what in God's name was that kid Eggler doing at shortstop? He was an outfielder! But you had to hand it to the Red Stockings, too. That Allison, who played "behind," had not dropped a tick or a toss. And no other Red Stocking had dropped a catch—except that scoundrel Waterman, who dropped the ball a-purpose. And if the umpire had called it right . . . ! Well, it had been a great game. Perhaps the greatest ever played—when the two best teams in the land had played nine innings with but six runs between them. Why, they'd be talking about this game for another fifty years! And if it hadn't been for Eggler . . . !

A writer for the *New York Sun* could not let Eggler rest. He suggested the Mutes might send down to Tennessee for old Andy Johnson, the former President. He, after all, was a member of Boss Tweed's Mutuals, too. And he couldn't have done worse than Eggler!

But this, strangely enough, was the beginning of the end of the Red Stockings' glory. Next season they actually *lost* a game. And of course when they lost a game, they were no longer champions. The very folk who had danced about in delight in front of the Gibson Hotel in Cincinnati when the news of the victory over the Mutuals arrived were the first to spurn the Red Stockings when they lost to the Brooklyn Atlantics—and when the local kranks dropped a hefty bundle in wagers. So just a season later the cast-off Red Stockings crept into Boston, seeking a new home and loving parents.

●

Boston, as few recall, was the center of great doings when the Civil War was over. Its capital had financed the opening of the West, with Boston money breathing life into the Atchison, To-peka, and Santa Fe Railway, and the Chicago, Burlington, and Quincy as well. Boston money set to working the picks and shovels that bored a tunnel through the Berkshire Hills at Hoosac to speed commerce with the grain farmers of the West and to ease the shipment of Boston's shoes and garments and fish and dry goods back. The city itself had doubled in size when it filled up the noisome Back Bay with ashes and rubbish from the far-off suburbs to make more room to build houses on. Newfangled steam shovels loaded crushed oyster shells, discarded wine bottles, and skeletons of hoopskirts into cars to be toted ten miles to create a wide empty space that for a while served no better purpose than for kids to play ball.

It was natural, then, that when the Red Stockings wore out their welcome in Porkopolis (Cincinnati's nickname), they sought support in Boston, where the local base-ball fancy had already turned away from the crudities of the Massachusetts game. These were not the complete Red Stockings by any means, but they had brought the best of the lot along, including doughty Al Spalding from the Forest City club of Rockford, Illinois, the team of "country boys" that had "spoiled the whole trip" for the traveling Nationals club from Washington, D.C. Colonel Frank Jones of the War Department, who had recruited the Nationals (and got them government jobs to keep them close), went into a sulk after that defeat, particularly when he heard the dark suggestions that the Nationals had thrown the game to improve the betting odds for when they moved on to meet Chicago's "big team," the Excelsiors, self-acknowledged "Champions of the West."

Spalding himself, his fame now secure after beating the fearsome Nationals by the score of 29–23, joined the fugitive Red Stockings when they came to Boston, and proudly identified himself to the census taker as "ball player." (He had been a make-believe grocery clerk before that, drawing a salary about ten times what other members of that profession took home.) Harry Wright, the great cricket player who had formed the Red Stocking team (named for the stockings a lady named Margaret Truman knitted for them), was a little uneasy about how the Boston blue bloods would take to a man who got paid for playing a little boys' game, and so he gave his own profession as "jeweler." Harry's kid brother, George, who had also been a professional cricket player with the St. George Club in Hoboken, New Jersey, came along to Boston, too, and allowed he was a ball player, sure enough. But he very soon set himself up in a shop on Eliot Street, where he sold "cigars and baseballs" to any in need of such items. (A half century later a lad named George Herman Ruth, who played for the team that had named itself "Red Sox" to revive the memory of the club that had gone before, also went into the cigar business, or at least allowed a cigar maker, for a share of the take, to name a cigar after him and feature his wide, happy countenance on the band.)

Cal McVey, the mightly slugger who had played right field for

Cincinnati, was another of the original Red Stockings to come to Boston. And Al Spalding persuaded his Forest City teammate Roscoe (Ross) Barnes to join them. Roscoe was a master of the "fair-foul" hit, the device that brought infielders to drink or to using, in public, language unsuitable to Boston. (Soon after, they changed the rules to judge a ball foul if it went foul before the bases, and poor old Ross was sent to the clubhouse to stay.)

Boston's first baseball park, where the newcomer Red Stockings (soon called simply the Reds) took up summer tenancy, lay in the salubrious stretches of the South End where Walpole Street met the tracks of the Boston and Providence Railroad, on a wide lot belonging to the Hammet family, not far from the Reformatory for Penitent Females and the Home for Aged Men. The Chickering Piano factory, the largest in the nation, stood hard by, too, but most of the rest of the area was given over to green trees, wide lawns, and comfortable homes for the rich. And there was a horse railroad handy to bring in kranks from Roxbury and the lace-curtain flats of South Boston, where the Irish, of all people (they were known to the swells as Hibernians and were generally to be shunned), had begun to filter in.

Irishmen by the drayload would soon begin to elbow their way into the blessed game—they having been trying at it on the dumps and back lots of many a city since shortly after the gentlemen's clubs sought stronger arms and swifter feet among the "greasy mechanics" of the day. Before that the teams had been peopled largely by men of British and Dutch ancestry, bearing names like Brainard, Waterman, Zettlein, Pabor, Polhemus, Laggett, Creighton, Kissam, Holden, Ketchum, Shelly, and Jones.

By the time the Boston Reds played the New York club, in 1874, they had on their side, playing at the first base, none other than Orator Jim O'Rourke, an Irishman from Connecticut, who some did say was the greatest in the world at taking a fly ball in one hand and, for that matter, the owner of the slickest tongue in the parish, a man who could talk the ears off a donkey.

The game itself was not really much of a contest by later

standards, although by this time base-ball had been sharpened a bit by making the "fly game" the rule, so that a fly ball had to be taken before it bounced if you were going to put the hitter out. (*Foul* flies taken on the first bounce still counted as an out.) And there were only nine men on a side these days, the ten-man dodge that lasted only a few months in 1874 having been done away with, in the National Association of Professional Base-ball Players at any rate. And only two thousand kranks showed up, no more than half what was needed to fill the small grand-stand, the weather being so cool and all. It was a tight game for those days, when two dozen runs in a game was not anything to run home and tell the folks about. The Reds beat New York twelve runs to four. Next day, the weather not having eased up a particle, there were no more than twelve hundred paying cus-tomers to watch. This time the Reds won 11–4.

And so it went, with the Reds beating all comers. Even when the great Hartford Dark Blues came to the South End to play, before the biggest crowd of the season—too many indeed for the dinky grandstand—only four thousand paid to watch. Why, there were more on hand when John G. Gough came to South Boston under the banner of the Women's Christian Temperance Union to enlighten the multitude on the dread effects of whiskey on kidneys and character. And a good prize fight would have pulled in double that number.

The fact is that baseball in the 1870s was still a game to *play*, as softball is today. And there was little enough about the game then to cause the blood to bubble. When the great "Lords" of Baltimore came to Boston to meet the Reds, they carried a catcher who could not throw to second base on the fly. And in the game with Hartford, the deed that sent hats wheeling into the air, to mingle with the howls of amazement and delight, was the "double catch" of a fly ball by George Wright, who had hustled in to home plate to stand beside catcher Cal McVey and made a one-hand catch of a soft fly that bounced off poor Cal's hands.

Baseball equipment had still not developed from its elemental form, when a bat and ball provided all a boy needed to get a game started. The bat was still a long, relatively thin stick. The ball, made largely of India rubber wound with yarn, could sail over a man's head on the first bounce. The only gloves in use would be worn by the catcher (who had originally played well behind the batter to take most pitches on the bounce) and then only when catchers began to move "up close." And pitchers, no longer required simply to serve the ball to the batter, as was done in rounders, were seeking new devices to keep the batter from hitting the ball at all. To take some of the sting out of the pitch, the catcher now was permitted to wear, without shame, thin gloves, like dress gloves with the fingers cut off. The rules by which the game was played outside the association were changed from season to season—and from game to game, when two teams met that had been playing by different rules.

The trouble was that the New York Game, from the start, had few written rules. It was simply agreed, without discussion, that gentlemen would not resort to tricks, evasions, or deceit. It was decidedly improper, in the early days, for the pitcher to try to keep the batter from hitting the ball, as it was ungentlemanly for the striker just to hold his place without even offering a swing. But once the game spread as it did among the less proper folk, it was the pitcher who first resorted to dark ways to undo the striker. First he began to toss the ball far to the side so the poor striker would be able to do no more than scratch it with the end of his bat. This wickedness was temporarily discouraged by allowing the umpire to call "wides" and to allow the batter, after a certain number of such indecencies, to take the first base free and be awarded a "hit" in the score book. (In the beginning it took three "wides" to give the striker a free walk.)

It soon became clear that the batter, too, could employ improper tactics, and the umpire was then empowered to deal with such unregenerate folk by calling "good pitch" when the batter ignored one too many deliveries. If the batter then continued to let good ones go by, he could, after what seemed to the umpire undue delay, be called "out."

Of course, by the time Harry Wright brought his professional club to Boston and the game was organized, albeit loosely, in the National Association of Professional Base-ball Players, it had come a long way from Knickerbocker days. Now it was standard practice for pitchers to try to deceive the batter and for the batters to do their best to bedevil the fielders. The game had nine innings now, when at its beginning it was played only until one or the other of the teams had scored twenty-one "aces," or runs. Generally, the batter was called out after three "strikes" were called, although for one season (1887) the authorities allowed him four.

All the same, on the vacant lots and beaches of Boston, on the West Side dumps of New York City, and wherever there was room in the vacant spaces along Grand Avenue in St. Louis, the rowdier and less restricted forms of the game persisted. I well remember the sting of a thrown tennis ball against bare skin on a beach near Boston when it was used to punch me out in a game of elemental "baseball" that was played there every summer day. And Rube Waddell, who became the best pitcher in the new American League after the twentieth century began, had a few years earlier delivered one of his fierce fastballs to a wandering base runner, hit him square in the anatomy, and sent him screaming to the ground. When the whole ballpark, including Rube's own teammates, rose up to shout their dismay, Rube simply explained, "That's *out* where I come from." And so it was still, in many a backwater baseball field.

Boston, no backwater, nor any breeding ground for rowdyism, still harbored, in its Irish ghetto, a certain hankering for physical excitement—especially among the undisciplined young males who sought most of their fun in the streets. Before the Red Stockings arrived, the only real "hero" the local Irish knew was a plug-ugly, Dick O'Brien by name, who was better known to his neighbors as the Irish Pet. He burnished his reputation by swaggering through the North End whenever he had a drop taken and belting out any dude or country jay who dared to try to share the public way. So the decent folk of the parish took deep comfort in the arrival of Jim O'Rourke, outfielder and first baseman, known as the Orator because he had such a lovely way with words and such a wondrous supply of them. For Jim was no plug-ugly, nor any country jay, although he did, it was true, come straight off a Connecticut farm. Jim was a sort of wonder in other ways than playing ball, for he was a truly learned man in that day when most professional ball players were unschooled in the commonest graces. Fred Dunlap, for instance, the "Sure Shot" second baseman who played in that day for Cleveland and St. Louis, could neither read nor write. But Jim could not only read and write fit for royalty, he could figure too and could talk finance with the best of them. Besides being a mighty hitter, Jim was a fine figure of a man who, with his tightly curled bank of black hair and his ten-dollar mustache, would stop in her tracks, at least momentarily, almost any colleen who chanced to spot him as he idled through the lobby of the Commonwealth Hotel, a swell among swells.

Jim's boss with the Boston Reds was one Arthur Soden, about as tightfisted a Yankee as ever squeezed the dust out of a dime. But he was no match for Jim when it came to arguing rights and wrongs.

Even by latter-day standards, Soden, who took charge of the Reds in return for an investment of forty-five dollars, was one of the all-pro tightwads of baseball history. He lived in a fine suburban home and owned pieces of several banks and half a dozen railroads, and had made a fortune in the roofing business. Yet, while he was running his stake in the Reds into many thousands, he still carried his lunch to work in a paper bag, and often stood outside the ballpark and sold tickets from his own pocket, while one of his players turned the stile. He kept baseballs in play until they began to burst at the seams, and when fly balls fell in the stands they were quickly recovered, even if they had to be pried out of a spectator's hands.

Soden's free list could have been written on the back of a grandstand ticket. His partners, James Billings, a shoe manufacturer, and William Conant, who grew rich from making hoopskirts, could come into a game without paying; they could bring their wives in free as well. But no one else. There was usually one sentinel, perhaps a spare ball player, stationed outside the fence to fight off kids who might try to capture a ball that dropped out there, or there would be at least some man charged with providing the description of whatever scoundrel tried to hide a baseball in his pocket and escape with it. An umpire who chanced to pocket a spare ball would be forced to disgorge it before he left the park.

Jim O'Rourke was no man to suffer more than briefly this sort of bush league penny-pinching. He was damned if, after being required to pay out twenty dollars for his uniform, he would still have to cough up fifty cents a day for meal money while he was on the road. (Soden's players, it was said, counted themselves ahead of the game if the boss didn't soak them half a dollar for taking time off to eat a sandwich.) So at the start of the 1879 season, Jim said yes to an offer from the Providence club. Arthur Soden, however, allowed that, by God, he would have the law on Jim to keep him in Boston. A group of fans hastily joined together to match the Providence offer. But Jim would have none of it. He had given his word to Providence and he would not go back on it. And as for Soden's imaginary "contract," tightfisted Art could go whistle for it. So O'Rourke went on then to put in one season with merry George Wright, Harry's brother, who had fled Soden's clutches the season before to manage the Providence club.

Soden had tried to strong-arm another outfielder and came in second that time as well. The outfielder, who went by the name of Charlie Jones (although his square moniker was Rippay), had been insolent enough one day to ask Soden for the money owed him. Common ball players weren't *supposed* to brace the boss in that manner. (Soden had previously fined a player who failed to doff his hat on meeting Soden on the street.) So Jones got a short answer:

"I owe you nothing!"

"By God, you do," said Jones. "You owe me a month's wages."

"You'll get nothing until I'm ready!"

"Then I won't play ball until I'm paid."

"You won't play ball because you're suspended and you're fined a hundred dollars!"

Soden then stalked away, leaving Jones penniless in Cleveland.

But Jones had a friend or two there who managed to stake him to the fare to his mountain home. And when Soden, back in Boston, discovered himself short a player who could tell right field from left, he wrote Jones and asked him how much Jones *thought* was owing.

Mischances of this sort prompted Soden to cook up a scheme to gain a tighter hold on key players, so he put a clause in his contracts with four of his mightiest lads that held them bound to the Reds for life—or at least until they were traded. And this device, adopted a few years later by all clubs in the organized game and applied to all players, became the notorious "reserve rule" about which Commissioner Landis, decades further along, warned the club owners, "Someday it will ruin you."

It never did. But Al Spalding, boss now of the Chicago White Stockings and spokesman for the league club owners, came up with a new idea, to tighten the reserve rule further by a $2,000 salary limit. Whereupon Monte Ward, representing the Brotherhood of Professional Baseball Players, asked for a chance to discuss this matter. Spalding then was involved in plans for a world tour with a team of selected players (including Ward) and he put Ward off by agreeing to consider canceling the salary limitation and then talk over the whole business when they came home.

When the tour was completed, the owners refused even to meet with Ward. They did, as Spalding had implied, repeal the salary limitation. But they came up with an even more offensive plan—a classification rule that would limit salaries all up and down the line, so that players on the weaker clubs would have no chance whatever of earning a better wage. As for meeting with any common ball players, those half-educated and impecunious characters who were given to drinking in low places and talking like farmers or (God forbid) like ditchdiggers, and actually *negotiating* with such subhumans, why the thought simply turned their stomachs.

The Brotherhood's response to this neat double cross struck the owners where it really hurt, for Ward and his followers set to work at once to build a new league that would put the old league out of business. In the fall of 1889, they announced the formation of the Players' League, in which the players, like stock-holders, would share directly in the take. Wealthy sponsors had been found for clubs in every major city. Nearly every player of any standing had signed with the new league and agreed to walk away from their old bosses in the spring.

They did, too, but alas, although the existence of the new league—which actually outdrew the National League in most cities—for a while seemed secure, its major backers were soon lured away by slick-tongued promises from Spalding and associates, promises that were never kept.

One after another, the sponsors of the Players' League surrendered, leaving Spalding and his cohorts in clear command of the field, with the classification rule still in place and many of the humiliated players hastening hat in hand to learn if there was still room on the payroll.

As in later rebellions, the best known and most widely loved ball players had stuck with their teammates. Mike "King" Kelly, perhaps the most famous of all, and a notorious soft touch and spendthrift, was offered a $10,000 check, made out in his name and put right into his hand, if he would sign a new contract, at a salary to be named by himself. Mike stared at the lovely check for several minutes, then placed it on the desk.

"I have to take a walk!" he declared and abruptly left Al Spalding's office. He returned in about twenty minutes to blurt, "I can't go back on the boys!"

Charles Comiskey, field manager for Spalding's White Sox, used exactly the same phrase in refusing to sign a new contract.

The sportswriters, however, or most of them, quickly lined up with the club owners, the notable exceptions being Tim Murnane of the *Boston Globe*, who had ingested a bellyful of Soden's parsimony when he played for the Boston Reds, and Jacob Morse, of *Baseball Magazine*, who always liked ball players better than magnates anyway. The big name among the writers, Oliver Hazard Perry Caylor of Cincinnati, greeted the formation of the Brotherhood by declaring that its creators were "a few porcine professionals who in their selfishness and love of gold tried to destroy the reserve rule."

"It is wonderful," Caylor went on, "that these poor oppressed souls could not arrange a procession under a red flag and go through the streets shouting 'Bread or Blood!' It is noteworthy that the men who kicked the most against the reserve rule are men from the slums, who were street loafers and idlers before playing ball; the men whose ignorance and loaferism made them a burden on the community and who would fall to the same level if baseball were wiped out tomorrow."

Other writers from different cities hastened to align themselves with the club owners, whom they deemed among the world's "better people," like their blessed selves. Some sample contributions:

"Not one ball player out of ten is to be trusted to keep his word, or even his bond if there is any pecuniary temptation."

"A more ungrateful set of people than the majority of professional ball players would be hard to find."

"Low drunken knaves have too long been allowed to hold positions on professional baseball teams."

(Among those loafers and idlers were not only their leader, John Montgomery Ward, who became a successful lawyer in New York and eventually bought control of the Boston baseball club, but also John K. Tener, who became governor of Pennsylvania, and Charles Comiskey and Connie Mack, who both became club owners in the American League.)

The only truly famous ball player who refused to join the Brotherhood was Adrian "Cap" Anson of Chicago and he declared, when the struggle was over, that the Brotherhood leaders "were never so crooked or deceitful as the owners were."

Despite the defeat of the Brotherhood, the battle did bring a few rewards, because club owners thereafter, when salary negotiations with the star players seemed to promise trouble, often proved willing to engage in under-the-table deals to bypass the classification rule.

What private deal kept Anson in the National League is not recorded. But Anson always put his private concerns up front. He seemed to be devoted, above all else in the world, not just to his own well-being but to his image, his physical prowess, his dominance, and his "honor," which to him meant recognition of his superiority over all other breeds.

Good manners on the ball field, however, were no concern of his. Indeed, Anson may well have been the one who turned professional baseball finally from a gentlemanly contest to a competition almost as fierce as business itself. Cap was a notorious "coacher," a dirty name then, applied to one who used loud and abusive language on the sidelines, comporting himself like the lowlifes who peopled the "coaches" (backless benches that ultimately became the bleachers). He applied his sandpaper tongue not only to the opponents but to his own teammates when they failed to perform to his standards. And if the fans dared taunt him, he would outbellow the bunch of them, detailing their doubtful ancestry, their personal failings, and their revolting facial irregularities. Umpires, of course, were regular targets of Cap's verbal abuse and more than one or two of them had been known to shade their decisions just a little in Cap's favor when they felt his hot breath on their necks.

But Cap was not really an angry man. His use of derision and name-calling was simply another weapon in his fierce struggle to come in first. He was as hard on himself as he was on his mates, avoiding hard drink, late hours, rich foods, and strange (or even marital) beds. He prided himself on his great physical strength, his moral purity, and his honest dealing. As the catchphrase of the day had it, he wore no man's collar. He even chased the Chicago club owner, Al Spalding himself, back to the owner's box ("Where you belong!") when stout Al undertook to join him in an argument with an umpire.

But it was the part of a real he-man in that day to flaunt his "manly" prejudice against all lesser breeds, and Anson played this role with relish. He once joined with two forgotten clowns to prance through a vaudeville turn wearing green whiskers and singing (or yelling) a song called "We're Three Chubelin [Shoveling] Tipperary Turks." The Irish in that day were accepted as comic targets, as were the Jews and especially the blacks, who stood on the very lowest rung of the ladder. Still, there were not too many folk in organized baseball who made a show of their bigotry. Anson was proud of his. There were in the 1880s about twenty black players in organized baseball, including Moses Fleetwood Walker, Oberlin College star who played with Toledo of the Northwestern League and later in the American Association—a major league then—and in the Western League. Walker entered professional baseball with his scholarly brother, Welday Wilberforce Walker, who had starred with him at Oberlin. Then there were Bud Fowler, who played second base with Keokuk and Binghamton; Frank Grant, Buffalo second baseman; Charles Kelly, first baseman in Danville, Illinois; and George Stovey of Newark, who still holds the Newark record of thirty-five victories in one season. Fleet Walker also played for Newark while Stovey was pitching there.

Anson and the Walker brothers had first met in Toledo in 1882 when Anson, spotting improper skin hues on the diamond, demanded that "that nigger" be removed, else he would take his club from Toldedo forthwith. The Toledo management invited him to go ahead and assured him he would also forfeit his guarantee. Anson backed down then, but five years later he brought his club to Newark for an exhibition game and saw their star pitcher, George Stovey, warming up. Again bold Adrian insisted that the field be purified by banishing the black man. And this time, too, the Newark club urged Anson to pack up and go. But Stovey, allowing that it was against *his* principles to play ball with a bigot, walked off and let the game proceed.

Soon afterward, John Montgomery Ward, captain (i.e., manager) of the Gotham Giants, completed a deal that would have brought Stovey to New York. This time, Anson, roaring his indignation throughout the league, found among the club owners allies enough who sported minds as narrow as his own, and the "unwritten rule" was established that kept black players out of the major leagues for almost sixty years.

Of course, among the "better people" of that day, there was

firm prejudice against Irish and Jews as well. Employers often made it clear that "no Irish need apply" and Jews were systematically excluded from clubs, college fraternities, and camps for boys and girls, as well as summer hotels throughout the land. But even Irish and Jews, particularly those who, in the New England phrase, "had an easy of making a living" often saw fit to adopt the bigotry of their self-styled "betters" toward black people. But Jews and Irish at least were white and so did not too vividly flaunt their difference. So, while there had been some resistance in the early years, Irishmen like O'Rourke, and Kelly, and Nolan, and McGillicuddy, and Comiskey, and Sullivan did finally find welcome in organized baseball. And Jews like Lip Pike (supposed to have been the first Jew to join a major league team) and Sammy Strang (his original name was Nicklin) were accepted as if they were practically human.

Of course, bigotry of every sort had long been a pet indulgence of the "better people" in this blessed land, and was still thriving late in the next century. A strong anti-Catholic cabal, as noted earlier, festered among the Boston National League players and was one reason the arrival of the American League team in Boston quickly won the devotion of the Boston Irish, who, led by Boston saloon owner "Nuf Ced" McGreevey, provided an organized cheering platoon, named the Royal Rooters, who eventually laid claim to a special section at the park.

In my own school days, Roman Catholics were carefully excluded from all college fraternities (except their own) and treated with marked suspicion even at summer hotels—many of which incidentally, even openly, without a blush, advertised that they catered to a "strictly Christian clientele." Whether Christ himself could have been cradled in one of their outbuildings was never revealed.

But, of course, blacks were different. *Everyone* knew they didn't belong. In fairly recent times when I made so bold as to suggest to a baseball executive that he might do well to add a certain black veteran to his broadcast crew, he exclaimed, "We can't have them *everywhere!*" (What will happen, I ask myself, when "them" becomes "us"?)

Chapter 4

THE GREATEST FELLER IN BASEBALL

1. "*The Greatest Feller in Baseball*" (self-acknowledged) never really knew how the game was played and in the beginning had to ask, after his team had completed a game, how it came out. Eventually he did learn to keep track of runs and he stopped urging his players to "hit all balls to right field." Still, everyone who dealt with him would quickly agree that, even if he was not the greatest "feller" in the game, he was surely one of the greatest club owners. No one begrudged him the statue of himself he had made to be placed, when the time came, on his grave in Bellefontaine Cemetery in St. Louis. And just about everyone agreed that there was no more openhanded, better-natured, or soft-hearted boss in organized baseball.

His name was Chris von der Ahe (pronounced, usually at the top of his lungs, "Aw!") and the baseball club he owned was named the St. Louis Browns. Alfred Spink, cofounder with his brother of the *Sporting News*, helped put the club together and Chris, owner of a prospering grocery store, put up the money, even though he did not know much more about the game than what it was called. He did know, however, that it drew large crowds of thirsty men who bought gallons of beer peddled by Chris's aproned vendors who marched through the stands with bouquets of flowing steins crying, "Give your orders, gents!"

Actually, Chris breathed life not only into the Browns of St. Louis but into the entire American Association, the brand-new league created in 1882 to rival the National League. And Chris, whose grocery business had grown from a corner store at Sullivan and Spring avenues to a resplendent market on Grand Avenue, sat among the rejoicing fans when, in the new league's first game, the Browns beat the Cincinnati Reds, a team created by Oliver Hazard Perry Caylor, the most famous sportswriter in Ohio. Chris rejoiced in the size of the crowd, in the amount of beer that was consumed, and in the fact that all the fans were happy. "What a big, fine crowd!" he cried to Al Spink. "But the game, Al? How was it? Was it a pretty good game?" And Al assured him that it had indeed been a pretty good game, particularly in the outcome.

The Browns were originally a "cooperative" club, like all the "semipro" clubs of a later day, that divided up the gate in shares, 60 percent split equally among the players and 40 percent going to "management," who paid all the expenses. Within a very few seasons the Browns were tightly organized, well coached, and profitable, so that with the take from his beer sales, the baseball income made von der Ahe rich. He did drop some large sums at the racetrack but hardly noticed the loss.

Chris lived the life of a millionaire—or at least the life he believed a millionaire ought to live, spending money as if it came out of a spout and sharing his wealth with everyone he took a liking to. At first the Browns, before the league was formed, took their foes where they found them—usually Chicago, from among a number of "prairie" teams, so called because they played all their games in the wide open areas outside the city. But these clubs were always put together helter-skelter, with no inducement other than a few trips to far-off places to beat down some city club. A player on such a team who was left off the lineup in one game might not bother to show up for the next one, or a pitcher might be lured away by the offer of some hard cash. One team came to St. Louis to play the Browns one day and had to report that they had neither pitcher nor catcher, whereupon Al Spink rounded up an unemployed battery and made the visiting team whole. The Browns still beat them. And the visiting team, which called itself the Chicago Eckfords, was voted by the local kranks the best team that had ever tried to beat the Browns. And the sixteen-year-old kid Al Spink had found playing catch on a vacant lot in North St. Louis and allowed to play for the Eckfords became a catcher in the America Association for seven seasons, known for all his career as Kid Baldwin.

St. Louis, from the time of the Civil War, was alive with able ball players, for the game had been played all over town since just before the war, when Jerry Fruin came from the East to scratch out baselines in a vacant lot that eventually became LaFayette Park. Jerry taught the local kids the "eastern trick" of letting the hands give with the power of a throw so as to keep the ball from bouncing away. And he took the bruises out of the old-time game as Alexander Cartwright had by eliminating the "corking" or "soaking" of the hapless base runner.

A number of amateur baseball teams had then taken root in St. Louis, and many a great name had flowered there. Once the city had grown out of its origins as a fur-trading post and a way station for the cattle trade, it built its own stockyards across the river from the town and seemed to grow a new building every day—despite the fact that the famous 195-foot Elm Street shot tower had collapsed into a heap of rubble two hours after some nameless genius and his associated architects and engineers had declared it perfectly sound, good for years. (A shot tower was used to make lead musket shot by dripping molten lead from the top of the tower so it would congeal into solid balls on the way down.)

The Civil War had not harmed St. Louis, although the citizens were sharply divided over slavery. The German contingent was all for freedom, even rebelling against the very idea of spoiling a Sunday by moping in a church. And while there were occasional rumors of a rebel gunboat in the offing, causing local Confederates to rejoice, none ever appeared and the city grew in peace—and apace. The miraculous Eads Bridge brought six railroads to town,

and even before Chris von der Ahe arrived there was good baseball played on every lot.

Among the great players who brightened the summer afternoons for the kranks of St. Louis in the early days were Dickey
Pearce, still (in the 1870s) acknowledged the best short fielder
alive; Lip Pike, a sure-handed fielder who had learned his trade
on the Capitoline Grounds in Brooklyn; Eddie Cuthbert, the
sliding man who still made kranks yell when he rode into a base
on the seat of his pants; and, when the "Only" Indianapolis team
came to town, there were Ed "The Only" Nolan, who one season
pitched thirty shutouts (and who had been the great Mike Kelly's
battery mate when they were teenagers in New Jersey), plus Silver
"The Only" Flint, the only man indeed who dared catch Nolan's
fearsome speed—bare-handed.

What St. Louis did seem short of until von der Ahe and the
Spinks appeared were kranks willing to pay enough for seats to
even buy streetcar tickets for the players, although the "Mound
City" (from which the mound had long since disappeared) *had*
been the scene of "the greatest baseball game every played" when
the St. Louis pros had played the Stars of Syracuse, New York,
for fifteen innings without a single run scored.

But the greatest independent club that Spink ever brought to
St. Louis to meet von der Ahe's darlings was a team put together
by Ted Sullivan, an Irishman from County Clare. This team,
named the Dubuque Rabbits, had played itself right out of its
own league by trimming every club in Dubuque and thereabouts
so badly that they all went back to hauling hay, or whatever they
had been up to before the baseball bug infected them.

Star of this team was a bricklayer's son from Chicago, by the
name of Charles Comiskey, who was center fielder, third baseman, first baseman, and occasional pitcher. A college teammate
of Ted Sullivan's, Comiskey, in the off-season, peddled candy
and magazines for Sullivan's news agency. His salary was $50 a
month, in that era when "a dollar a day was very good pay."
Sullivan's club was no match for von der Ahe's, but Spink decided
that he had to have Comiskey on his side, so he wrote to Com-

iskey after the game and suggested he apply to von der Ahe for a job with the Browns. "Put your price as low as possible," he wrote, for the Browns now had graduated from divvying up the gate receipts and were paying steady wages. Comiskey, having just married a young lady from Dubuque, steeled himself to ask for $90. Von der Ahe, who believed that even a ball player was worthy of his hire, agreed at once (because Spink urged him to) and Commy came to help turn the Browns into champions. After one month Vondy raised Comiskey's pay to $150. They came home first in their first season and promptly issued a challenge to the Chicago White Stockings, now managed by Al Spalding, who had taken the championship of the National League. The purse for such a series was $1,000, donated by the *Mirror of American Sports*. Spalding quickly accepted and the series was played in Pittsburgh and Cincinnati, as well as in St. Louis and Chicago, on the theory that everyone in the nation would naturally wish to be on hand when the "Championship of the World" was at issue. Alas, the crowds outside St. Louis and Chicago were meager indeed and the "World Series" was completed in the cities most concerned.

Still, those who did attend the games saw a new style of baseball, invented and practiced by the man from Dubuque, Charles Comiskey, who would one day become Mr. Baseball in Chicago, where he was born. For Comiskey was the man who set the infielders free, who taught the pitcher to cover first base to allow the first baseman to leave his post and capture a grounder. In early baseball the baseman used to keep one foot on the base, or close behind it, guarding it against capture by a foeman. And first basemen generally were stout fellows, not given to sprinting into the outfield to grab a short fly, or to scuttling out on the baseline to intercept a daisy-cutter. A few of them indeed had little taste for bending over.

The series left neither Spalding nor von der Ahe completely happy, for it was declared a tie after Comiskey pulled his Browns off the field in Chicago because the hometown umpire refused to alter a decision that Commy found improper.

"Comiskey," Spalding declared, "is a quitter! I'll have no more to do with him!"

So when von der Ahe, in 1886, with both teams once more having finished first in their leagues, challenged Spalding to another go, the great man angrily spurned the bid. And when von der Ahe, his jolly nature not one whit embarrassed, persisted in pressing the challenge, Spalding thought to put an end to the business by offering to play a home-and-home series, with the winner to pick up *all* the marbles. (He did not realize he was dealing with a man who would bet his only clean shirt on a horse race.) "Sure thing!" von der Ahe replied and the series was quickly scheduled for Chicago and St. Louis.

Involved in the deciding game, played in St. Louis, were a number of players whose names would echo down the years (and finally be forgotten). Playing for Chicago was probably the greatest ball player alive, named the King by sportswriters and fans, as well as the players—the Babe Ruth of his time, whose name was shouted or sung for two or three generations until hardly anyone could recall who he really had been. This was Mike Kelly, the man who loved to slide and who did it better than anyone else of his time. "Slide, Kelly! Slide!" some songster wrote. "Slide, Kelly! On your belly! Slide, Kelly! Slide!" And fifty years later, small boys would holler to each other, "Slide, Kelly!" without owning the smallest notion of just which Kelly they were invoking.

Kelly was the catcher for the Chicago club that day—one of the several positions he could handle with consummate skill. At first base stood (he seldom moved from his position) the mighty Cap Anson, no longer called the Marshalltown Infant, as he had been when he first came East from Marshalltown, Iowa, where his father and a bushel of other Ansons all played together on the local baseball team.

At third base for the Browns was the tiniest man on the field, if not the tiniest in all organized baseball—Walter Arlington Latham, from Lynn, Massachusetts, called Arlie and acknowledged everywhere as The Freshest Man on Earth, a title awarded him by an anonymous songwriter who wrote a jingle for Arlie to sing in a show called *Fashion*. (Arlie had to pass up a round-the-world trip with Spalding and a squad of ball players to appear in this show.) He sang:

> *I'm a daisy on the diamond;*
> *I'm a dandy on the stage.*
> *I'd ornament a horsecart*
> *Or look pretty in a cage. . . .*
> *I'm a Hustler from Hustletown,*
> *The Freshest Man on Earth.*

When I met Arlie Latham he was still in baseball, although his active career had ended when he ruined his wonderful throwing arm in winning a $100 bet for long-distance throwing. Now, at age eighty-eight, he was in charge of the press box at the New York Giants' Polo Grounds and he could recall every bright moment of that great game against Spalding's White Sox. What he recalled most vividly was the $15,000 slide by Curt Welch, so called because that was the value of the purse in the winner-take-all contest. Welch, on third base, had taken a long lead and Mike Kelly, behind the plate, had signaled for a pitchout in hopes of nailing Curt before he could get back to the base. But Curt, in typically reckless fashion, instead of diving back to third, kept right on for home. The pitchout came in high and wide. And when Kelly got the ball, he turned just in time to see Welch sliding in to score the winning run. Whereupon Kelly hurled glove and mask high in the air and sent a garland of ripe curses after them.

A. G. Spalding, you may be sure, begrudged the loss of the $15,000 purse with all his money-worshiping soul, and probably blamed Cap Anson, who had first urged the winner-take-all arrangement because he *knew* the Browns could not possibly win. I doubt if Spalding would have been the least bit comforted to know, as Latham explained to me, that the crafty players on both clubs had "stood in" with each other, agreeing to split the shares fifty-fifty, no matter who won.

Chris von der Ahe, had he known about the scheme, would not have given a damn. It was not the purse he was after but the victory. Money to Chris was just something to spend or give away, a token that he was a very rich man. Every one of his champion Brownies shared in the club's success. He even believed in sharing it with the losers. When he learned that a few of the Chicago players, having bet on themselves, were broke and far from home, Chris peeled enough cash off his roll to see them safely back to Chicago. He also blew a good portion of his share on a champagne party for everyone. (He had offered to bet Spalding $10,000 on the game, but Al, never a man to put too much money where his mouth was, immediately chickened out.)

Spalding was sufficiently stung, however, by the evaporation of the gate receipts that he challenged von der Ahe to set his Browns against the White Sox in a six-game "championship" series to be played in the spring. His White Sox had lost this series, he complained, because Mike Kelly had led them all on a tour of St. Louis hot spots. His star pitcher, Jim McCormick, had showed up for one game so thoroughly soused that he could not have struck out the batboy. He gave up thirteen hits and six runs. And when his next turn came he could not even find his way to the "pitcher's point" (now called the mound) and had to be led away to safety.

For the rematch, however, Spalding took all his boys to Hot Springs, the resort of choice in those days for wealthy drunks to soak the alcohol out of their veins, and Anson mother-henned them all safely and soberly to their celibate beds every night.

Not so von der Ahe and Comiskey. They turned their lads loose for the winter and gathered them in the spring to find them all overfed, overdressed, and far out of condition. The White Sox this time took four out of six games from the Browns. But the series was quickly forgotten and no one, except perhaps Spalding and Anson, considered the White Sox champions. They did not even come in first that season.

Chris von der Ahe, however, had the time of his life and didn't even call this a beating. He never knew for sure if a game was won or lost until someone told him. And he spent his spare hours dreaming up new excuses to go riding in style from one big city to another with a party of some sort every night. He could not think of much else his money could give him. He wore the finest and flashiest clothes of any man in town: a top hat, a dazzling waistcoat, a cravat as wide as a towel and brilliant as a flag, a diamond as big as a bullet in his stickpin, and two-toned button shoes. His large mustache generously waxed, his bright eyes a-shine, and his amazing nose dominating his face with its nearly supernatural glow, he was the center of every room he entered.

Chris wanted no tinge of the second-rate around him. While other ball clubs might carry their players from the train stop to the ballpark in a secondhand omnibus drawn by two wind-broken plugs, Chris carried his boys to work in a convoy of open carriages drawn by prancing horses, each one of which wore a blanket emblazoned "Browns." He built a row of apartment houses, naming each one after one of his players. (And he added a saloon on either corner.)

In 1888, having by this time twice taken the measure of the White Stockings, and having that spring "championship" series erased from his memory, Chris arranged a game against the great Gotham Giants of New York City. (They were really the New York Metropolitans and some people even called them the Mets.) And the trip to New York, Chris decided, would be a celebration in itself. Having taken himself to Columbus, Ohio, when he got the idea, he wrote Al Spink and instructed him to arrange for a special train to take his ball players, all the sportswriters, a collection of loyal fans, a few friends, and his regal self to the big city in presidential style. Al dutifully applied to the local agent of the Vandalia Railroad for the accommodations. Said the agent, "Why that's nonsense! A special train from here to New York will cost Vondy twenty thousand dollars! Tell him I'll arrange regular transportation."

Al Spink dutifully reported the news to von der Ahe and the

big man almost exploded. "I didn't ask you what was the price! I asked you to get me the train! So please do me the favor and get it! Get everybody on board right after the game on Sunday and bring the train to Columbus. I meet you there and we go right to New York. Take care of this and someday I do as much for you!" Al could not imagine his ever wanting to arrange a special train to anywhere for himself, but he began at once to round up the crowd. So every sportswriter in St. Louis, all of Chris von der Ahe's best friends, all the coaches and players, and all of the club officials boarded the Browns' Special and set off for New York. With one stowaway—Augustus Thomas, who within a few years would be the most famous playwright in America. Thomas now worked for the *Missouri Republican*—but not as a sportswriter—and he begged Al to get him on board. "Put me down as a sportswriter for the *Republican*. I want to get to New York." So Al, against his better judgment, took Thomas on. And when Chris joined them he spotted Thomas at once as an interloper. Chris knew *all* the sportswriters. But Al allowed that he would stand good for Thomas's expenses. (Chris had agreed to pay all the hotel bills at the Grand Central Hotel in New York.) So Thomas got to the big city, promptly found himself a job at the *New York World*, shook hands with Chris and all the rest of the party, thanking them for their indulgence, and went on to fame. (By Al Spink's reckoning, he owed it all to von der Ahe.)

The special train drew cheers and excitement all along its route, for it sported on the side of every coach banners with the proud device: "St. Louis Browns. Four Times World Champions."

In New York, the Browns lost the first game 2–1, with the great Tim Keefe pitching for the Giants against the Browns' Silver King. But in the second game, Mickey Welch held the Giants scoreless and the Browns took the game 2–0. And that, Al always maintained, was their undoing. For big Chris, alert for any excuse for a celebration, ordered up a carload of champagne and joined his boys at the great Grand Central bar in gulping down goblet after goblet, royally toasting everyone, including the batboy. As a result they did not win another game until they got back to St. Louis, to finish the ten-game series, and managed to add three more victories—two less than the Giants. But the players were not downhearted. After their New York victory, and their regal banquet, Chris had sent them all out to buy a new suit of clothes apiece with orders to send the bill to him.

And, apparently because he had all the new suits he had any room for, Chris then had himself built into a statue.

The mere fact that Chris von der Ahe's glorious excursion to New York had ended in defeat did not temper his taste for travel and excitement. That celebration was still echoing in his head when he got word of another club owner who was as devoted to flaunting his renown as Chris himself. His name was Stearns and he was a wholesale druggist—by no means from the same mold as the frolicsome Dutchman but a merry fellow all the same who, when he had made a score, wanted all the rest of the world to know about it and rejoice. Stearns owned the Detroit club in the National League (the only big league club without a nick-name) and his team had just licked the mighty White Sox to take the National League pennant. Too exuberant to keep this triumph to himself, Stearns immediately wired Chris von der Ahe to outline a scheme for a tour that would rattle every window from the Atlantic to the Mississippi—a fifteen-game series for the championship of the universe to be played in fifteen different cities. That sounded good to Chris, except that he wanted at least two games to be played in St. Louis and Detroit, out of fairness to the local fans. So they settled finally for games in Philadelphia, Brooklyn, New York City, Pittsburgh, Baltimore, and Washington. And of course there would be a special train to cover the whole circuit, carrying ball players, sportswriters, loyal fans, and club officials and friends.

The series began in St. Louis, where each club won a game. In Detroit, the first "World Series" game ever staged in that city was a thirteen-inning victory by Detroit. Then it was on to Pittsburgh, where Detroit's famous left-hander "Lady" Baldwin (so nicknamed not because he was effeminate but because he was so polite) beat the Browns 8–0. By the time they reached Washington, Detroit had won seven games. A morning game was scheduled for Washington and an afternoon game for Baltimore. Detroit won the Washington game, and you'd have thought that would have ended it. But the two hearties would have none of that. They had agreed on fifteen games and they were not going to stop short of the whole bagful.

Back, then, went the whole caravan to Detroit where a *real* celebration was scheduled. A parade of open carriages drawn by plumed horses, with banners flying, carried the teams and their company through the Detroit streets to accept the plaudits of the multitude. Then the entire host sat down to a banquet that would very likely have felled the entire Roman senate. There was wine of every origin, six or seven varieties of roast meats, and hard liquor enough to fill a diving pool. How the players ever managed after that to haul themselves into the ballpark, let alone to play baseball there, no one could divine. But they did put on a show of sorts and Detroit came out the winner, 6–3. The real feature of the game, however, was the appearance, in the fourth inning, of a man with a loaded wheelbarrow who pushed it from the outfield straight to home plate, where it was handed over to Charlie Bennett, Detroit's beloved catcher. It contained 427 silver dollars, donated to Charlie by his local admirers. Charlie accepted the gift with a joyous yip, grabbed up the handles, and wheeled the whole load completely around the baselines, while the crowd of four thousand made racket enough for ten times that number.

The two clubs then returned to St. Louis, with the championship long ago decided, and played out the string before a meager crowd. Detroit won this one, too, making the final score Detroit eleven games and St. Louis four. That was all right with von der Ahe. He had never had so much fun before in his whole life, and he promised himself at once that he would keep on winning pennants and keep on taking the entire assembly—players, writers, and fans—around the whole nation to finish every season in a burst of glory.

History does not make it clear whether von der Ahe ever *did* find out how to keep score in a baseball game, or even how to tell who had won. But he did observe that his great rival, Al Spalding, made headlines and a bankroll for himself by selling his greatest ball player, Mike Kelly, to the Boston Beaneaters for $10,000, and his prize pitcher, John Clarkson, to Boston for another $10,000. Well, if that was the way the business was run, Chris did not see why he could not do just as well as Spalding. He had pitchers and catchers as good as anybody's. Without troubling himself for a minute over whether he could find anyone to replace them, Chris set out to peddle his own stars on the open market. He had made many an extra penny by selling crockery beer mugs with the name "Browns" emblazoned thereon and by hawking little imitation "pennants," fashioned after the "whip pennant" that was awarded to the winner of the championship. (The original pennants had been scarves, in the college colors, tied on to canes by the fans at college football games.) But obviously the big money lay in making baseball stars and selling them when they were ripe.

So Chris sold his prize battery, pitcher Dave Foutz and catcher Doc Bushong, along with another pitcher, Bob Caruthers, to Brooklyn at $10,000 for the bundle. And he sold, in a package deal, tough Curt Welch, whose $15,000 slide had first beat the White Stockings, plus shortstop Bill "Kid" Gleason, to Philadelphia. The Browns were then left with two pitchers, Nat Hudson and Silver King, who had indeed won thirty-six games between them. But Silver had won thirty-two of those. For a catcher Chris had a .240 hitter, Jack Boyle. To play shortstop, he had nobody. On the glad news of his employer's sudden enrichment Charles Comiskey's temper shot skyward. And fans from all around the area screamed at each other in outrage. Had von der Ahe finally gone clear off his rocker? But Chris sat down with Comiskey, applied part of these unexpected capital gains to Comiskey's own salary, and assured himself that big Charles could surely find enough ball players around town to people the playing field as well as he had done before. It *was* a fact, after all, that

Dave Foutz had needed a watch set on him to keep him sober, and Caruthers had earned the name Parisian Bob when he had fled to Paris to conduct his own celebration.

And it was not too long before earnest Charles Comiskey had managed to round up practically a whole new team that seemed as good as the one that had been sold. He unearthed two twenty-year-old pitchers—Jim Devlin, whom he lured back from Philadelphia, and "Ice-Box" Chamberlain (who would have been named "Refrigerator" today), a squat and solid lad who had been playing for Louisville. To fill the hole at shortstop Commy found a sore-armed local sandlotter named Ed Herr and kept him until he made a deal with Louisville for Bill White, who could at least throw a ball to first base without a bounce. Behind the plate, Comiskey put big Jocko Milligan, who could just about drive a baseball through a board fence. And from Boston he summoned another Irishman, Tommy McCarthy, who could run so far and so fast to capture a fly ball that the kranks came close to forgetting their hero, Curt Welch.

Not that local fans would ever stop telling stores about Curt, who seemed always to be on the lookout for the man he couldn't lick—and who found him one day in an undersized but ironfisted young second baseman named Fred Dunlap, called Sure Shot because, using either hand and always spurning use of a glove (it would have interfered with his left-handed throws), he never failed to hit the target in the dead center. Sure Shot Fred at the time was managing and playing for the St. Louis Maroons, a "cooperative" team in a new league called the Union Association, invented by a wealthy man named Henry Lucas. The St. Louis club became, to friends and enemy alike, the "Onions," and besides Sure Shot Fred Dunlap, they carried a shortstop called Pebbly Jack Glasscock, who earned his name by his eternal groundskeeping at his position, picking up pebbles tirelessly and flinging them out onto the grass. And they also listed Charles Sweeney from California, a hot-tempered man who was reputed to be the fastest pitcher the town had ever seen. The Onions were openly and heartily despised by their rival Browns. And in furtherance of their feud Curt Welch swaggered into their park and dared *anyone* to put up his dukes. Sure Shot Fred was first in line and he beat poor Curt so bloody that Curt needed help to get home. It was probably just as well that Sweeney had not volunteered to deal with Welch, for Sweeney wound up *his* career in San Quentin prison after killing a man in a brawl.

Von der Ahe's new Browns went right on to win another championship, while Chris continued to look for new places to spend all the money he was making. Spurred, apparently, by his success, St. Louis businessmen sponsored a "city league," as most other towns large enough to support a daily newspaper eventually did in the first decades of the next century. In Chris's city there grew the Sultan Bitters, the Jolly Nine, the Home Comforts, and the Dimmicks, all named and outfitted by one local business or another. These clubs played in the late afternoons, when work was over, and, as the Browns had done at the start, were paid a share of the gate—if there was any. Often there was no money to split except that collected in a hat from the onlookers.

One of the stars of this short-lived league was a future big-leaguer named Ted Breitenstein, who was eventually rated, for a time, "best left-handed pitcher in America." Ted became a full-time professional with the Grand Rapids team of the Northwestern League. Von der Ahe heard of him and decided he should be working in his hometown. With the Browns he teamed with another local, Heinie Peitz, to form the "Pretzel Battery," beloved of every German fan in St. Louis.

But Chris von der Ahe and his Browns had by this time been doomed by the Brotherhood strike, in which Charles Comiskey walked away from his $8,000-a-season job to join his charges in their vain struggle against the bosses. Comiskey came back to St. Louis after the strike, but von der Ahe's love for his doughty manager had grown cold, and Commy found a job in Cincinnati. The stars von der Ahe had gleefully peddled about the league finally came back to town in their new guises and began to clobber the Browns with dismal regularity. The American Association folded and the Browns joined the National League, whose other

owners deemed the high-living Dutchman a freak and spendthrift. The kranks' devotion had flagged during the Brotherhood
strike. Chris moved his ballpark to a new spot across the road
from a race track (where he naturally found help in thinning out
his wallet). Chris, who probably was never quite sure what a
manager *did,* failed to find even a feeble substitute for Comiskey.
He started with a part-time undertaker named Joe Quinn, who
also played second base. Then he gave the job to frisky Arlie
Latham, who was too merry a man really to ride herd on a
collection of tough ball players.

Next he turned the job over to a favorte sportswriter, one Joe
Diddlebock, whose very name suggested frivolity. Finally he settled on Tommy Down, famed throughout St. Louis as a devotee
of hard liquor and jokingly named, by krank and player alike,
"Buttermilk Tommy." After Tommy had dragged the Browns
down to tenth place in the eleven-team National League, Chris
decided to go with no manager at all.

He tried to lure in extra fans now by hiring a cornet band,
made up of pretty young ladies in striped skirts; installing a chute-
the-chute to hold the kranks' attention between games; staging
some boxing matches; and sponsoring horse races across the
street. But nothing availed. The team lost games; the park drew
fewer fans. Extra money put up by the streetcar company to keep
the show going did not help. Chris sold his great "Pretzel Battery"
to keep the ghost walking, then moved his living quarters into
the park to save on rent and turned the active operation of the
Browns over to his assistant, a man who had a hard time
convincing the sportswriters his name was really and truly
Muckenfuss.

The new boss hired some better players, including the league's
only left-handed catcher, John Clements, but still the club kept
losing both games and money. In 1897, they made it all the way
to the bottom of the league. And to put a sort of operatic finale
to the whole adventure the park caught fire one day and, while
four thousand fans in the grandstand kept yelling "Play ball!"
until the heat drove them out, the whole shebang, including

poor Chris's home and all of his trophies, was turned into junk and ashes. That final disaster put Chris into bankruptcy. His beloved Browns were sold to pay off his debts. His glittering jewels had long been in hock and his priceless clothes had gone threadbare. And poor Chris himself, who may have been the only man in baseball of whom it could truthfully be said he did not know third base from a certain part of his anatomy, ended his days operating a second-rate saloon on a side street in St. Louis. But Al Spink, who had first lured him into baseball, remained his good friend until the last. For Al, like others who had known Vondy well, always declared that professional baseball had never known a warmer-hearted club owner than the "Great Feller" from St. Louis.

Chapter 5

DISORDERLY CONDUCT

1. *Through the 1870s and 1880s* baseball fans grew accustomed to gore—especially after catchers in the professional game began to move up close to the batter and take the pitches raw-handed, right off the bat. The mightiest catchers, working with some of the most fearsome pitchers, caught without gloves or protectors—some of them spurning all protective gear even after the "patent safety glove," the "patent safety mask," and the "patent safety chest protector" had been authorized by the league for game use. It was a part of the "dead-game sport" in that day to avoid even the least appearance of babying their flesh.

Pay in professional baseball immediately after the Civil War was scanty, but glory was great and players relished the admiration they earned through their toughness as well as for their skill. About 1870, in a game between the "old" Philadelphia Athletics and the St. Louis Browns, a doughty young man named Dockney, catcher for the Athletics, engaged in acrimonious debate with a tough character from the St. Louis Kerry Patch who brought the talk to a sudden close when he drew a razor and sliced Dockney across the chest from shoulder to shoulder. Dockney was carried to a hospital, his shirt soaked in blood, and a doctor closed the wound with stitches and plaster, then put poor Dockney to bed. The next day, scorning all protest, Dockney appeared at the ballpark to team with his pitcher, the powerful Dick McBride, in facing down the Browns. Catchers in Dockney's day—even those like Dockney who dared stand close behind the batter—caught with both hands and fingers outstretched toward the pitcher. Naturally, many a sizzling pitch, or foul tip, broke through the catcher's hands and struck his chest. About halfway through the game that day, Dockney's wound broke open and his flannel shirt (his only protection) was dark with fresh blood. Yet, despite the warnings of his doctors and the appeals of his mates, Dockney hung tough. With blood darkening the dust all about his feet, he caught every pitch for the full nine innings. Then barely able to keep his legs beneath him, he allowed himself to be carried back to the hospital.

Lesser wounds than Dockney's were routinely sanitized with tobacco juice, of which there was an ample supply at every ball game. A sprung thumb could be yanked back into place, and broken fingers simply ignored, so that the hands of a professional catcher in that era often resembled dead cypress roots that had been pulled out of a swamp.

But spectators did not really gather at ball games just to see blood. The bloodiest scenes and, it must be granted, the most alluring in that age, were the bare-fisted prizefights, where "first blood" was a prize to be counted toward victory. Indeed, while ball games might often draw four or five thousand paid customers, a great prizefight would pack in double that number for a costlier ticket. When the Louisville baseball club played A. G. Spalding's Chicago White Stockings in 1876, local seers predicted that a crowd of ten thousand would pack the small park to watch the struggle between these giants. Actually, only two thousand kranks bought their way in, while an even greater number, unwilling to drop a half-dollar to sit inside, gathered on a small hill that provided a fine view, over a low fence, of all the doings.

But more than two thousand fight fans crowded into McCormick Hall in Chicago a few years later to see the Boston

Strong Boy, John Lawrence Sullivan, fresh from his murderous conquest of the Troy Terror (whose real name the sportswriters had forgotten), take on all comers with a fifty-dollar purse to the man who could stay three rounds with big John (he weighed 180 pounds at ringside). The only volunteer was a Michigan lumberjack named Jack Byrnes, who weighed 200. Rounds in this fight were to be three minutes each and the fans grew impatient when Sullivan simply fended off for two rounds all the blows Byrnes could deliver. But with the third round just one minute old, John, in response to the howls of his followers, first numbed his man with a hard right to the jaw and then, with a left uppercut, sent the poor man into a backward somersault that carried him clean out of the ring. Now *that* was a prizefight! Fans hastened to shove Byrnes back in the ring, but the poor man just stood there, palms open, arms outstretched, as if he were begging for mercy.

"Hit him!" the crowd yelled.

"Don't hit him *again!*" cried the referee.

"Of course not," said John.

And Byrnes's seconds jumped in to carry poor Jack to seclusion. It was forty minutes before Jack knew just where he was or whether it was today or the night before.

But that crowd was actually a tiny one for a good prizefight. The Sharkey-Maher fight in the Palace Athletic Club in New York, where bare-fisted fighting, as in most of the civilized world, was against the law, drew ten thousand. And they saw a spectacle none of them would ever forget. The two men fought evenly for six rounds. Then in the seventh Maher, after mocking Sharkey to his face, knocked him to the floor. Sharkey, apparently taking instant leave of his senses, jumped right to his feet and took after Maher like an outraged tiger. "Knock *me* down, will you, you bastard?" Clawing with both hands and roaring with anger, Sharkey ignored the bell and piled into his opponent. The referee jumped between them and Sharkey belted him out of the way. Sharkey's seconds tried to grab their man and he belted them, too. Now timekeepers and handlers all rushed into the fray and Sharkey set out to take on the lot. It required a whole squadron of cops, with drawn billy clubs, to persuade Sharkey that the fight was over. The referee screamed out his decision. A draw! And the cops arrested both fighters. The howling spectators felt they should have arrested the referee.

But a truly gory fight that kept the fans screaming would be one between the great heavyweights, who could cut each other up to the crowd's taste even with the "modern" gloves on. For the gloves were just thin leather coverings that were mostly useful in keeping the knuckles from bleeding. When Bob Fitzsimmons, in what he vowed (falsely) would be the final fight of his career, took the championship from Gentleman Jim Corbett in Carson City, Nevada, the whole city seemed to have turned out, along with a horde of visitors. While the old system of calling a round when one man went to the floor had been discarded, this was still a "fight to the finish." It lasted fourteen rounds and along the way Jim Corbett had two of his precious gold teeth knocked out and had to struggle to keep the blood from escaping, lest Fitzsimmons be granted "first blood." But there was blood aplenty before the fight was half done. By the fifth round, Fitzsimmons was bleeding at the mouth. In the sixth his nose was running red. And after Corbett had been counted out in the fourteenth round, and Fitzsimmons had retired to his corner, Corbett broke away from his seconds and kept raging after Fitzsimmons, spitting blood and profanity. ("Vile blasphemy," Fitzsimmons reported.) Corbett beat poor Bob (who was about thirty pounds lighter) about the neck and head until the handlers pulled him away. Said Fitzsimmons, the gentleman from Cornwall, "Jim simply lost his head and his manners." A few minutes later, Corbett sent word he would like to shake Bob's hand. Bob agreed and the two solemnly congratulated each other. Except that when Corbett, agreeing that Bob was the best fighter he had ever faced, asked for "another go," Bob said he would never fight again. (He did and was beaten by Jim Jeffries.) Corbett blew his top once more and allowed that, should he ever meet Fitzsimmons on the street, he would, by Jesus, beat him to death. "Try it," said Bob, "and I will kill you." Having thus exchanged vows, the two men parted, never to meet again.

While the blood in baseball flowed less freely as the century grew old and bare-fisted prizefighting became a mere legend of a barbarous age, rough stuff in the major leagues (the National League and the American Association) did persist and did prompt many a well-raised young man—one who was devoted perhaps to the more seemly sports of his kind, football and rowing—to name baseball "a mucker's game." Yet it did take hold in colleges and a few colleges did begin to produce young men who could play the game well enough to get paid for it. Holy Cross, in Worcester, Massachusetts, actually set up special classes for ball players, some of whom could not have finished high school with credit.

One such was the original Cleveland Indian, Louis Sockalexis, a strapping young man who could run like a racehorse and who, on the sandlots of Maine, had learned to drive a pitched baseball from here to eternity. In 1896, when he batted .444 at Holy Cross, big leaguers began to take notice of him. That summer, Notre Dame borrowed him to go to New York with them and play in an exhibition game with the New York Giants, who owned the admittedly fastest pitcher alive—Amos Rusie, "The Indiana Thunderbolt." The New York fans greeted Sockalexis with war whoops and watched gleefully for the mighty Rusie to bring home his scalp. Rusie fed the Indian his famous curve— faster than most fastballs, and the fastest ever seen in the league up to that time. Sockalexis measured it coolly and drove it straight to the distant fence. Then he sped around the entire base circle for an inside-the-park home run.

That was enough to convince John Ward, the Giants' manager, who wrote that very day to his friend, Patsy Tebeau, chief of the Cleveland Spiders, who had already been told about the Indian by the Holy Cross coach, Jesse Burkett. On the strength of these endorsements, Pat offered Sockalexis a job.

In his first practice game, Sockalexis drove two pitches to the fence and, playing in deepest right field, threw out two runners at the plate. He promptly became the regular right fielder with the Spiders. In the first game of the regular season, however, the mighty Indian went hitless. But the next day he fulfilled all promise. Batting against Still Bill Hill of Louisville (a deaf-mute), Sockalexis made two long hits. And from that day forth, he hit almost every day, until he came up against Ted Breitenstein, front end of the "Pretzel Battery" (with Heinie Peitz catching), a graduate of the St. Louis sandlots and now rated the best left-hander in all baseball. Ted struck him out three times. But the next time Sockalexis faced the powerful paleface, the Indian got three hits.

By this time, Sockalexis had become the most talked-about person in Cleveland. He was an attractive man, in looks and manners—notably handsome, gentle, happy, given to laughter. Sports cartoonists everywhere pictured him with a mighty war club in hand and a head made glorious with feathers. One sports-writer was inspired to invent a poem in "Hiawatha" rhythm, about "Sockalexis, Chief of Sockem." For Sockalexis, by the end of July, was batting .400, with never another strikeout. (No one in the league except Breitenstein ever did strike him out.) But his popularity finished him. Like many another instant hero, he could not say no—to an invitation to a party or an offer of a drink. He never went sober to bed and often carried an unhealed hangover to the ballpark. His batting average grew slimmer by the day. Long before the season was out, he made sixteen errors in the outfield. Tebeau, weary of lecturing him and fed up with broken vows, finally, sent his beloved Indian down to the minors, where Sockalexis failed to locate the trail to sobriety. But that winter he wrote numberless letters to Tebeau, describing his reformation, foreseeing a life of total abstinence, and promising to destroy every pitcher he faced. Pat gave in and brought Sock-alexis back for the 1898 season. But he soon wished he hadn't, for the merry Indian simply could not resist taking every drink that was thrust upon him, nor was he the sort who could spoil a party by ducking out before the fun was over. Once he even missed the train to the next city. He managed to make the scene

for only twenty-one games and collected but fifteen hits. Again
Tebeau sent him away. And again Sockalexis sent letter after
letter vowing that *this* time for *sure* he would not tarnish his
throat with one *drop* of liquor. Pat Tebeau had heard it all before.
But Cleveland owned a new manager, Lave Cross, who was finally
persuaded to bring the great Indian back. For a moment, it did
seem that the spell was broken. Sockalexis, who had never in
all his career been known to lose his temper, exploded in his first
at bat when pitcher Jack Powell of St. Louis, who had been the
Indian's teammate the previous season, very nearly scalped his
old friend with a beanball. Sockalexis pounded the plate in a
rage and drove the next pitch to left center for two bases. He
hit safely in his next four times at bat and once more he owned
the world. But the celebration that marked his triumph was his
last. In the six more games in which he could make it to the
plate he managed only one hit and Lave Cross could bear him
no longer. Sockalexis did not make the train when the club left
for St. Louis. When he came home he was arrested for "creating
a disturbance" in a Cleveland theater. Then it was back to the
bushes.

In the lesser league he did no better, and began to drift lower
and lower. He played for a time in Lowell and in Hartford, then
sank back to the New England sandlots. He took to begging in
the streets for drink money. And I met an old man years later
who vowed he had met Sockalexis, frowsy and tattered now,
crouched by a fire in a hobo jungle. Sockalexis played no more
baseball. He ended his days running a ferry back home in Old
Town, Maine, where he died at age forty.

●

Drink, of course, has wrecked the lives of many folk in every
profession, but throughout the 1890s, what with hard times and
cheap booze, it seemed to wreak a special devastation on some
of the instant heroes professional baseball created. The great Mike
Kelly was ruined by drink. (Once, when wobbling unsteadily
under a fly ball, before muffing it, he consoled himself by as-

serting, "By God, I made it hit me glove!") After losing job after job in baseball, he died of pneumonia at the age of thirty-seven in a Boston hospital (a town where he used to sport about in an open carriage drawn by "spanking greys" given to him by his admirers).

More tragic still was the death of one of the century's greatest heroes whose name now is practically forgotten, except for those who see it in the baseball Hall of Fame and wonder about him. That was Big Ed Delahanty, one of five brothers, all of whom played big league baseball (and all of whom spelled their surname differently from other Delehantys.) Big Ed was the mightiest of the family. He was the first man in the league ever to hit four home runs in a game. (In pre–Civil War baseball, home runs were commonplace, the ball being so lively that it would speed off like a cannonball when squarely hit.)

Ed made his record when he was playing for Philadelphia against Chicago in 1896. In his first time at bat, he drove one of Adonis Bill Terry's fastballs into the right-field bleachers. Next time up, he sent a ball far out on the right-field sod and ran all the way home before the fielder could get the ball back. In his third at bat, he smashed a line drive that struck shortstop Bill Dahlen square in the chest and knocked him flat. That went for a single. His next blow was another home run, hit so deep into center field that even fleet Bill Lange could not recover it in time to heave it home. By this time, the Chicago fans were as excited as Ed's followers.

"Another one! Ed!" they yelled. "One more!" Bill Terry made ready to pitch with, one imagines, a trickle of fear in his heart. But Bill Lange shouted to him, "Hold it a minute!" And while Terry stood waiting, Bill ran as far out into center field as space allowed and took up his position right between the two club- houses. This was no-man's land, where no baseball ever fell and where the groundskeeper did not bother to keep the grass trimmed.

Big Ed, never a patient man at the plate (pitchers were warned that his favorite was a wild pitch), laid into the first ball Adonis

Bill offered him and drove it on a whistling line a sight farther than poor Bill had ever seen one of his deliveries travel. The ball, with distant Bill Lange gaping at it, bounced off the roof of one clubhouse, landed on the other, and rolled down into the deep grass, where Lange recovered it. He would have needed a cannon to get it back even close to the diamond to manage a play on Ed. So he simply hid it under the floor of his team's clubhouse so he might have a souvenir of the event.

The fearsomeness with which Big Ed could hit a baseball has probably never been matched. He once broke the ankle of a third baseman who got in the way of one of his daisy-cutters. Another time he broke a baseball right in two when it dared to come within reach of his bat.

Ed Delahanty was a handsome man, whom both men and women found attractive, for he was outgoing, happy, and obviously ready for anything. He loved a good time (which always meant good drink) and he loved excitement. He never wanted to be out of the lineup and he was ready to play almost any position. At different times he was left fielder, shortstop, and catcher, and he played all three bases.

Ed's salary, regardless of his drawing power, was never much above the minimum, so when an ex-sportswriter named Byron Bancroft Johnson turned his Western League into a new major league and set out to lure National League players his way by urging them to escape the bonds of the reserve rule, Ed was one of the first to jump. In his first year with the new Washington club, Big Ed led the American League with an average of .376. Being free, he thought, from the reserve rule, he accepted a fat offer from John McGraw with a $4,500 advance, to jump back to New York in the National League. New York! That was where a man could really turn a fast dollar. And where good times were to be had on every corner. Alas, Ed's dream never came true, for the two leagues made peace and Ban Johnson's boys were all bound again by the reserve rule. So here was poor Ed stuck with the same bush-league salary, owing McGraw $4,500 and not daring to count up the cost of all the horses that had failed him at the race track. Even his priest might have agreed that it was enough to make a man say many bad words out loud. There was probably no word in the devil's dictionary that Ed could not define, and he found employment for them all in discussing this turn of fate with his teammate, George Davis, who had just made a deal with Chicago that also had to be called off after the reserve rule was sanctified by both leagues. Both George and Ed, promising each other that they would never again play for Washington, made a move to report to New York, but were promptly rebuffed. Ed then wired the "outlaw" league in California, asking for terms, but found no comfort there. Eventually Ed returned to Washington with the understanding, some of his friends said, that he would be traded to New York before the season ended. But there was no forgiveness of his debt to McGraw and Ed sulked his way through game after game. He kept himself hopelessly broke by investing in red whiskey with whatever cash came his way. And he brooded every night over what his wife could be up to while he was on the road. After he had turned up drunk at one too many games, manager Tom Loftus suspended him. This was the very last procedure Big Ed's affliction called for and he immediately devoted his full time to the bottle. For some reason, Loftus took Ed along when the club traveled to Detroit. But Ed walked out of the ballpark before the game was over and he was, as the British say, "making his own arrangements" more merrily than ever before. He wired his wife to meet him in Washington, hastily jammed a few things into his bag—leaving most of his clothing, including his uniform, behind—and took off to catch the 4:25 P.M. Michigan Central train for the East.

In the train dining car, the waiters apparently could see no reason why the big man could not have a drink, or even five, if he desired them. As a result Ed took more whiskey aboard than he had ever before tried to carry.

Intent now on involving all his fellow passengers in the party, Ed was dismayed to discover there was almost no one awake. Well, that difficulty could be quickly mended. Shouting happily, Ed walked through the sleeping car and set out to yank some

potential playmates out of their berths. The row that followed
brought the whole train crew running and it took all of them to
get a good hold on Ed and move him to the door. The train had
come to a stop at Fort Erie, Ontario, the last stop before crossing
the bridge at Niagara. Ed was dumped forcibly out on the empty
platform and the train started off at once. Ed, recovering some
sort of balance, set out in pursuit, daring the sons of bitches to
stop and have it out with him. As the train lights disappeared
in the dark, Ed stumbled wildly after them. It was rough going
on the ties, even for a sober man, for as anyone who has tried
to walk them knows, they are spaced just the wrong distance for
a normal footstep—"too short for one, too long for two." It must
have been a good twenty minutes before Ed, never doubting he
would capture the bastards at the next stop, came to the beginning of the bridge across the Niagara River, and there someone
appeared with a lantern—the watchman, a man named Kingston,
a husky man, but of course no match for Big Ed.

Kingston held up his hand.

"Hold it there!" he cried. "The draw is open!"

The words meant nothing to Ed and he surged on. When
Kingston took hold of Ed's coat to stop him, Ed grabbed the man
and set out to throw him to the ground. The two wrestled there
in the dark until Ed finally pulled away and took off full speed
after the train.

"For God's sake!" Kingston yelled. "The draw is open!" Then
he bent over to retrieve his hat and jammed it on his head before
starting in pursuit. But long before he came close, he heard a
wild yell from Ed. Then a silent minute or two. Then a cry from
far, far below him: "Help! Help!" But Kingston could offer no
help. He could merely hurry to retrieve his lantern as the faint
cries came—five times, he said. Kingston stumbled back to the
station and panted out his story to the first man he met. Then
he took off his hat and discovered it was not his hat at all but
the one the big man had been wearing. But who the big man
was neither he nor anyone else could say.

It was days before anyone learned Big Ed's fate. The train crew said nothing of it. He was just a nameless drunk who had been shoved off the train.

In Washington, Ed's wife tried frantically to learn where he had gone. She wired everyone in Detroit, New York, and even in Cleveland, Ed's boyhood home, whom she thought Ed might have gone to see. She had almost no money left, because Ed had been paying back the money he owed McGraw. And she had a small daughter to keep. Ed's teammates just laughed and said not to worry, that Ed was just off on a bender somewhere and he would turn up soon enough, never fear, all sobered up and full of remorse. Tom Loftus, however, was not so sure and he too sent inquiring telegrams to Ed's possible companions. But no one had any word.

It was a whole week later before Ed's mangled and bloated body was found against a wharf twenty miles below the Horseshoe Falls. He was identified by his teeth and his injured fingers. By this time, the railroad had got around to checking the drunken man's baggage and identifying Ed as the one who had been pushed off the train at Fort Erie. He had, the railroad reported, been threatening passengers with an open razor. But Ed's friends and family knew Ed had used a safety razor all of his life.

Almost half a century later, another angry ball player met a fate as shocking as Big Ed's—and under similar circumstances. Len Koenecke, an outfielder with the Brooklyn Dodgers, enraged when he was sent down to Rochester after failing to live up to his promise in Brooklyn, was traveling to Chicago on a plane with two teammates who had been similarly demoted. Seeking comfort from a bottle of whiskey he had carried on board, Koenecke, a solidly built young man, gradually developed a grudge against his whole immediate world. He wandered the aisles, despite the protests of attendants, snarled at fellow passengers who might complain when he bumped them, offered to punch out any who snarled back at him, and even sought entry to the pilots' compartment to comment on their lack of flying skills. When an attendant took hold of him and tried to gentle him back to his seat, he knocked her to the floor. At this, one of the pilots, along with the two ball players who had been in his company, took hold of him and restrained him until the plane landed in Detroit, where they deposited him on solid ground and left him. But this did not slow Koenecke in the least. With the craftiness of a drunk, he managed to hire himself a private plane and two pilots to carry him to Buffalo, where perhaps he meant to even the score with those who had disowned him. Almost as soon as the plane was airborne, Len began to take issue with the pilot's decisions as to height and direction, and the pilot, perhaps aware for the first time that Koenecke was more than just slightly "tiddley-boo," tried to brush him off. Koenecke tried then to force his way into the copilot's seat and was soon engaged in a wild wrestling match during which he made an effort to snatch the controls. The pilot then abandoned control long enough to grab the fire extinguisher and deal Koenecke a solid blow to the head that silenced him. When the plane landed, a doctor declared Koenecke was dead. "Well, if he's dead," the pilot allowed, "then I killed him."

Most of professional baseball's champion drinkers came to far less dramatic ends. Some managed to fight the demon to a draw and a few even finished him.

Nearly everyone's favorite batter throughout the 1880s was the original Louisville slugger, Louis Rogers Browning, called Pete by friends and fans and The Old Gladiator by sportswriters. There was probably never a ball player born who loved to hit any more than Pete Browning did. It was, as a matter of fact, the only part of baseball that Pete really had command of. Even though he played just about every position in the game—including a very brief spell of pitching—he could never have held a job even on a minor league club on his fielding. For Pete was really terrified of being hit by a baseball. Some players were convinced he fielded ground balls with his eyes closed. After he joined Louisville, his hometown club, and through some strange stroke of fate the home of the company that made all the bats, Pete was given a chance at every infield position and was equally inept at all four. In his fifth season he was moved full-time to the outfield. But even there his performance was enough to make his manager close his eyes in despair. For Pete was determined not to risk his precious health by running too fast, or to court chilblains through stepping into a puddle. On base, he would rather be put out than take a chance of skinning his hide or twisting a joint through sliding.

At the plate, of course, he *had* to hold his position or he couldn't hit, so he became a champion at twisting, squirming, bending, and ducking to avoid close pitches. But if the pitch came into the strike zone, or even into the general area, Pete could hit it. And he could hit it far. In his first season with Louisville of the American Association (then a major league), Pete batted for an average of .378, the best in the league. In 1890, his ninth year in professional baseball, Pete joined the striking players in the Players' League to play outfield for Cleveland and led *that* league with an average of .373.

If you asked Pete where his batting skill resided, he would tell you it was in his feet and in his eyes—and mostly in his eyes. He never failed to report to his fans in the bleachers, all of whom he counted as his good friends, that his old dogs were in great shape and his eyes just full of base hits and sunshine. His method of ensuring the brightness of his eyes and the sharpness of his vision was to stare at every opportunity straight into the sun for as long as his eyes could stand it. No one ever told him that he might very well, by this process, be inviting early blindness. Pete had already been partially deafened by an abscess in his ear and he habitually talked in a near shout because that is the way people talked to him.

Every baseball fan in town, it seemed, liked to talk to Pete. He was an attractive man—six feet tall, lean, and broad-shouldered. He had a mustache as large as a hairbrush that gave him a permanent expression of friendliness that drew even small boys to him. He took good care of his mustache, waxing and combing it with care and, to his mind, he was taking special care of his eyes by never allowing soap and water to endanger them.

Naturally, whenever Pete walked abroad, he met friends, or

found them following in his wake. Having been awarded the title of The Old Gladiator for his murderous ways with his mace, he liked to refer to himself, always in the third person, as Gladdy. To any he met he might declare, "The old Gladdy's fine today! He's going to line them out today!" And naturally, although he took special care all winter long to avoid the fried foods he loved and the "German tea" (his pet name for beer) that he doted on, when friends urged him to raise a glass in their company, Pete could not resist. However, it was never a glass, but a stein. And too often it was followed by an invitation to a dinner featuring fried pork chops or fried chicken enriched with fried potatoes. And poor Pete, a sociable man by nature, lacked the heart to refuse.

A saloon in that day, when they grew on almost every corner, often with an extra one tucked into the middle of the block, was the workingman's club, as the corner cigar store was the workingman's betting parlor. A saloon had swinging half doors, wide open above and below, like the doors that mark off the pharmacist's quarters in some drug stores. They opened at the touch of a finger and provided an uninterrupted invitation to stop in and join the hilarity that could be detected from the street. Some saloons might even place a small mechanical figure in the window that would tap sharply on the glass, at frequent intervals, lest passersby neglect to pay heed to the standard signs inviting them to stop in and deal with their thirst.

Beer could be had for taking home in tin buckets, called "growlers," at a nickel a fill-up. But the real fun was found in the glowing companionship, the dice games, and the barroom harmony. There was usually a free lunch set out for the taking: pretzels, sausages, even cannibal sandwiches (raw hamburger—the junk food of the day). To most men the place held more attractions than home (William Blake once wrote that if they could but meet in a tavern, "God with the Devil no longer would quarrel/But kiss him and give him both drink and apparel"). How could the best-loved ball player in town resist the beckoning fingers and the sleeve-clutching hands of the men he loved most—the ball kranks who cheered him daily at his work? So Pete's physical condition deteriorated almost by the day during the playing season. Yet his bat eyes continued to shine, his skin to glow, and his mighty bat to send baseballs flying. Hillerich and Bradsby, the chief builder of bats, and a neighbor to the ball club, made a special bat for Pete to his own specifications. (Most clubs in the day bought bats by the dozen and allowed each player to saw or whittle his down to suit himself.) Pete was continually fondling, honing, and sandpapering his weapons, and sometimes trying to copy the bat of some hitter he admired. It was said that Pete at one time owned more than a hundred bats and treated each one like a pet.

But, despite his winters of self-denial, Pete's appetite for German tea began gradually to affect his comportment. By the season of 1889, his batting average had sunk to .256—the first time it had fallen below .300 (he had batted a listed .471 in 1887, but that was the year that bases on balls were counted as hits; leaving out the free walks, Pete's average was .402). The shift to the Players' League in the Brotherhood strike of 1890 brought Pete's bat back to life and he led that league. An average of .373 was the figure statisticians gave him, but Pete liked to figure his own averages with pencil and paper and he was likely to announce to his loving bleacherites, "Old Gladdy is batting .395." Or he might even pass that intelligence on to a stranger he met in the street.

Pete, like a latter-day batsman named Ruth, had no known enemies, nor ever wanted any. If he hurt anyone's feelings, he was instantly penitent and quick to make amends. He even apologized to his manager one day for hitting a home run. He had been instructed to bunt, but as he stood at the plate and a pitch came down to him, someone in the cheap seats yelled out, "Hit it in the canawl, Pete!" So Pete laid into the ball and drove it not quite into the water but clean over the fence, into a backyard where it frightened a poor lady who was hanging out her clothes. Pete completed his tour of the bases at good speed and hastened to face his manager, his hands held out in appeasement. "I know!

I know!" he cried. "You said bunt. But that goddamn bug in the bleachers got me rattled!"

When Pete earned his highest average (.471, until the modern statisticians got hold of it) his bleacher fans chipped in to present him with a big gold watch, such as men of great wealth carried, a turnhip, in the slang of the day, and staged a dinner party to present it to him. Pete, who was by no means an untalkative man, was struck near speechless when he accepted the package and uncovered the prize. He turned it over and over in his hand while the crowd yelled, "Speech! Speech! Let's hear it, Pete!" Finally, after swallowing hard, he blurted, "Where the hell's the chain?" And this set the whole roomful to howling and pounding the tables. That was Pete for you!

Before Pete walked out, with all the other strikers, in 1890, he suffered a real scare. He showed up for play one day, so far gone from the effects of German tea that his manager would not let him take the field and fined him $600. At that very moment Pete took the pledge of total abstinence. And he kept it for two whole seasons. His transfer to Cleveland in the Players' League made it easier for him to forgo German tea, for he had no army of adoring hometown fans to coax him clear of sobriety.

When the Brotherhood strike ended, Pete was awarded to the Pittsburgh club, which traded him, after fifty games, to Cincinnati. Here, the German tea flowed from a thousand spigots in beer gardens throughout the town. And here Pete found two merry companions, pitcher Billy Rhines and catcher Jerry Harrington, who helped Pete find his way from beer garden to beer garden every night all season long. Here, too, Pete made a habit of studying every bat of every enemy hitter and ordering copies of all those he liked, until he had those hundred new bats to choose from. And he once more posted an average above .300. But manager Tom Loftus grew weary of Pete's toting of hangovers to the park and abruptly turned The Old Gladiator loose to find his way home to Louisville, where Rhines and Harrington, having been suspended by Cincinnati, soon joined him. Pete felt sure the home kranks would rejoice as he assured them the old dogs (which had carried him to 121 stolen bases in his greatest year) were in fine shape and that his lamps were still full of base hits.

But, despite the worshiping fans and the fact that he did manage to keep his average high, Pete could make it to the diamond in only fifty-seven games during the season of 1893 and he and his two playmates were handed their releases once more. Pete did manage to talk himself into tryouts then with Brooklyn and St. Louis but played only one game for Brooklyn and two with St. Louis. After that, it was down to bush league Allentown, where the great Mike Kelly, ending his own career, was serving as playing manager. Pete hit home runs there and showed speed on the bases. But one day, when a tall fly was driven his way by an enemy batter, Pete, running to get under it, found a wide rain puddle in his way. Was he going to risk his priceless old dogs in some nasty, cold puddle? You think he was crazy? Pete pulled right up on the near shore and glumly watched the ball drop safely on the grass. Well, he had hit a home run, so what did it matter? Well, it mattered to Mike Kelly, who promptly fired Pete from the team. So Pete went back home to Louisville, where he explained that Kelly had fired him out of jealousy— just because the old goat hadn't hit as many homers as Pete had.

But this time, there was no one to pay heed when he reminded them that the old lamps were "still full of sunshine and base hits." Pete, whenever a new team came to Louisville, would hasten to the ballpark to assure the visiting manager that his dogs and lamps had lost none of their transcendent skills. But no manager could find any spot for Pete on the roster. So ultimately poor Pete, who could not endure life without baseball, and who would look for someplace to hide when he was not knocking out base hits, accepted a job with a local semipro club, where he found folk who would still shout their devotion to The Old Gladiator. But that didn't really console him and he finally applied to Nick Young, president of the National League, for a job as umpire—a lowly spot indeed in those days when pay for umpires was piddling and respect almost nil. But Young was not convinced Pete's old lamps were equal to the task of calling balls and strikes and he turned Pete down. By this time Pete was really sick. His abscessed ear had worsened and the doctor urged an operation. Old Pete, reduced to a skeleton by illness and despair, never recovered from the operation. He was only forty-seven when he died.

●

There really were few jobs then that superannuated baseball players could prosper in, and other players besides Pete Browning fell upon evil days indeed when their skills began to dwindle. The standard fee for an umpire was five dollars a day—enough at that time to keep a man fed and sheltered, had he been able to hibernate through a long winter.

Most professional baseball players through the 1880s and 1890s were anything but "gentlemen in the highest social sense." While the great colleges all sponsored baseball teams, few indeed of the players developed there found baseball a proper calling when the day came for them to start earning their own bread. Of course, to black players, like Fleetwood and Welday Walker, who starred in baseball at Oberlin, baseball seemed to offer a relatively bright future, brighter at least than most "colored" jobs of the day.

A few professional ball players passed as college men, from having at least worn the uniform of a college team. But Sockalexis had attended "special classes" at Holy Cross, where he studied what he ought to have learned in secondary school and he earned no degree. Another supposed "college man" was the famous "Old Hoss," Charles Radbourn, who was the best of them all when he won the pennant for Providence in 1884 by pitching twenty-seven games in a row and winning twenty-six of them. But the closest Old Hoss ever got to college was the locker room of Illinois Wesleyan, when he served as a "ringer" in a game the college played against a team of pros.

The school most great players of the nineteenth century attended was the sandlot, where baseball was played in all its different forms even long after the New York Game had been adopted as the *real* game in every city. Town ball, obviously a more regulated form of rounders, was far closer to the Massachusetts game of baseball than the New York Game, for it had four bases, in addition to the home base, and hitting the runner with the ball was the proper way to "tag" him out. When Mike Kelly, the future "King" of the game, first started to play ball as a small boy in Washington, D.C., where his soldier father was stationed, town ball was played on many a vacant lot and boys often chose it because of the delight they took in soaking their playmates with the ball. But the game itself was relatively unorganized with no definite positions for any player and with most players scattered over the field as "scouts." The pitcher was just the "feeder," as he had been in the very beginning of the New York Game. And he was required to change places with the catcher every few innings. What surely attracted Mike Kelly to the New York Game, besides the fact that it was the game the professionals played, was that in the New York Game now the pitcher could fire the ball (from fifty feet away) with all the power his muscle could produce, and players would play in the same spot from game to game.

Mike's personal hero, among the pros, was stalwart Joe Start, the "Old Reliable" (he hardly ever dropped a throw) who played first base for Hartford and New York. When Mike was in Washington, he organized a club he called the Keystones, made up of schoolmates, and when the Kellys moved to Paterson, New Jersey, Kelly gathered another club together and called them the Keystones too. One of his new teammates sported a fifteen-cent baseball cap exactly like the one Joe Start wore. And young Mike, who was acknowledged the swiftest runner and the best batsman in the crowd, allowed that he would not play with the team unless he could have that cap. There was no argument; they had to have Kelly. Actually, Mike at that time had no ambition to make his living at baseball. He wanted to go on the stage, where the real money grew—an ambition he did not realize until after he won fame as a ball player.

With his sandlot club, Kelly played catcher because he was the only boy who dared stand up to the fiery pitching of a lad named Ed Nolan, who would become famous a few years later as "The Only" Nolan, the only man ever to pitch thirty shutouts in one season. Nolan and Kelly were the Keystone battery for three years and they traveled all over New Jersey, taking on whatever team chose to face them—amateur or semipro—and beating most of them. Like most teams of this type throughout the years, the Keystones played for a divvy of the gate—which was usually collected in a hat. Sometimes the full take would be three dollars to be divided among the lot. To keep breath in his body, young Mike had to find regular work, so like most young men in the area he set out to learn silk-weaving in the local mills. Pay: three dollars a week, with no time for baseball. Mike's father and mother both died soon after the family moved to New Jersey, so sixteen-year-old Mike was his own sole support, and he could barely buy bread on the silk mill wage. Besides, the workplace was like a jail. Happily, he landed a job bringing New York papers to town on the early train. That meant rising with the roosters at four A.M., but it left the whole bright afternoon to give to baseball. His battery mate, Ed Nolan, who earned his keep as a fireman on the Lackawanna line, after three years with the Keystones was offered a paying job on the independent team at Columbus, Ohio, so Kelly had a new battery mate, a rugged young Irishman named Jim McCormick, who would eventually star with Pittsburgh. Kelly and McCormick became "the Keystone battery" and their fame spread throughout the entire area, for the Keystones were quick to accept a challenge from any club, near or far, sometimes with only their round-trip fare guaranteed. But mostly the gates were fat enough to justify making baseball Mike's full-time summer job. In the winter, it was back to the silk mill, to be sure, as all the books taught him he must have a trade to live by. But one more season in confinement was all Mike could take and when a team in Port Jervis, New York, offered Mike a regular pay envelope, baseball became his full-time profession. Then Mike, before the first season was done, moved up to a better-paying job with the Buckeyes of Cincinnati, where all of his skills seemed to desert him. In his first twenty-one times at bat, Mike reached first base but once, and that time on an error. So Buckeye manager Cal McVey, former star of the Brooklyn Atlantics, sent to Manchester, New Hampshire, for a new outfielder. Mike promptly smelled his own doom; in desperation he went to bat next day and produced two doubles, a triple, and a home run. That was enough to put a clamp on his job. When the club went to Chicago a few days later, Mike won the ball game by batting in all the runs. In the fall he and a number of his mates, plus a few from the Buffalo club, traveled to California, where they put to flight the famous "Hop Bitters" traveling club—a team named after a patent medicine. Kelly's mighty slugging in that game impressed Cap Anson, captain of Spalding's Chicago White Sox, and Cap, after arguing for a week over $100 difference in salary, gave in and signed Mike Kelly. Now fully grown (he was twenty-two), Mike said what seemed to be a final good-bye to the sandlots.

Ed Nolan had a similar but much briefer experience. His first regular-paying job, with an independent team in Columbus, Ohio, led him to Indianapolis, where W. B. Pettit, owner of the Indianapolis club (which had not yet joined the National League), saw Ed strike out twelve and give the big leaguers but four hits. So Pettit offered Ed $2,500 to come play for Indianapolis next season. Ed had just turned nineteen and this was the richest payday he had ever known, and one of the fattest salaries most ball players had seen. And Ed, along with the rest of the club, went south the next year, on the first "spring training" trip any team in organized baseball had ever scheduled. Starting in New Orleans, Indianapolis won eleven straight games in the South, and Ed Nolan pitched them all. From that time forth he was "The Only" Nolan. When the club got home Nolan pitched seventy-six complete games, won sixty-four, and tied eight. And he set his record of thirty shutouts. In thirty-three games, to rest his arm, he played right field—as the "change pitcher," in the days before substitutes were allowed, except for injury. One of his games was a no-hitter, and two of his wins came on the same day in a doubleheader against Columbus.

Although he stood only five feet eight inches, Nolan had mighty shoulders, developed in his fireman job, and he threw the scariest fastball of his day, as well as a sharp curve—at a time when only about twenty pitchers managed to put a curve ball into the strike zone more than four or five times in a game.

In Nolan's day, a ball player who spoke out of turn to his boss could be barred from the National League for life. Nolan missed a game one day and was promptly suspended by Pettit. That meant that Nolan was finished in organized baseball. No club in the league would dare deal with him, nor would any of the clubs that had entered into a compact with the league to have exclusive rights to a certain territory. The Indianapolis fans—and fans from every other league city—set up such a yowl of outrage, by voice and by mail, with sportswriters joining in to swell the chorus that Pettit offered Nolan his forgiveness after two seasons and took him back, then shipped him off to Cleveland, where Nolan tried in vain to recover the smoke he had owned in his great days. Still "The Only," but without his stout catcher, Silver "The Only" Flint, Nolan hung on, pitching a few games for Pittsburgh in the American Association, and winning eight out of twenty-two. Then he was moved to the Wilmington "Onions" (the Union Association entry), where he won but a single game of the five he pitched. (He played four games in the outfield.) He ended his big league career in Philadelphia, where he lost five of the seven games he started.

After that, at the age of twenty-seven, he took his unmatched record back to the sandlots and remained the only pitcher who had ever won thirty shutouts in one season, the only one to win his first eleven games in a season, the only one to allow four hits or less in seventeen games in one season, the only one ever to post an earned run average of half a run per nine-inning game—The *Only* Nolan.

●

There were greater pitchers to graduate from the sandlots in the 1880s. One who might well have been tapped by the Hall of Fame, and for a short time as the best in baseball, was Thomas Ramsey, called Toad for some reason now lost to history. He was certainly the strikeout king of his era, when the pitching distance was still but fifty feet. And some think that he might have been utterly unbeatable had he pitched in the days when a pitch had another ten feet to work its wiles on the batter. But Toad's big league career was only two seasons longer than Nolan's. Hard feelings and hard drink and a shouting match with Chris von der Ahe cut Toad's career short when he was still the strikeout king of the organized game.

Toad probably was the first knuckleball pitcher, although he had no name for his bewildering pitch, which he acquired in a minor accident. Toad, as a teenager, was an apprentice bricklayer who loved to play ball beside the firehouse in his native Indianapolis. One day, while inexpertly wielding his trowel, he sliced a tendon in his right hand, his pitching hand, and he could never again straighten out his index finger. After that he pitched with one finger perched atop the ball, so that it was impossible to make the thing spin as a fastball should.

The pitch, thrown with a fastball motion, was almost unbelievable, for it seemed to come to a halt on its way to the plate, then drop suddenly just as it got there. Toad, although he often missed the strike zone, could make his pitches drop exactly where he wanted them to, usually just as they crossed the plate. Once, after he had dazzled batters in the American Association for three seasons, he stood before a "jury" of ball players and newspapermen and, to win a bet, bounced three out of four pitches squarely on home plate.

Toad had been "discovered" in the lot by the firehouse when he was sixteen years old. A dressed-up dude named Jack Kerins, who managed a semipro club named the Whens (after the When Clothing Company) stopped to watch the kid teams perform. One long look at young Ramsey, and Kerins called him over to the side.

"Where'd you ever learn to pitch like that?"

"Nobody learned me. I just do it."

"How'd you like to do it for money?"

What sixteen-year-old would answer no to that? Kerins promptly signed Toad on as a relief pitcher for the Whens. The next season Toad was the regular full-time pitcher. (In that league the same pitcher would usually start every game.) Toad Ramsey within weeks was the number-one pitcher in the whole league, and stayed that way until Jack Kerins was made manager of the Indianapolis club in the brand-new American Association, a major league then. Kerins wanted to bring Toad along to the big club, but the club owner, a wholesale liquor dealer, said "Nothing doing! No kids on my club!" Well, Toad was twenty years old then and Jack Kerins didn't consider him a kid. So he took Toad with him when he became manager of the Louisville club—just added to the league. Poor Toad had a difficult time locating the strike zone his first season. But the next year, 1886, he recovered his sandlot form and pitched in 67 games, winning 38 of them and posting an earned run average of 2.45 in 589 innings. He struck out 499. But alas, he led the league with 207 walks. (Some fans did say that most of the walks were gifts from the umpires, who were as thoroughly bamboozled by Toad's amazing "drop ball" as the batters were.)

In his first big league game, against the Pittsburgh Alleghenies, Toad struck out twelve. Two days later, against Cincinnati, Toad struck out fourteen. His next opponents were the St. Louis Browns, Chris von der Ahe's darlings—if not the best, at least the best-publicized club in the Association. Toad set them down for ten innings, struck out sixteen, and promptly became famous throughout that part of the civilized world that knew beans about baseball. By the end of the season, Ramsey had pitched two seventeen-strikeout games, three with sixteen, and three with thirteen. He actually pitched a no-hit game that season, rare indeed in those days when a base on balls counted as a hit, but the official records do not give him credit for it. Not a single ball was hit out of the infield that day and all the outs, including strikeouts, were accounted for by the first baseman, the catcher, and the shortstop. The *Baltimore Sun* reported the game as a no-hitter and described the game as "the greatest ever seen in Baltimore," inasmuch as the losers made not a single safe hit. But somehow, perhaps through the dark doings of a friend in the composing room or in the editorial office of the official "guide," outfielder Pat O'Connell, the man from Maine, slipped a base hit into the box score.

Two days later Toad Ramsey went after Baltimore again. This time he did give them one hit, but he struck out seventeen and had the spectators howling with laughter at the sight of their very own darlings stumbling, wildly waving their bats, or going to their knees as they tried vainly to connect with that goddamn drop ball. One or two batters were almost ready to swear the ball had *disappeared* at the plate because it had been right *there* when they swung at it.

Toad Ramsey might have achieved a record that would have lived until today had not the league authorities for the next season decreed that each batter should be allowed *four* strikes. (It seemed fair to baseball's prophets that there should be just as many strikes as balls.) In June of 1887, Toad pitched against the sorry Cleveland club, last in the league, and struck out seventeen, giving them all four strikes apiece. One should be permitted to wonder how many more batters he would have fanned if the three-strike rule (which came back the next season) had been in effect. Five more batters, to make twenty-two? Six more, to put the record out of sight?

But even this startling deed did not make the Louisville management's face to shine upon poor Toad. He asked for a small boost in salary and they told him no. So, like too many folks who have begun to feel sorry for themselves, Toad sought comfort in hard liquor. And he threw himself into this new interest with such fervor that even his teammates turned on him.

In 1889, when the American Association had already begun to stagger toward its demise, Toad contrived to stay drunk for three solid weeks. But he had a new boss now—the Louisville Chamber of Commerce had taken over the ball club to keep it from utter collapse, and they did not feel they could do without

the man who had been their star. When Toad sobered up, they
assessed a very small fine against him and added a gentle repri-
mand. But Toad's teammates roared in anger and dismay. A few
of them had been docked a hearty chunk from their pay for
carrying hangovers to the park and they were not going to stand
for this sort of raw discrimination. Toad, when he had taken a
drop (or two), was, as they say nowadays, "no day at the beach"
and it is doubtful he could have found a friend in the whole
league or one who would admit to his friendship. So the Chamber
of Commerce boys shopped him around and knocked him down
for $3,000 to Chris von der Ahe's Browns. This sudden left turn
on Toad's fortunes very nearly sobered him. He did take a pledge,
or part of one, and limited his drinking enough to enable him
to win three games (out of four) for kindly Chris. And the next
season he actually won twenty-four games and struck out 257
batters.

Then in 1891, the year after the Players' Brotherhood strike,
Toad had trouble getting a good start. Old Chris himself was
beset with woes, not just the strike but also some misbehavior
of his own: choices at the race track and the collapse of a few
of his sidelines. So he had no patience with Toad Ramsey's
frequent inability to zero in on the strike zone, and he told Ramsey
so. And Toad, whose own temper was never securely balanced,
yelled back into Chris's face in terms no one in that day would
have dared to print. So Toad was almost instantly looking for
another job.

He found one in Montgomery, Alabama, a long way from the
big leagues. But drinking once more became his principal oc-
cupation and he gradually lost control of his famous pitch. He
was chased out of one bush league after another throughout the
South and finally found himself back home in Indiana, where
the candlelights may or may not have beckoned to him through
the sycamores. The only baseball job he could find was with the
Indianapolis Admirals (of what? one wonders) and there in a
game against Lebanon he issued fourteen walks.

The next year, he did find work as an umpire in the Western

League. Fed up with that, Toad came home and tried to put together a league in Indiana, with himself as pitcher of the Kokomo team. When that venture collapsed, it was back to the sandlots for Toad, with a job at bricklaying to keep up to date on his barroom bills. Nobody knew him now. Even the record books failed to celebrate his one-time greatness. And in 1906, when he was only forty-one, he died of pneumonia. Baseball by this time had turned into something like the modern game. All the players wore gloves. The pitching distance was sixty feet six inches. A walk no longer counted as a hit. Nor did a sacrifice bunt count as a time at bat. And no pitcher lived who could make a pitch behave like Toad Ramsey's.

●

Sandlot baseball did not change as the major league game had. In the 1880s kids still played without gloves. Basemen still hung close to their positions. No one ran out to the outfield to help relay a ball home. Because space was so limited in town, "over the fence was out"—always—for sometimes there was no getting the ball back.

Still, this was a time when *everybody* played baseball, or tried to. Even girls were known to cook up contests resembling baseball, in which a token—not necessarily a ball—was kicked or hurled away and the one who propelled it had to scurry to touch a base and return. This was very close to the game of catapult ball, or trap ball, in that it did not require a whole company of kids to get a game started. The batter just popped the ball into the air by stepping on a trap, or catapult, and then tried to get back safely before the ball was returned. (In Scotland, perhaps through native thrift, the game was played without a catapult, the ball being tossed up by the batter and then struck off. This was fungo, "fung" being Scottish for snapping into the air.)

Naturally, most boys in that era selected a professional player—like Joe Start in Mike Kelly's case—and tried to fashion himself in some way after him, posing at the pitcher's point like Al Spalding of the Boston Reds with the ball held up in both hands as if he were about to eat it. Or pointing his bat almost straight at the pitcher, in the manner of the day's mighty batsmen. And this was about all the actual "training" boys might go through on their way to professional ball. Because the real object of the game was to have fun, many developed an intense love of the sport that would never diminish. And more than one or two persisted in playing, regardless of physical handicap, as Toad Ramsey had.

Indeed, one young man insisted on playing baseball even after he had lost an arm. That was Hugh Daily, who began to throw baseballs when he was a schoolboy in Baltimore and had both his arms. Like some other great pitchers he spent hours, when there were no mates to play with, simply throwing a ball at a target—a tin can that he had nailed to a fence behind his house. By the time he was fifteen Hugh had become the only pitcher of his parochial school team. He, like Ramsey, was a strikeout king, and often struck out half the side in schoolboy games.

But Hugh had to work to support his widowed mother, so he took on almost any odd job that was offered. One job was helping the stage carpenter at the Front Street Theater, and one task he was awarded was arranging "red fire" (candlelike sticks with wicks that would burn red, such as were used to signal danger on the railroad). Monkeying with these to simulate a house on fire off-stage, Hugh managed to burn himself so severely that his left arm had to be amputated at the elbow.

Stop playing baseball just because one arm was gone? Not young Hugh. He got himself a baseball bat and whittled it down so he could wield it with one hand. Then he persuaded a playmate to pitch to him hour after hour. Eventually Hugh, who had great shoulder strength, developed a sort of half push, half swing that would really drive out a fine daisy-cutter. Now he felt he could play ball with the best of them. He needed only one arm to pitch. And he had developed pinpoint control by throwing at that tin can.

When he was nineteen years old he joined a collection of neighborhood youths who called themselves the Quicksteps and he led them in clobbering all the sandlot clubs in and around Baltimore. But he often ran into difficulty in fielding. After stopping a number of ground balls with the tender stump of his arm, he designed a leather extension to fit on his elbow, with a square pad on the end of it to stop a ball. With that he developed unusual dexterity and seemed as able as any two-armed athlete.

From the Quicksteps, Hugh graduated to the Newington club, a profit-sharing combination that traveled all over the East—to Washington; Richmond; Newark; Jersey City; Columbus, Ohio; and Springfield, Massachusetts, playing not only sandlotters and semipros but National League clubs as well, and earning a decent dollar. Two seasons like this and Hugh was known in a dozen cities, more than one of which tried to entice him to come play in their yard. But Hugh was happy with the money he was making and he preferred home cooking to anything he had sampled on the road. He did give in finally to an offer of a regular salary from the newly created Baltimore club in the so-called National Association, itself newborn. He could play with them and still have supper at home. But the new association foundered after one season, during which Hugh, like most "relief" pitchers of the day, played right field when he was not pitching. And he won local fame at least for his timely and solid hitting as well as for his control and his sizzling curves.

With the evaporation of the National Association, Hugh accepted an offer from the New York Metropolitans—the team that manager Jim Mutrie had called "My big ones! My Giants!" And Hugh Daily pitched in the very first baseball game played in New York City by acknowledged professionals. (All other clubs, from the Brooklyn Atlantics to the Cincinnati Red Stockings, earnestly pretended to be amateurs.) Facing the Washington Nationals in the brand-new Polo Grounds that Mutrie had rented for the season, Hugh won his first big-time victory. Because the Washington club did not make the scene until late afternoon, there was time for only five innings before daylight died. In that time Daily beat the Washingtons 4–2. He permitted them only three hits and knocked in a run with a single to left. And he kept the twenty-seven hundred spectators yelling happily; Jim Mutrie was happy, too, although he did not yell, because now he knew professional baseball was firmly established in New York, where the game had been born.

In 1881 Jim Mutrie (known throughout the city as Truthful Jeems for his astounding habit of telling the truth about whatever he might be trying to sell) rented the Polo Grounds again. And with Hugh Daily doing practically all of the pitching, the Metropolitans beat nearly every top team in the nation, including the great White Stockings of Chicago and the slick teams from Harvard, Yale, and Princeton.

That season with the Metropolitans was the beginning of a career that, in better-scrutinized times, would have put Daily in the Hall of Fame. He was sick all the month of June, but once he recovered, he went on to win thirty-eight games, including eight shutouts and five two-hit games. He played fourteen games in right field, four in center field, and one at shortstop, fielding ground balls by stopping them with his leather pad and quickly grabbing them up to fire them to first.

The next year Hugh moved into the big leagues—not really faster company but better paid and better organized. He first joined Buffalo in the National League, where he and "Pud" Galvin pitched all the games and won forty-three between them, and where he shared the locker room with Big Dan Brouthers, the best first baseman in the league and one of the largest ball players, and with Jim O'Rourke, the famous "Orator," who managed the club.

Hugh, looking for a better payday, moved to Cleveland next, where he pitched a no-hit, no-run game, most of it in a drenching rain, and walked only three batters. In 1884 he joined the Chicago "Onions" (the Union League entry), apparently seduced by founder Henry Lucas's plan for dividing up the take among the players. With the Onions, Daily struck out 464 batters in fifty-four games, in a season when fouls were not called strikes. Later against Boston, Daily struck out twenty batters but was credited with only nineteen strikeouts because John Krieg, his catcher,

George Wright.

Below: Dickey Pearce, in 1871.

Harry Wright.

4

Above: The Oberlin College baseball team of 1881; Moses Fleetwood Walker is seated, middle row, far left; Welday Walker is standing, top row, second from right. *Left:* Cap Anson.

5

Mike "King" Kelly.

7

Orator Jim O'Rourke, with his son,
James Stephen "Queenie" O'Rourke.

8

9

Charles Comiskey.

Left: Amos Rusie.

Chris von der Ahe.

Fred "Sure-Shot" Dunlap.

13

Above: Lou Sockalexis, with Lowell of the New England League. *Opposite:* Pete Browning.

Ed Delahanty.

15

Cozy Dolan, in 1902.

16

Deacon McGuire, in 1900.

Above: The Royal Rooters, at the 1903 World Series.

Rooter's Souvenir
BOSTON - PITTSBURG
Oct., 1903.   M. T. McGreevy

TESSIE,
You Are The Only, Only, Only.

CHORUS.

Tessie, you make me feel so badly;
    Why don't you turn around.
Tessie, you know I love you madly;
    Babe, my heart weighs about a
    pound.
Don't blame me if I ever doubt you,
You know, I wouldn't live with-
    out you;
Tessie, you are the only, only,
    only, -ly.

3d Base.   Nuf Ced.

Who Kidnapped the Pittsburg Band
Nuf Ced—McGreevy.

19

20

Big Jim Corbett towers over John McGraw.

John McGraw towers over Tod Sloan.

Left: Waite Hoyt, in 1918. *Below:* Hal Chase, in 1919.

23 Kenesaw Mountain Landis, in 1922.

Opposite, top right: Howard Ehmke, in 1923.
Opposite, top left: Connie Mack.
Opposite, bottom: Pepper Martin after his game five home run in the 1931 World Series. Frankie Frisch is congratulating him; Chick Hafey is the next batter; Mickey Cochrane is the catcher.

24

25

26

Smoky Joe Williams.

Frank Crosetti, with the San Francisco
Seals, 1928.

Satchel Paige, in 1942.

29

28

Babe Ruth and friends.

let a third strike get by and the runner made it safely to first. He allowed one hit in that game and three days later he faced Boston once more and struck out ten, again allowing but one hit.

Before Daily quit the professional game, at age thirty, he had never sought a single concession because of his handicap—except once, in 1880, when he was pitching for the New York Metropolitans against the Jersey City team. Tom Deasley, the catcher, had worn a large hangover to the park that day and he very soon grew weary of snapping the ball all the way back to the pitcher's mound and instead began to roll the ball to Daily on the ground. But Daily got a damn sight more weary of leaning over to stop that ball with his pad. After an inning or two he summoned Deasley to the mound. Deasley trotted obediently out to confer with him and Daily meanwhile unlaced the extension from his arm. When Deasley come within reach, Hugh lifted the false arm and brought it down full force on Deasley's unsuspecting head.

"Arch 'em, God damn it!" he yelled. "Arch 'em!"

You may be sure that Deasley took care after that to arch them.

●

There was one sandlot player who went to no other school than the sandlots and entered professional baseball when he could not read or write. That was Sure Shot Fred Dunlap, mentioned before as the man who beat tough Curt Welch in St. Louis until Curt needed help to stand on his feet.

Fred's parents both died before he was ten years old and he was taken in by a kindly German couple who apparently thought boys were born just to have fun. Fred's only chore was fetching a daily bucket of beer and, that errand done, he could go out on any fair morning and play all day. Like nearly every other boy in or near Philadelphia, what Fred liked best to play was baseball, as the big guys played it. So whenever the weather smiled on him, Fred and a few friends would hurry out to the nearby meadows to throw and bat the ball. Unable to read any instructions or advice, even on baseball, Fred believed that you should throw with either hand. His one ambition, which lasted all his life, was to win the current ball game. To this end, while his mates were at school, Fred would keep playing, throwing the ball and catching it, or scooping it off the ground with one of his tiny, girl-sized hands. It mattered not to Fred if his playmates were big or small. Fred would take them all on—in a fistfight if need be—although he was far from being a quarrelsome lad.

Fred started playing ball for money when he was eighteen years old and signed a contract with the Philadelphia Acmes, a club of little renown and short life. But the signing mortified poor Fred beyond speech, for when his signature was needed, he could only make an X. Immediately after that he found a teammate who showed him how to write his name. He learned too to recognize a few words in print. But he had no knowledge of the alphabet and could not read a book. Still, he was acknowledged as one of the smartest and the best-conditioned men in the game. Having concentrated on baseball as his "major," he might have earned a doctorate in the subject. He was never known to throw to the wrong base, was never caught out of position on any play, and seemed to be thinking a play or two ahead of the enemy at all times. And unlike too many professional ball players, Fred was an athlete all year round, seven days a week. He was not a big man, only five feet seven, but he was trim, erect, and strong-looking. He was also, once he could afford the necessaries, one of the best-dressed ball players in the land. Mike Kelly, who prided himself on his own splendid wardrobe and his ability to flaunt it, always maintained that Fred Dunlap was the best-dressed man in the world. He was also charming socially and an adornment to any company, with his gleaming top hat, his beautifully cut suit, and his glistening stickpin. His manners were faultless, and his bearing graceful, as if, some said, he had been raised by royalty. Fred's physical appearance was striking, too. He was as lean and as brown as an Indian from year-long living in the sun. He had an Indian's straight nose and deep brown eyes. But he was muscled like a tiger, enormously strong, and quick as a cat on his feet. He habitually ran close to the ground as if he had a nose for the ball. And of course he could field and throw it with either hand. His real specialty, however, was the accuracy of his sizzling throws. He earned his nickname Sure Shot because he never missed a target.

By the time he reached twenty-one, Fred had joined the Cleveland club of the National League and was on his way to becoming the best-paid player in the league. Like most great ball players of his time, he played nearly every position, including pitcher. When he left Cleveland in 1884, to manage the short-lived Maroons of the "Onion" League, he served as manager at a salary of $6,000 a year, a figure that amazed the baseball world, for that was very nearly a rich man's wage.

In Cleveland Fred was part of the "stonewall" infield that was deemed the finest of the century: Big Bill Phillips at first, Sure Shot Fred at second, Mike Muldoon at third, and Pebbly Jack Glasscock, the acknowledged king of his position, at shortstop. The real "King" of that era, of course, was Chicago's great Mike Kelly, named by many observers and writers the king of them all. But Dunlap was a "king," too, and as long as he lived, there were fans who argued that he was greater than Kelly. Kelly himself agreed that Dunlap deserved the crown. For Dunlap could outrun a jackrabbit and could place a batted ball neatly through a hole (he led the Union Association in home runs, thirteen, and batting average, .412). And of course his powerful and accurate arm could throw out runners from almost any spot in the field. Even sprawled on the ground, Fred could get off a throw that seemed to skim the turf and beat the runner to the bag. As a base runner, Fred was a terror to the opposition, a reckless, headfirst slider who scared more than one baseman almost out of his pants with the fierce and fearless way he would come into a base.

Fred, wherever he went, played his heart out for his team. He was the individual star of the fifteen-game "World Series" in which he played second base for Detroit. He left that job to join the series' enemy, Chris von der Ahe's Browns, and he played his heart out for them. But it was with Cleveland that Fred enjoyed his greatest thrill, the memory of which dwelt with him all his short life. Playing against the Chicago White Sox, who had just won twenty-one games in a row, Fred came to bat after Jack Glasscock had doubled and drove a fastball over the fence for two runs, winning the ball game 2–0 and sending the Cleveland fans into near delirium with joy. That was in 1880 and Fred still had eleven seasons to go in baseball.

When Fred left baseball, it was said that he had more than $100,000 in the bank—and he looked it: neatly barbered, spiffily dressed, his button shoes always a-shine, his top hat set at a perfect angle. Eleven years after he retired from the game to go into the building business, Fred died, penniless and alone, in a cheap Philadelphia rooming house. Some men recalled having seen him, shabby and disconsolate, a short time earlier, walking the Philadelphia streets alone. There was talk that he had lost his entire fortune in the stock market. But some wondered if perhaps poor Fred had signed too many contracts that he could not read.

There was no one to admit kinship or to claim Fred's body. When it was brought to the city morgue, a policeman who had been a long-time baseball fan thought the body looked like Fred Dunlap, and he persuaded Lave Cross, who had played against Fred Dunlap in the Players' League, to come look at the body. "That's Fred Dunlap, all right," said Cross. But there was no one else to come tell Fred good-bye, and he was hustled off to a pauper's grave.

Chapter 6

CROSSING THE LINE

1. *The first black baseball player* to reach the major leagues in our land was not Jackie Robinson. It was Moses Fleetwood "Fleet" Walker, a lithe and learned man who studied baseball, and other subjects, at Oberlin College in Ohio. Along with Welday Wilberforce, his kid brother, Fleet Walker joined the Toledo club of the Northwestern League and became a major leaguer when Toledo was gathered into the American Association (then the "other" major league) in 1884. Welday played only five games in the outfield in the American Association. But Fleet, a catcher, played the full season, except for some time out to mend a broken collarbone.

In 1885, Toledo was dropped from the American Association and taken into the Tri-State League, a minor league where the Walker boys played out their string.

In 1888, the Tri-State League adopted a regulation barring "members of the colored race" from playing on any club in the league. Welday Walker thereupon wrote a letter to the president of the league, saying, "The law is a disgrace to the present age and casts derision on the laws of the state of Ohio that says all men are created equal. I would suggest that your honorable body, in case the law is not repealed, pass one making it criminal for any colored man or woman to be found in a ball ground."

The law was immediately repealed.

This move by the directors of the Tri-State League was by no means an isolated incident. Black players had been specifically barred from playing in the National Association in 1867. And of course there had been "agreements" from time to time to remove a black player from the roster in certain games. But once Cap Anson took charge of the Chicago White Stockings he gathered enough bigots around him to establish the unwritten (and unspeakable) rule that barred black players from organized baseball for six decades.

And even when the "unwritten rule" was finally wiped off the board with the signing of Jack Roosevelt Robinson to a Montreal contract, there were cries of outrage from players, magnates, and sportswriters as well as fans. Joe Williams, of the *New York World Telegram,* who counted himself the voice of New York fans, set the style for all the polite protesters when he expressed the friendliest of feelings for Robinson but hastened to remind Jack of his "responsibilities"—by which he clearly meant his duty to avoid acting as if he were white. Williams, out of his own shallow experience with such matters, offered his private observation that black players had been barred from organized baseball chiefly because they could not play well enough to perform on an equal basis with whites. It had been his discovery, he solemnly averred, that "the Negro's demands bulked larger than his capabilities." This was apparently the polite way of declaring that "the goddamn nigger should learn to know his place."

Not all of Williams's colleagues, however, joined the cry. Dan Parker of the *New York Mirror,* a very large and very outspoken man, and perhaps the sharpest of the lot, calmly observed: "Why a good, respectable Negro athlete shouldn't fit as well into organized baseball as he does into college football, basketball, boxing, and cricket (to drag an ally into the argument) is something I have never been able to figure out in view of the record of amicable race relations in these sports."

A number of sportswriters, like Williams, assumed an air of neutrality but privately encouraged a festering revolt among Robinson's teammates-to-be. (Dan Parker later on assured me that "you have to know Joe Williams really well in order to dislike him.")

Of course there had been great black baseball players in every corner of the land since before Jackie Robinson was born, many of them whose abilities bulked larger than those of their white counterparts. We have already marked the existence of George Stovey (a teammate of Fleet Walker in Newark), who established the Newark pitching record that no white player has ever matched: thirty-five victories in one season.

In the years when Stovey was working, there were some twenty black players in organized baseball, all of whom owned abilities more than equal to the demands. As noted earlier, a black second baseman named Bud Fowler played for both Keokuk, Iowa, and Binghamton, New York. In Buffalo another black man, Frank Grant, played second base, while Charles Kelly, a black first baseman, played for the professional club in Danville, Illinois. But even then there were cradle Confederates and their sympathizers throughout the Union struggling to rid the Great Game of any trace of racial equality.

Most black players, naturally, sought places in the "Negro leagues," rather haphazard structures that could at least provide a reasonably decent payday for hundreds of the nation's great black athletes. The first all-black teams were hippodroming outfits, many run by white promoters, that often played up to the white man's prejudices by cavorting minstrel show–style on the diamond. But the greatest of the all-black baseball clubs that earned some serious national recognition was the team built around the dining room crew of the Argyle Hotel in Babylon, Long Island, and led by the headwaiter, Frank Thompson. They called themselves the Cuban Giants, although few of them had ever been much closer to Cuba than Charleston, South Carolina.

The Cuban Giants, as their fame spread and as they began to offer regular salaries to their players, set out to find top players from everywhere. Eventually they featured two of the finest baseball players, black or white, that the country had ever known—

Sol White, a batsman as mighty as Cap Anson himself, and Shep Trusty, who had no equal as a pitcher. In their first year (1887) as a straight professional club that could pay a man as good a wage as he could earn in a first-class dining room, they took on both the all-white Indianapolis club and the Cincinnati club of the International League and beat them both. And they threw a scare into the championship Detroit club of the great National League by playing them almost even—losing 6–4.

The success of the Cuban Giants spawned the creation of a dozen or more "Cubans" and "Giants," some of which were still run by white promoters, and many of which paid dining room–size wages: eighteen dollars a week for pitcher and catcher, fifteen dollars for infielders, and twelve dollars for outfielders. But the hours were better and the fans often tossed extra tribute onto the field. By the end of the century there were the Cuban X Giants, the Genuine Cuban Giants, the Mohawk Giants, the Elite Giants, the Leland Giants, the Royal Giants (who were sponsored by the Royal Cafe in Brooklyn), and the Lincoln Giants of Lincoln, Nebraska, who eventually moved to New York.

The truly elite of all the "Giants" were the Page Fence Giants, sponsored by the Page Fence Company of Adrian, Michigan. They traveled in a private railroad car and usually offered a parade on gleaming bicycles before a game. But even they, for all their style, often had to trudge the streets until late at night to find a place to sleep and could never enter a first-class restaurant or even earn a polite welcome at a one-armed lunchroom (so named for the table-armed chairs where you'd sit and eat your lunch). No matter that they, and other Giants, could outplay many of the best white professionals, and despite the relaxation in the northern states of some of the cruelest aspects of segregation, they were still required to "know their place"—which was always several notches below even the lowliest white man.

Sportswriters, on the few occasions when they had to acknowledge the existence of a black baseball player, did not boggle at referring to him as a "coon" or "dinge" or "nigger" or rendering him to their readers as an ignorant or comic figure, as black people were invariably presented on the stage or in magazine fiction. Even well into the twentieth century, black people could be reminded at every turn that, law or no law, they were not to consider themselves as wholly human. In one enlightened corner of New England, in the 1950s, a black man who had dared to order a sandwich at a lunch counter saw the plate he had used conscientiously broken into small pieces before his eyes. And the lunch counter owner, who had performed the symbolic deed, was solemnly congratulated by his customers.

On a hot day in New York, about this time, a black woman who had been asked to bring a pound of butter home to her employer had the butter handed to her in a flimsy single sheet of wrapping so that long before she reached her kitchen melted butter was running in a stream down her arm. If a black man carrying a briefcase was seen moving at a trot along a midtown street in New York, he was certain to be stopped and questioned by a cop. And one day a newspaper story told of a bank manager whose uniformed messenger had been stopped at the door and questioned by a couple of apparent nobodies. When the manager ran to a nearby policeman to report, "They're holding up my man!" the policeman thereupon hurried to the scene and shot the messenger. After all, he was the only black man in sight.

A teenage baseball player, farmed out to a club in a small southern city, had his stomach violently turned one day when a car full of angry white men sped by, dragging behind it the severed head of a black man. The guy had attacked a white girl, the boy was told. He also learned later that the lynchers had "got the wrong man" and were sorry.

This is the sort of world many black ball players were raised in, during the first decades of the twentieth century. And white children, even after two world wars had produced black heroes by the score, still learned from their story books and from the "jokes" told by their elders that black people were put into the world to be laughed at.

Even the very President of the United States who had issued

the order to integrate the armed forces (an order the great General MacArthur refused to obey) turned on a reporter one day, during talk about the effects of integration, and snapped, "Would you want your sister to marry one?"

This was during the Korean War. In an earlier war, another president, Woodrow Wilson, prompted a number of black Democrats to change their registration to Republican when he ordered the black officers of black troops headed to France to be replaced by white officers—who, it was solemnly rumored, had been given permission to shoot any soldiers under their command who, in the officers' own judgment, deserved shooting. While no such horror obtained in the Korean War, General Edward M. Almond, MacArthur's personal favorite, did, in a top secret memo, offer his judgment that black troops could be useful anywhere except in the front lines and preferably even then to be under white command.

All the same, black baseball was thriving and there were black performers everywhere who were clearly the equals and often the superiors of their white counterparts. By the time the twentieth century had begun, black baseball clubs were operating winter and summer, often playing against all-white clubs from the organized leagues and frequently beating them.

As in the white leagues, the pitchers in the black leagues were usually the heroes. In 1914, the mighty Walter Johnson, who had been accepted by white fans everywhere as the greatest pitcher alive, was outpitched by a black man who had been raised in Johnson's own hometown (Coffeeville, Kansas). He was a pitcher named Wickware, a skinny, seemingly many jointed man who because of the odd shade of his skin was known as The Red Ant. Wickware faced a team of major leaguers led by Johnson in Albany, New York, after the season was over, and struck out seventeen of them, not allowing a single run.

While permitting black men and white men to play in the same park was a sin against nature in the southland, in other parts of the country such doings, while not exactly commonplace, caused very little public alarm, even when the black team came in first, as it often did. And in Cuba, where some of the first organized black clubs played all winter in a regular league, all men, at least on the ball field, seemed to have been created equal in everything but skills. The Cuban Giants, as well as two other "Giants"—the Quaker Giants and the Philadelphia Giants— played regularly there and mighty batsmen like catcher Clarence Williams, first baseman Sol White, and second baseman Johnny Hill earned islandwide fame, as did a pitcher who was known as Kid Carter.

But it was not until the 1900s, when baseball had finally grown up—with fouls counted as strikes, the pitching distance settled at sixty feet six inches, and the catcher required to play up close and permitted to use a well-padded glove—that the greatest black pitchers appeared. Most notable, perhaps, was Rube Foster, pitcher for the Philadelphia Giants, who created (in the Midwest) the first Negro league. Rube, who spent most of his life in the game as player and manager, was a natural showman, who continually dressed up his games by adding such features as ordering every man who reached third to try to steal home, and promising that his club would provide at least six home runs. Rube managed the Leland Giants of Chicago (later named the Chicago American Giants) and earned fame for, among many other talents, giving signals from the bench with puffs of smoke from his pipe.

Still, peaceful and friendly competition between whites and blacks did nothing in the early 1900s to win the bigots of the day to ways of decency. A newspaper writer in 1905, gleefully reporting how some black men were bumped off a freight car and chased away with a club, referred to them in print as "dinges" and "boogs." And after a game in which a black team defeated the white World Champion club, there were protests in the white country newspapers about this "disgraceful exhibition" and insistence that it should never be allowed to happen again.

As a matter of fact, it was *not* permitted to happen again because the baseball deities decreed that henceforth no major league baseball club could compete, as an entity, against a black club. No more than *four* players from any one club, they ruled, could take part in such a performance—perhaps for fear that little white children might grow up to suspect that black daddies were sometimes the equal of white daddies.

The game that prompted this rush to the barricades was staged at Olympic Field at 136th Street and Fifth Avenue in New York, in that area known then and now as Harlem. It was the second game of a doubleheader scheduled for October 17, 1915, and over nine thousand fans, almost equally divided between black and white, had crowded into the scanty stands to watch.

The first game apparently posed no threat to the social structure because in it the all-black Lincoln Giants faced only a bush league white man's club from New London, Connecticut, so it was not as if some white father figure was likely to be demeaned. The feature of this game, which was taken by the Giants 7–1, was the pitching of Ad Langford, the spitball artist of the Giants, who, had there been such an institution, would have eventually been memorialized in the Black Hall of Fame.

In the *big* game, the Giants were to face the National League champion Philadelphia Phillies (or most of them), with the great Joe Judge of the Washington Senators on first base for the Phillies, in place of Fred Luderus. And pitching for the Phillies was George Chalmers, himself a native of Harlem, which was not an all-black enclave then. The pitcher for the Giants was Cyclone Joe Williams, a tall, powerful Texan who had earlier faced the Phillies' thirty-game winner, Grover Cleveland Alexander, and beaten him 9–2.

Joe Williams, who depended largely on his smoking fastball, was a pitcher who, like Christy Mathewson, liked to work well within himself. He granted the big leaguers but seven hits and struck out ten. And he contributed to the only score in the game when he followed Frank Forbes's base on balls in the eighth inning with a single that put Frank on second. Right fielder Earle sacrificed, moving Forbes to third. A single by third baseman Bragg brought Forbes home with the run that won the game.

The Phillies were convinced that the game was tied in the ninth inning after Bert Niehoff, the Philadelphia second baseman, drove one of Joe Williams's curves clean over the right-field fence, into an adjoining tenement. But that fence was almost directly behind first base and, according to the ground rules at Olympic Field, the hit was good for only one base. (In Joe's boyhood, it would have been "out.") Joe Judge came up then and bounced a hard drive right off the fence in front of the center-field bleachers. The ball rocketed high in the air, headed for the street beyond. But the lad who was attending the score-board grabbed the ball before it fell and tossed it to the Giants' center fielder.

Niehoff, meanwhile, had lit out from first on the blow and made it all the way home before the ball was returned to the infield. Judge reached third. It was a home run, by the Phillies' reckoning. But the umpire, quoting the ground rules again, de-clared that inasmuch as the ball had been "handled by a spec-tator," it was good for only two bases. That put poor Niehoff back at third, and he was nailed at the plate when he tried to score on a roller by Hank Eibel, a bush leaguer from Atlanta borrowed by the Phillies.

Cyclone Joe always counted that game the best of his long career, although his version, offered some thirty-two years later when he was tending bar in Harlem, differed from the way the papers of the day told the story. Joe "recalled" there had been men in the field whose presence was not noted by the reporters. But their names had obviously been treasured by Joe from other times long past. Joe's dream box score listed a left fielder named Bloney Hall; a second baseman called Polly Mangin; and a catcher named Doc Wiley; in center field Julius Thomas, Bill Pettus at first base, and Phil Cockrell in right, with Todd Allen at third. Frank Forbes he put at shortstop and that was correct, as was the presence of Wabishaw S. Wiley, known as Doc because he was studying dentistry. Bloney Hall and Julie Thomas were also in the real lineup that day. The others had played, obviously, in long ago fields where roses fade.

Joe's fondest memory was of Doc Wiley, who had died ten years before Joe and I talked together. Doc had practiced dentistry for a decade in Orange, New Jersey, and before joining up with Joe had been a star with the Lincoln Giants. Doc was the one Joe was proudest of, and missed the most. Good old Doc Wiley, who had an arm like a gun.

Joe's arm, too, must have been mighty. "I never threw a 'heavy' ball," he said. "My pitch started just above my head and let go about my shoulders. I most used fastballs and a change of pace. My control was good, so when I used a curve it would break right around the man's knees. I never used no freak balls, less I seen the other feller doing it. Then I might take a piece of emery and rub a spot on the ball about the size of a dime. That pitch would do tricks. Did I use that pitch every game, I'd *never* have lost. Not once. Once in a while I tried a knuckler, but no spitter. I just didn't like that pitch. I pitched a lot of good ball in my time." Joe's grave handsome face was softened by a gentle smile. "I'da been in the majors, too, if'n my hair wasn't so curly. Anything but colored, I'da made it. I don't know why it is they give us such a hard time. We all the same really. We all sit on that old common denominator."

Joe, six feet five inches tall, broad-shouldered, deep in the chest, was still straight and strong at sixty, still a handsome man people would turn to look at. His skin was bronze, almost butter-colored, and his eyes were large and brown. His close-clipped gray hair set off Indian features.

"They tell me I was born in Wimmia, Texas, in 1886," said Joe. "A little place. Only four stores in it. But I was raised in San Antonio. I was fourteen when I started pitching for the San Antonio Black Broncos, for money. My mother lived thirty miles off, but she never missed a game. She'd sit on them rocks, which is what the bleachers was called, and keep a-yelling 'You can't beat my son!' And, you know, mostly she was right. I won a lot of games."

Joe left Texas after his first season with the Broncos and he never went back. First he went to Cuba with an "all-star" team of semipros (as he did every winter thereafter). But mostly he played ball around Chicago with different semipro clubs before joining the Lincoln Giants. He was twenty-six then and one of the best pitchers in the country. The Giants were owned by the New York State boxing commissioner, Charles Harvey, and managed by two other white men, Jesse and Ed McMahon. They made Joe their leading man and started him off in New York, on Lincoln Field, against an all-white semipro club named the New York Ironsides. Joe sank the Old Ironsides "six to nawting," he said, for he remembered the game well.

That same year Joe for the first time took on the big leaguers—the New York Giants, who sent George Wiltse, their veteran pitcher, to face him. Joe beat that bunch, too, and once more it was "six to nawting."

Joe took on the entire Pacific Coast League in the wintertime, pitching for Rube Foster and the Leland Giants. He won nine games out of eleven, tied one, and got beat only by Portland. Joe laughed out loud when he recalled the time he had to pitch two games in a row against Seattle.

"I beat them already two to one on Saturday. Gave them seven hits. Then on Sunday I'm sitting on the bench with my sweater on and Seattle fills the bases in the first inning. Old Rube Foster begun to sweat. He looks at me a long time. Then he says, 'Give you fifty if you get me out of this crack.' I says, 'Another fifty if I win it?' 'Sure,' says Rube.

"Well, that old sun was beating down and I felt good all over. I start to warm up in front of the grandstand and first thing you know, it starts to rain real money. Silver dollars, half-dollars, come pelting down and I pick them all up and tells those fans thank you. Then I give Rube the money to hold and I went in to pitch. Beat them one to nawting, too. They only got one hit."

One pitcher Joe had little to say about was Cannonball Dick Redding, who played as Joe did, with various "Giants" among the black clubs. But there was a clipping in Joe's scrapbook that recorded the game, in 1918, at Olympic Field in Harlem, when Joe met Cannonball Dick head on and beat him by throwing a no-hit, no-run game against him, allowing but one base on balls and winning the game 1–0. Redding, according to the clipping, was "Joe Williams's great rival." But all Joe had to say about Dick was that he was no longer living.

There was another Williams pitching for the Brooklyn Royal Giants in Joe's day—a left-hander named String Bean Williams whose fastball was the equal of Joe's and whose curve had no equal. And String Bean had another left-hander for a team-mate—Lefty Harvey, whose curves and fastballs did not match those that the mighty String Bean delivered, but who was of big league caliber, too. Both String Bean and Harvey died young.

Any of these strong-armed young men, had their hair been straight and their skin less dusky, would have earned, on the record of their deeds and the length of their service, a place in baseball's Hall of Fame, as a few of them did. Joe Williams never made it, but he did have a hand, or at least a few fingers, in making a place for another black man, younger than himself. That was Buck Leonard, surely one of the game's mightiest hitters. Buck, who learned his trade, like many black players, in the barren lots of Baltimore, made his living, until he was in his mid-twenties, by working in the railroad shops. Like thousands of others, Buck lost his job in the Hoover depression and found a baseball job that paid barely enough for him to keep himself fed, playing first base for the Baltimore Stars. Buck came to New York with the Stars and was left there almost penniless when the Stars went bust. Buck had been in the city just long enough to make friends with Joe Williams, at the very bar where Joe was working years later, when I first knew him. And after Buck had found a job with the Brooklyn Royal Giants, Joe urged him to hook up with the Homestead Grays, the best black club in the nation, where the pay was steady and the future bright. Joe got Buck an offer from the Grays, whom he used to manage, and Buck took over there as the regular first baseman. He quickly became the second-best hitter in the league and perhaps the niftiest fielding first baseman in the country, black or white. He could field, men who saw him said, as deftly as Hal Chase and could hit as hard as Lou Gehrig. But Chase, who was probably as well met and jolly a man as Buck, was one of the me-first types who seldom passed up a chance to grab an honest or dishonest dollar, while Gehrig, in his early years, was socially awkward and not much given to laughter. But Leonard, as James Whitcomb Riley might have said, just held out his warm heart in his own two hands to everyone.

With the Grays Buck teamed up with the number-one hitter in America, by most observers' lights. That was Josh Gibson, who always felt that he, rather than Jackie Robinson, should have been first across major league baseball's "color line."

With the Grays, whose home base was Pittsburgh, Gibson and Leonard were the Ruth and Gehrig of the black leagues, with Gibson, the home-run hitter, batting third and Buck Leonard, the extra-base hit man, batting fourth. Occasionally they would swap places, with Josh often coming to bat with Buck already on second base.

Buck, like most of the black stars, hastened to warmer climes in the winter, to play in one of the Latin leagues in Cuba or Puerto Rico, where fat and steady paydays awaited. As indestructible as Satchel Paige, Buck Leonard played baseball for pay until he was nearly fifty. When Buck was forty-five, Bill Veeck, then operating the sorry St. Louis Browns, invited him to come aboard. But Buck decided he was too long in the tooth to hold his own in the big leagues now. When he was forty-eight, he reduced his age by ten years and secured a job in the Mexican League, "where the pitchers didn't throw so hard." (But the fans threw firecrackers.) Returning to Cooperstown on a visit after he had himself been elected to the Hall of Fame, Buck Leonard at sixty-eight was as spry as more than half the other Hall of Famers who had made the scene, far sprier than some, and a damn sight easier to meet.

Another great ball player, and a teammate of Joe's on the Lincoln Giants, was John Henry Lloyd, who played third base and shortstop. A hero in Cuba, where the fans tagged him Cucharra (meaning "ladle") because of his out-thrust chin, John was often compared to Honus Wagner, Ty Cobb's rival for the "greatest ball player" of his day. Like Wagner, Lloyd had enormous hands that could scoop up a fast ground ball (along with a handful of gravel) as neatly and as swiftly as if he were scooping sugar and then fire the ball at rifle speed to the first baseman. Like Wagner, Lloyd ran bases with a loping stride that ate up some six feet at a clip so he moved far more swiftly than he seemed to. He resembled Wagner in nature, too, although physically he was somewhat leaner and a few inches taller. Like Wagner he was a gentle man (but fearless and aggressive as a base runner) who never owned an enemy.

Then there was Joe's batting hero, Charles "Home Run" Johnson, who hit a good many more home runs than Frank "Home Run" Baker, the hero of the 1911 World Series when he hit two home runs for Philadelphia. Alas, no musty records exist to record the number of times Johnson performed the same feat.

Joe recalled Buddy Petway, too, the catcher who was supposed to have taught the great Johnny Kling of the Chicago Cubs how to snap a ball to second base from a crouch—a deed for which Kling became famous. And there were two other long-ball hitters in Joe Williams's private Hall of Fame: Pete Hill and Frank Duncan, contemporaries of the great Jap Payne, who used to set fans to screaming by his amazing throws from right field to capture runners trying to score. Jap could put topspin on the ball, Joe declared, so that the ball would take one long, low, sizzling bounce inside the baseline and streak, only inches from the ground, straight into the catcher's glove.

In the days when Cyclone Joe was doing batters down in city after city, there was one more black man who came close to slipping into the big leagues in disguise. This was a muscular little shortstop named Haley whom John McGraw (who probably thought a black man was "just an Irishman turned inside out") spotted and lured into trying to dodge past that "unwritten rule." Legend has it (and it must be partly true) that McGraw spent many thousands of dollars trying first to establish Haley as a Cuban in Havana, and then endeavoring to slip him through Ellis Island as an immigrant. Getting him settled in Havana was simple, but bringing him back without revealing his true identity and derivation proved impossible. So Haley returned to the Dakotas, where McGraw had discovered him, and continued to startle the natives with the big league caliber of his play.

One wonders what uproar might have exploded had tough John McGraw sat in years later when the assembled club owners met to bar the door against Jackie Robinson and fifteen of them, lacking only Branch Rickey (who was strongly, and correctly, suspected of plotting a violation of the "color bar"), all voted that it was against the interests of "baseball" and probably a violation of the laws of nature to permit a black man to play on the same team as whites. When Rickey, with Robinson safely inside the gates, revealed some seasons later that such a vote had been taken, there was a scattering for cover—as some executives pleaded loss of memory, some said they weren't even there, and one or two were struck dumb. Said Rickey, "I would like to see the color of the eyes of any man who denies that vote took place." And he explained how the "eyes only" memorandums preceding the vote had been handed out to each executive to be read and handed back, with each name checked off the list as the memos were returned. At the same meeting, Happy Chandler was named commissioner of baseball, succeeding Kenesaw Mountain Landis, deceased. When questioned about Rickey's charges, Chandler refused comment. But years later, after his term was over, he imparted to me in a letter that he had given Rickey the word to disregard the vote and sign Robinson. And of course it came to pass that, within weeks of Robinson's arrival in Brooklyn, there was a gathering rush to sign black stars to the big league contracts. After all, they could possibly be had for less money.

It seemed only natural that one of the first to follow Robinson should be old Satchel Paige—old, that is, in the lexicon of many sportswriters who liked to pretend that Satch's birth date was unknown and that he might well be past fifty, instead of forty-two as his easily available birth record in Mobile, Alabama, would have revealed. Although some of the first (often imaginary) interviews with Satch managed to fit him into the fictional mold of the shuffling, slow-talking, barely literate stereotype of the southern "darky," common to the minstrel shows and the vaudeville jokes of the day and the fiction of Octavus Roy Cohen,

Satch was an articulate, voluble, sophisticated man with a solid sense of his own value to the world and, when he felt himself put upon, a steaming temper. He was also one hell of a pitcher, quite possibly the best who ever lived. Had there ever been a research project to decide that question, Dizzy Dean and Connie Mack, two who might well have served as judges and who had often seen Paige in action, would have cast votes for Satch. Dizzy Dean allowed, with forgivable (and typical) exaggeration, that Paige's fastball "makes mine look like a change of pace." And Connie Mack declared that he would have given $100,000 for Satch "if he were white."

Paige, be it known, was not enriched by his acceptance into the ranks of the elite—or of the "ofay" (*au fait*), as the white folks were categorized by the blacks in Satch's day. Satch was already rich.

But Satch started out poor. He was the seventh of eleven children born in a four-room house in the black quarter of Mobile, Alabama, just a barefoot "nigger kid" who developed his arm, as all his playmates did, by throwing rocks, and collected spending money by picking up thrown-away nickel bottles in the street.

He was not named Satchel for the size of his feet, which were indeed, when he got his growth, bigger than most men's. (He wore size fourteen shoes.) LeRoy earned the nickname by carrying satchels for travelers at the railroad station at ten cents a satchel, very poor pay if you could lug only one bag at a time. But Satch, by fitting several ropes to a long pole, could handle four or five bags at once. For that, his mates named him Satchel-Tree or just plain Satchel.

Satch started throwing baseballs instead of rocks when he was in primary school and quickly earned a reputation as the best kid pitcher in town. But, like Babe Ruth, he got into so much devilry on the streets that he was sent off to an industrial school. There he learned to pitch, or learned the difference between pitching and just throwing. (It is an irony seldom noted that "pitching" at the start of ball playing meant tossing underhand, as in pitching pennies.)

Satch came out of industrial school having grown to his full height of six feet four inches, and having developed a good share of common sense. This was in 1923 when little LeRoy had become a grown man of seventeen, ready (and expected) to earn a living. There were not many jobs open for black kids just out of reform school. But Satch found a home with the local black semipro club, where his brother played, and where Satch could pick up about a dollar a game. To fatten his wallet a little he started pitching for other clubs around town and took on a steady job helping the groundskeeper at the local minor league stadium, home of the all-white Mobile Bears.

In 1926, after having beaten practically every team afloat in the Mobile Bay area, Satch joined the Chattanooga Lookouts of the Negro Southern League, where he discovered a regular payday—fifty dollars a month—and where he learned what nearly every traveling black baseball player in a white man's world had to learn: to sleep on his suitcase.

With the Lookouts, Satch's pay within two years grew to two hundred a month. In 1928, he was sold to the Birmingham Black Barons, where he drew nearly three hundred and where he began to sample big-city nightlife, a taste for which lasted throughout his career.

But Satch also discovered Latin America after that first year with Birmingham and from then on, like so many of the great black players, Satch pitched all year round. He pitched his first game against major leaguers when he signed up with the Baltimore Black Sox in 1930 and went on tour with Babe Ruth's All-Stars, who featured great hitters, besides the mighty Babe, like Hack Wilson, Chicago's home-run hero, and Babe Herman, flaky darling of Ebbets Field. But even though Satch was hungering for a go at the Babe, it always seemed that when Satch was pitching, Babe was needed on the bench. He *did* have a reputation to think of.

Satch makes it plain in his autobiography, written with the aid of the talented David Lipman, that he was not a man much concerned with the affairs of his friends. He was quick to shift allegiance to whatever pasture produced the richest crop of green. Ultimately he joined Gus Greenlee's Pittsburgh Crawfords, one of the strongest and classiest of all the black clubs, where Satch's salary rapidly climbed to major league stature. And there he teamed with the man who was, to many people who had seen them all, the greatest hitter of the age, black or white, Josh Gibson. With these two on the same team, major league parks began to open up to make room for the crowds that gathered to watch them. And black teams everywhere began to prosper from their presence. Still Satch was an old man, by major league standards, by the time civilization caught up with organized baseball and black players began to appear on nearly every roster. Fairy tales about Satch's age, perhaps abetted somewhat by Satch himself, or his promoters, caused some big league club owners to shy off, while a few of the clubs that could have used that limber and accurate arm—the Boston Red Sox, for instance—were quietly determined that *their* organization at least would never be so lost to social grace as to put a black man in their uniform. The Red Sox, yielding to local political pressure, had earlier made a show of offering black players, including Jackie Robinson, a tryout (along with a collection of white high school kids), watched them power a box of baseballs out of the park, then, sniggering to each other at the very notion of actually *signing* a "dinge," allowed that they would "let them know."

By the time Bill Veeck, a man who had something of Satch's own gift for showmanship and loyalty to the high dollar, invited Satch to come join the Indians, there were a dozen black ballplayers, including Cleveland's own Larry Doby, already adorning big league rosters. Even the lordly New York Yankees, the team all ambitious young baseball players were supposed to dream of joining, deigned to sign, after much blather and hesitation, a brilliant black catcher-outfielder who could drive baseballs from here to there with startling regularity. Elston Howard seemed to have been born to be a Yankee and it was said by those close to him that the Yankee locker room became the one place he most wanted to be. (A sudden temporary shift to the Red Sox nearly broke his heart.)

But the Yankees, according to the people who were supposed to be privy to such matters, had at first undertaken to sign Vic Power, a first baseman from Puerto Rico, but quickly backed off when it was reported that he had been "involved with a white woman." (Elston Howard was, happily, involved only with his beautiful wife—who sometimes dealt baseball's hard-core white supremacists a few uncomfortable moments. Indeed, at one meeting with baseball's brass she pinch-hit for Elston, describing some of the burdens black players had to bear, in southern cities especially—traveling miles for a haircut, living apart from their mates and sometimes unable to share a table with them, forced to make way for whites at every corner, and frankly barred from many stores. One league president, left without an answer, kept sliding down in his seat until Arlene Howard feared he might be making ready to crawl under the table.)

But it must be noted that it was Ford Frick, who presided over the National League when Robinson joined the Brooklyn Dodgers, who had really made sure the "unwritten rule" was dead. When a number of St. Louis Cardinals were planning to "go on strike" when Robinson stepped on their field, Frick brought that plan to a sudden stop with a statement that still does him honor. "I don't care if half the league strikes," he told the conspirators. "If you do this, you will encounter quick retribution. All will be suspended from the league."

Of course this had no effect on the thousands throughout the nation who had been brought up to believe that it was the duty of good Americans everywhere to shame or frighten black people into "knowing their place." And there remained throughout organized baseball itself an unregenerate cabal who would not be reconciled. As late as the 1960s, when every club in the game carried at least one black player on its roster, one club owner, after assuring himself that there were none present at a news conference who might take issue, bitched to the group about his ballpark's being stuck "in the middle of jig-town." And one practiced bench jockey appointed himself the chief producer of vicious, obscene, and bitter insults to Jackie, until Commissioner Chandler shut him up. One of the Boston scouts who had observed Jack's phony "try out" with the Boston Red Sox announced (for publication) that the entry of Robinson was "the worst thing that ever happened to organized baseball." The great Rogers Hornsby, who, unlike Will Rogers, seemed never to have met a man he really liked, growled to the press that "Negro players should play in their own leagues."

But the doom foreseen by all these ancestral voices never did eventuate. Black players actually began to dominate the game in some places, with no damage done to shrinking Dixie maidens nor any crack appearing in the social structure. Willie Mays became the most valuable and most valued player in the game. Roberto Clemente earned a spot in the baseball Hall of Fame, posthumously and ahead of time because he had died a hero— trying to fly food and medical supplies to the hundreds made homeless by an earthquake in Managua. And many a haughty restaurateur who had thought to maintain the "purity" of his establishment by barring black folk suffered a sudden conversion when white ball players walked out, too—as a group of Yankees, led by Roger Maris, did when Elston Howard was given a cold reception at one favorite eating place.

It took a long time for the Red Sox management to abandon the hope that the day was coming when all "nigras" would quietly crawl back to their own leagues, but at last, twelve years after Jackie Robinson had crossed the line (and actually erased it), the Sox signed a rugged twenty-five-year-old switch-hitting black infielder from California named Pumpsie Green. And the State House remained standing. (No one at the time seemed to recall when *Catholics* were also among the unwanted on the Boston baseball club, causing all the Boston Irish, led by "Nuf Ced" McGreevey, to switch allegiance to the new American League club as soon as it was invented.) But the blotch was finally removed from the Red Sox escutcheon when Ted Williams, their own all-time all-star, offered on his admittance to the Hall of Fame, instead of the usual resounding platitudes in his acceptance speech, a straightforward demand that black players be given their proper places there, too.

Chapter 7

HALL OF LESSER FAME

/. *When Amos Rusie* was a schoolboy in Indiana, his teacher used to rap his knuckles with a ruler if she found him writing with his left hand, as nature had intended. So little Amos wrote his lessons right-handed and when he was in the schoolyard he took care to throw with his right arm. Once he had been set free from school, however, Amos went back to writing left-handed. But he found it was too late to learn to throw properly with his left arm, so he became the only lefty right-handed pitcher in the Indianapolis City League— or perhaps in the nation. He was seventeen when he joined the Grand Avenue Never Sweats semipro club in the city league, but he had got his full growth (six feet one inch) and had built up a solid share of muscle. When he joined the Grand Avenues he was an outfielder, but after four games he had to take over the pitching when the regular pitcher failed to get anyone out. Immediately he began to blaze through the league—a flaming redhead with a fastball that could break a fence.

One afternoon, Pebbly Jack Glasscock, acknowledged the best shortstop in professional baseball in the 1880s, chanced to see Rusie as he was scaring semipro batters in a city league game. Jack promptly asked his boss, John T. Brush, owner of the Indianapolis club in the National League, to come see big Amos in action. One look and Brush invited Rusie to pitch for Indianapolis in an exhibition game against the Chicago Maroons of the Western Association. Rusie trimmed them 7–3. The next day he signed a contract with Indianapolis.

The big team had three catchers. But only one, George Myers, was willing to work out with Rusie. The big redhead just threw too damn hard! The catcher in those days used a small five-fingered lightly padded "wafer" glove such as outfielders used at a later date. It took a tough character indeed to stand up to Rusie's cannonball throws with a flimsy glove like that. It was bad enough in a game, when some of these bullets would be intercepted by a bat, affording a moment's respite from the pain. But to take those thunderous pitches hour after hour—who was crazy enough for that?

Apparently George Myers was, despite the fifty-foot pitching distance and the rule that permitted the pitcher to take two forward strides. But even with George's coaching, Rusie—as Amos himself freely admitted—was "wild as a March hare." It took a whole month of hard work by Rusie and Myers to get the boy so he had a reasonable notion of where the plate lay. Then Manager Frank Bancroft of Indianapolis decided to start him against the Cleveland Spiders.

The Spiders did not hit Rusie much. They didn't need to. Rusie gave almost everyone, at least once, first base free, and the Spiders beat him 9–3. Twice big Amos forced runs across with a base on balls. Two days later, Bancroft started Rusie against the Spiders again. This time poor Amos blew higher than Killian's kite, throwing more wild pitches than he did strikes. That finished him with Myers, who urged the manager to ship the big lad to the minors, to remain until he had learned the strike zone—and perhaps until George's hand had healed.

Jack Glasscock, however, urged Bancroft to keep the redhead around a little longer and let him learn his lessons in friendly surroundings. But by midseason Amos was as wild as ever, and he was shipped off to Burlington, Iowa, to waste his wild pitches in the boondocks. He returned a year later, a real big leaguer now, and took on the Spiders once more. This time, with his loving parents and some two hundred friends and former teammates in the stands to yell for him, Amos responded by beating the Spiders bowlegged.

The next season Rusie was in New York, with all the rest of the Indianapolis team, to replace the Giants, most of whom had joined the Brotherhood strike. There Rusie met John J. "Dasher" Troy, the first paid, full-time "coach" in organized baseball. Dasher taught Amos to watch the batter's feet for signs of nervousness, to use his high hard pitch to "loosen up" a nervous batter, and then to slip the next pitch over the outside corner of the plate for a quick strike. Another ancient, Tim Keefe, who had walked out with the strikers, showed Rusie how to throw a slow pitch, to make his fastball look all the faster. Under this tutelage, Rusie became the best in the league for several seasons.

Control was never Amos's specialty. But this may have been all to the good. Any fastball pitcher is a notch or two more effective when he is (as players in an earlier day used to put it) "pleasin' wild," so that the batter is never 100 percent sure that the next pitch may not separate his head from his neck. (Ty Cobb used to take advantage of Walter Johnson's unwillingness to dust off a batter by leaning just a little over the plate to provide Johnson less room to work in.) Rusie set—and still holds—the record for most bases on balls issued in one season: 218. (At this writing, Nolan Ryan holds the "lifetime" record, but he has been at it longer.) Before the pitching distance was lengthened to sixty feet six inches Rusie contrived to hand out 289 walks in a single season.

When he returned to the Giants, Rusie had a new catcher, Dick Buckley, who invented a way to stand up to Rusie's speed: He slipped a thin sheet of lead inside the glove to absorb some of the shock. But by this time Rusie had added a curve to his collection, a curve that batters swore was every bit as fast as his fastball, so it seemed to snap like a whip in the batter's face. The secret of this not even Rusie could explain. He did have, he noted, arms that were noticeably shorter than those of other men his size. But what did that have to do with it? More muscle packed into a smaller space? A quicker release? There were no physicists about at the time willing to peer into this petty mystery. All that the batters knew was that the big redhead pitched nothing but fastballs—some straight and some crooked.

Equipped with the change-up (he called it a "slow ball") and a frightening curve, Rusie, from the time he came to New York, never had a losing season. Batters now could be completely unbalanced as they braced for his speed and got his easy stuff instead. But he did continue to distribute free walks by the basketful. In 1893, the year he led the league with 208 strikeouts, he also set the record of 218 walks. Some observers insisted that many of Rusie's walks were the result of the umpire's inability to follow the break of that frightening curve. Still, Rusie did lead the league five times in strikeouts and twice struck out more than 300 in a season. After his first year as a major leaguer (his only losing season), Amos liked to recall the fact that he *never* lost a game against Chicago in Chicago's home park.

But Amos, alas, noted all over the nation as the mighty Hoosier Thunderbolt, the flaming redhead who set the baseball world on fire, won much of his fame through his holdouts. The New York Giants were purchased in 1895 by Andrew Freedman, a Tammany stalwart, a close friend of the notorious Boss Croker, and a smartly got-up gentleman, with neatly groomed black hair, a piercing eye, a bristling mustache, an easily unbalanced temper, and a tight fist. You might have thought that Freedman would have secretly relished owning a pitcher like Rusie, who, while he might have been drawing somewhat more than the minimum salary, was willing—even eager—to pitch every day. (When the previous manager of the Giants, Truthful Jeems Mutrie, wanted to stir Rusie into putting his whole soul into every pitch, he would promise that if Rusie won the game, he *might* let him pitch tomorrow's game too.) But under Freedman, Rusie became a little more sparing of his strength. One day he divided his salary by the number of innings he pitched and discovered that he was being paid less than $6 an inning. For the best pitcher in baseball? Rusie promptly suggested to Freedman that, as the club's winningest pitcher, he really should be picking up a more fitting paycheck. Freedman flushed red at the very suggestion. "A raise? Never!" he decreed. Why, with his "secret" bonus, Rusie was perhaps the best paid player in the game! (He was drawing a little over $3,000.)

Soon afterward, Freedman observed that Rusie had taken to frequenting barrooms and staying out late at night, as so many young men did in that day as well as this. Freedman was prompt to punish such derelictions by a $100 fine. And even though Rusie was just as prompt in venturing forth to trim the Giants' next opponent, Freedman was unforgiving. And the next season he undertook to enhance the punishment by cutting Rusie's salary to $2,000. Rusie felt he had already borne too much and he refused to work for such a wage.

In his defiance, Rusie was supported by a number of other club owners in the league, who urged Freedman to relent. But these guys were just the opponents of his scheme to establish a baseball "syndicate," Freedman noted, and he would not budge an inch or even a dollar. The league by this time had been split into two factions over the "syndicate" issue—a plan to establish a single ruling body that would own and operate the entire complex, to divide the whole take among the assembled owners and to assign the players according to where they might attract the richest gate receipts. The stars would then be divided among the top few cities and the least talented laborers dumped on the vineyards where the picking was poorest. So Rusie decided to remain in his tent.

Far from sulking, Rusie issued a forty-page pamphlet reprinting all the correspondence between himself and Freedman. This impertinence, Freedman and his cohorts told each other, had certainly been prompted and paid for by the anti-Freedman faction.

The leader of the antisyndicate crew was A. G. Spalding, former owner of the Chicago club. Freedman led the syndicators. And that damn Spalding was of course just bent on wrecking the

New York club to drive Freedman out of baseball. (Spalding had already declared he wanted Freedman out.) How much truth there was in this theory, earnestly promoted by Freedman, history does not record. What is a fact is that Nick Young, the fretful president of the league, who just wished the whole trouble would blow away, gathered the club owners from both sides and charged them all to urge Freedman to relent. (Meanwhile, many of the leading ball players in the league had been calling for the establishment of a "Rusie fund" to keep big Amos in coffee and cakes while he played ball in the back lots of his Indiana home.) But not all the league's horses nor all the league's managers could win Freedman to reason. So the Giants, who had the year before beaten Baltimore in the Temple Cup contests (that day's equivalent of the World Series), dropped, without Rusie, to sixth place in 1896.

The next year the united club owners did kick in to a fund to underwrite a $5,000 stipend for Rusie that would lure him back to the Giants. Rusie returned in 1897 to win twenty-eight of the thirty-eight games he worked in. Neither he nor Freedman would reveal the conditions under which Amos returned. But Freedman did note that the next season Rusie won "only" twenty games and did not deserve to draw that manager-sized salary again. Furthermore, Freedman vowed, he would continue to deny courtesy passes to any member of the Cincinnati club "as long as that club is in the hands that it is"—those hands, velvet-gloved or no, were the hands belonging to John T. Brush, former owner of the When Clothing Company, the man who first brought Rusie into the major league, and they were the hands, Freedman was convinced, that had produced Rusie's forty-page broadside and paid for its distribution. (Brush had deserted the "syndicate" cause to make a deal with the enemy.) This holdout lasted two years. When it was done, Rusie was only thirty years old, but he had preserved not an ounce of his fearsome speed. He pitched in but three games for Cincinnati, won none and lost one.

By the time Rusie was done, Freedman was nearly done himself—in baseball, at least. He had made himself a fortune in the insurance business and other enterprises in which the bless-ings of Tammany were tokens of good luck. And he had run the Giants very nearly into the ground. For a while he tried it with two managers—only one of whom, George Smith, actually wore the title; the other, Horace Fogel, just spooked about from bench to dressing room, offering advice when it was least needed, to the utter dismay of the entire roster. Preceding this unholy pair, Freedman had tried six managers. Eventually, he managed to win Cap Anson away from Chicago to put the Giants back on track (they had just lost six games in a row). Anson lasted three weeks, then went into permanent retirement. *Nobody* really managed the Giants, Anson discovered, but Freedman, who was ready, without notice, to leap from his private box to the playing field to argue with an umpire, dress down a player, or vilify an op-ponent. Freedman, everyone agreed, owned the skill to unleash, with no prompting at all, a string of foul, abusive, unprintable words (in the current phase) "to the bloody far down." Largely through this talent Freedman succeeded in ridding himself of uncounted numbers of friends and companions.

But Freedman seemed to share one personal oddity with Rusie: His left arm and his right arm were not completely in synch. For greedy as he was, grasping as he could be, tightfisted as he seemed, Freedman did, before he died, endow a home for aged and in-digent women. And when he heard one day that Jim Mutrie, most beloved of all old-time Giants, was ill and in need, he promptly sent Jim a generous check, although he had never met the man.

Freedman also, when the end of his baseball career was in sight and a plump price in view for his stock in the New York Giants, turned suddenly sweet, even to the point of making peace with Spalding. His final season in baseball—marked by a smart deal that brought John McGraw out of the new American League to become the greatest manager the New York Giants had ever known—was peaceful, even dull, with the Giants sinking quietly to seventh place. But fans for years afterward best recalled the time Andy Freedman said, of a sportswriter who had long be-

deviled him, that the man was "on the brink of an 'abscess' "
into which Freedman might one day shove him.

As for Rusie, while he did not fall into an 'abscess,' he did
withdraw from baseball altogether and landed back home in Indiana, where he found a job as a common laborer at a dollar and
a half a day. Eventually he worked himself up to four dollars a
day—a good wage then for a workingman but damn thin soup
for a professional ball player. When Rusie did come back to
baseball, he came back at John McGraw's behest, to take a place
as an attendant at the Polo Grounds. His red hair had gone gray
by then and there were few indeed to recognize him or even
recall his name. But John McGraw remembered, as he often did
when men who had given much to baseball fell upon hard times.
(Arlie Latham was press-box attendant at the Polo Grounds into
his late eighties.)

In the early days of the new century, another young man rode
out of the West (in a railroad car) to become the first baseman
of the newborn American League baseball club in New York—
named the Highlanders, after their lofty home park on Washington Heights, and called the Porch Climbers and even the
Burglars by many sportswriters and fans because they had crept
stealthily into town before crafty Andy Freedman and his Tammany helpers could run a street through the area. (Freedman had
often bragged that if any rival baseball club tried to play in New
York, he could have their chosen site cut into streets and alleys
before the sun went down.) The young arrival, handsome, well-
met, self-confident, and college-educated, was Harold Harris
Chase (who became Prince Hal to the press for his proud bearing
and his transcendent skills). He had been pried right out of the
grasp of his protesting "owner," James Morley of the Los Angeles
club of the Pacific Coast League. Morley had spotted Hal Chase
when he was playing in the outfield at Santa Clara University
and had immediately offered him a job playing first base for
money.

"I never played first base," said Hal. "But I'll give it a try."

The Los Angeles playing field had scarcely any grass, so there

was no distinct border marking off the infield. For this first practice, Chase, who was used to playing on barren fields, took up
his "first base" stance in short right field.

"No! No!" Morley cried. "You can't play *first base* out there!
You have to cover the bag! You have to get in to take the throw!
They'll bunt you to death!"

"Don't worry," said Hal, "the batter is even farther away. I'll
beat him to the bag!"

And Chase did indeed outsprint every runner to the bag, sometimes so swiftly that the man who had fielded the ball threw it
behind Chase and Hal would be charged with an error. More
often, however, Chase came charging down the baseline and
snagged the ball in time to put a tag on the bunter. He seemed
to have the reflexes of a spider, and could sometimes grab the
ball before it struck the ground. He also set the style in taking
throws—stretching high in the air with his right hand to take
the ball in his glove. This sort of play was frowned upon by some
big leaguers, who felt one-handed catches were just showing off.
Johnny Evers of Chicago thought Frank Chance did it properly,
taking most throws in two hands. He was a better player than
Chase, according to Evers, because he "doesn't take chances."

But the first big league scout who saw Hal Chase's supposedly
"reckless" play decided he was needed in New York, and he told
the New York American League club to claim him. Morley was
outraged. He would *never* let go of Chase! He was the best player
in the league! But the baseball deities said no. By the terms of
the national agreement Morley would have to let Chase be
drafted. So Chase moved on to New York and was very soon
rated by most writers the finest first baseman in the game. And
old men who could remember him, at his death in 1947, still
maintained he had been the finest first baseman of all time.

With the New York Americans, Chase set the fans to screaming by the way he would charge the plate to scoop up a bunt,
often so quickly that he had time to fire the ball to second or
third and catch the runner there. This was actually a rare play
in baseball, for even though bunting was frequent in this dead-

ball day, few infielders had learned to anticipate the way Hal did. With Hal it became commonplace. Hal even turned an attempted squeeze into a double play one day when he grabbed the bunt before it hit the ground and then threw to third to double the runner who was trying to score. And he once outfoxed Cleveland's mighty Nap Lajoie when Lajoie thought to annihilate Hal by faking a bunt and then trying to drive the ball down Hal's throat. Hal, charging in at top speed, snagged the drive in his glove and made a double play out of *that*. This was the sort of thing that started fans by the hundreds to make the long trek out to Washington Heights to watch the Porch Climbers perform. (Sometimes they actually lined the baselines, so it was a marvel no one was killed.)

Hal himself was a champion bunter who could place a ball as craftily as he could aim a pool ball (a skill at which he also excelled). Clark Griffith allowed that he had never known Hal Chase to fail to lay down a good bunt on a squeeze play, no matter what sort of pitch was thrown to outwit him. And Hal could hit the ball hard, too; in 1916, when he was with Cincinnati, he led the National League with a batting average of .339. He also set fielding marks: thirty-eight chances in a doubleheader at St. Louis, top mark for first basemen. And twenty-two putouts in one game to tie Tom Jones of St. Louis for the lead. But Hal also set new records in errors. In four different seasons he led all first basemen in the league in that competition. But most observers agreed that many of Hal's misplays resulted from his willingness to try for ground balls other fielders would have merely waved at. Only a few realized that Prince Hal was missing some of those ground balls because he *wanted* to.

Hal Chase was an attractive man, cheerful, talkative, full of jokes, and openhanded. Yet he was not much of a man to make friends. As a college graduate, he tended to look down on ballplayers, and he seemed devoted first of all to his own enjoyment of life, eager to pick up a dollar wherever it was offered and just as ready to hand it to the next man he met who needed it. When the Highlanders were idle, as they always were on Sunday, Hal,

regardless of rules, would take himself on a trolley to some un-
paved hamlet to pick up a small payoff with a semipro ball team.
He loved drinking, playing pool, shooting at targets, and playing
cards for money. He was a skilled horseman, a clever boxer, an
excellent mimic, and an inveterate joke-teller. But he always
danced to his own drum, seemed to have no ties to any place or
person, and recognized no commitment except to his own delight.
He writhed under the snarling rebukes of his manager, Kid Elberfeld, a former Detroit shortstop known as The Tabasco Kid
because of his rasping tongue, and a man who felt that the only
way to keep mules moving was to feed them regular doses of the
whip. Hal, weary of the Kid's sarcasm, simply walked off the job
one day and went back to California, where he could always pick
up a few dollars playing ball—and, it was whispered, earn even
more dollars by betting against his own team and making sure
they came in second.

On the loose in California, Chase used "Schulz" as his baseball
name, in a sort of acknowledgment of his illegitimate status. And
he felt free to indulge himself by taking a job he had always
yearned for: pitcher. As Hal Schulz, he won many a game for
the San Jose team in the California winter league.

Hal had actually worked as a pitcher in the East, too—once
in Elizabeth, New Jersey, for a semipro team called the Invaders
against another local outfit, the Argonauts, in a Sunday game
when the Highlanders, of course, were idle. Hal helped the Invaders beat the Argonauts in the first game of a doubleheader.
Then he played first base for the Argonauts in the second game.
Anything for a dollar.

But Chase did not confine his search for the dollar to ball
games. Almost on his arrival in New York, he appointed himself
official betting promoter for the club's locker room. That was a
day when the making and taking of bets on everything from
prizefights to ponies was a part of every male with even a trickle
of sporting blood. Baseball players openly bet on themselves
against their opponents. Train trips from game to game would
involve even the managers in endless poker games, often financed

by IOUs. One manager had to put a fifty-cent limit on all poker playing in the locker room after one of his players found himself in debt to his mates by more than a season's salary. There was neither rule nor custom to persuade baseball players to shun games of chance. And merry Hal rejoiced in carrying his mates' bets to his pet bookie. Early in his big league career Chase observed that there was a horse named Clark Griffith entered in a race at a handy track. The Highlanders' manager at that time being Clark Griffith himself, the old-time Chicago pitcher, Hal picked up betting slips from every man on the roster, including Clark. Clark the horse ran, alas, out of the money. But Hal Chase retained his job of carrying bets to market.

Hal came back to the Highlanders after his self-sought exile in California as soon as his nemesis, Kid Elberfeld, had, in the British phrase, been made redundant. In 1910, Hal himself was given the job of manager. He lasted through two seasons, in which he succeeded in dragging the hapless Porch Climbers down from second place to sixth. Thereupon the club owners—two ex-bartenders named Bill Devery and Frank Farrell—replaced Hal with Harry Wolverton, a third baseman of moderate attainments, who outdid Hal by sinking the club to the very depths. After that came Frank Chance, the first base end of the Tinker to Evers to Chance double-play combination. Hal Chase, who had often been irritated by the occasional suggestion that it was Chance who was the greatest first baseman in recent memory, thought old Frank was a joke.

Frank Chance was deaf in one ear, so Chase took care, when they were on the bench, to sit on Frank's deaf side. Here he could mimic Frank's throaty commands and imitate Frank's facial expressions, a pasttime for which Hal had a real gift. Not all of Hal's mates were amused, however, and one of them finally told Frank what Hal had been up to. Chase very suddenly then found himself traded to the Chicago White Sox, who rejoiced as Hal amazed mates and fans alike by his startling abilities. Chase's moves always looked awkward, for they were the result of sudden instinctive reaction rather than planning. Yet few ground balls eluded him and hardly any throw escaped him unless it was heaved into the stands.

When the Federal League was formed and began to entice players with better pay (and fans with twenty-five-cent admission) Hal, following his instincts as usual, hopped aboard the Buffalo club. The White Sox yelled bloody murder and promptly sought a court order to keep Hal in their corral, but the court noted that the standard contract gave the ball club the right to dismiss a player "on ten days' notice" and did not see why this arrangement could not work both ways. Chase *had* given the White Sox ten days' notice of his departure. So Hal stayed in Buffalo, batting .347 in seventy-five games. The next season, 1915, Hal's average sank to a mere .291, but he led the league with seventeen home runs.

Twenty-five-cent baseball proved profitless for the Federal League and it succumbed at the end of the 1915 season, leaving Hal, unwelcome now in New York, to find a place in Cincinnati, where, in his first time at bat, he hit a double, stole third, and scored on a double steal. From that moment he was the star of the club, and his salary of over $8,000 seemed to signal that he had reached very close to the top of the heap. His popularity soared until there were strong rumors that he was to become manager. But no such thing! In midseason, 1917, manager Buck Herzog was traded off to the New York Giants for Christy Mathewson, the Giants' famed "Big Six." Mathewson's great pitching career had been ended by an incurable sore shoulder and John McGraw had let him go so he might stay in the game as manager. But Matty's appearance in Cincinnati actually foreshadowed the doom of Hal Chase's major league career. For Matty soon observed that Hal, the peerless fielder, was occasionally something less than peerless on the field. Now and then, Matty noted with alarm, Chase, after some spectacular stop of a ground ball, instead of timing his throw with his usual exactness to put the runner out, would hold the ball just a second or two longer so that the ball arrived too late. Chase *never* made dumb mistakes like that—unless, goddamnit, the bastard was *trying* to louse up the play! Matty kept a wary eye on Prince Hal after that and counted more than enough such foul-ups to convince him that Chase was undertaking every so often to lose a game on purpose. And that's how he explained it to Cincinnati owner Garry Herrmann.

Herrmann, who knew that if anybody knew how that first base play should be completed Mathewson did, promptly announced that Hal Chase had been suspended without pay. Hal left town. And very soon afterward, Christy Mathewson accepted a commission in the chemical warfare division of the United States Army and was ordered to France, where American troops were already engaged in that "war to end all wars."

At season's end, Herrmann filed with the president of the National League, John Heydler, formal charges against Chase of deliberately throwing games. In January 1919, Heydler held a closed hearing, which two Cincinnati pitchers, Jimmy Ring and Mike Regan, attended as witnesses. New York Giants' manager John McGraw and one of his pitchers, Will "Poll" Perritt, were also summoned, along with Sid Mercer, a New York sportswriter. But the star witness, Mathewson, was still in France and there were only his affidavits to bear witness to Chase's evil deeds. What actually went on at the meeting no one alive can tell. But in a statement acquitting Chase of all the charges, Heydler declared: "In one game in which it was intimated that Chase had bet against his club, the records show that in the sixth inning, with two men on base and the score two to nothing against his club, Chase hit a home run, putting Cincinnati one run ahead." Heydler did not reveal how that game ended and he may have been unaware that baseball bets are sometimes made inning by inning. No matter, Chase was declared innocent and John McGraw, who had already announced that if Chase were cleared he would immediately welcome him to the Giants, did just that, acquiring Chase in a trade for Bill Raridan, one of the Giants' spare catchers.

But Chase's season with the Giants, where he batted .284 in 110 games, was his last in organized baseball. For Heydler, uneasy about his decision, had kept his investigators nosing around and they had come up with information, including some canceled checks from a Boston bookmaker, that showed Chase on at least two or three occasions betting against his own club. That finished him with John McGraw, who dropped him from the roster and warned all his charges that Chase was not fit company for man or beast.

When the Giants next saw Hal Chase, he stood in a hotel lobby wearing no necktie and no socks, his feet in sandals, his hair awry, a happy smile on his face—a premature hippy—come to greet his old teammates. But if anyone dared give him much more than the time of day, McGraw warned, he would have a fat fine to pay.

Although Hal Chase was barred from even the grandstands in the Pacific Coast League, he found "outlaw" teams all over the Southwest who could grant him a payday. He began to drink more heartily than ever, so that sometimes he would accept a place in a sandlot lineup for the price of a highball. He played softball—known as "indoor baseball" then—with touring teams from everywhere. He appeared at rodeos, for he was a champion horseman, and he spent many an active day at a race track, conscientiously "improving the breed" by laying greenbacks on a horse's nose. His wife had long since been abandoned and Hal's diet consisted largely of free lunches and booze, even during the days when liquor was illegal. He finally began to nurse a hope that he might be taken back into organized baseball, now that it had been cleaned up by Commissioner Landis. He wrote letters to Landis, admitting "mistakes" and inquiring what his status was. Landis finally replied that the commissioner's office had never listed him on its bad books and he asked Chase just what his "mistakes" had been. Hal was never able to think of an answer to that one. (Actually, his name had been among those brought up in the Black Sox investigation, but just what part he was supposed to have played was never made clear.)

Hal lived a surprisingly long time for a man so devoted to drink. It may be that he had adotped the "long-life" formula of an old man I knew: "You gotta keep moving!" Hal kept moving.

He tried a dozen different ways of making a dollar: gambling, boxing, shooting, playing ball winter and summer, and even riding horses. Until he became too old to play baseball, he clung to a dream that he might again one day hear that roaring tide of cheers he could remember. He expressed sincere admiration for Kenesaw Mountain Landis and named him the best thing that ever happened to organized baseball.

But poor Hal was one of the worst. As Oscar Wilde might have said about him, "He could resist anything except temptation." Ultimately, the abuse he awarded his body made him easy prey to a vitamin-deficiency disease: beriberi. He was sixty-seven years old when he died. And as great a player as he was, he will never be listed in the baseball Hall of Fame, where many a lesser performer has long been enshrined.

●

In the 1880s, and after, a ball player who didn't drink, or chew tobacco, or say bad words out loud was likely to be named Deacon or even Lady—not really in belittlement, but as a sort of friendly acknowledgment of his daintiness. And by an odd coincidence a pitcher called Lady and a catcher whose nickname was Deacon became one of the best-known, and mightiest, batteries in the land.

Lady Baldwin was no lady. (His mother named him Charles.) He was a solidly muscled pitcher who could probably have knocked down a horse with his fastball. And just about the only catcher, in those days of bare hands and "wafer" gloves, who dared stand up to Lady's speed was a hard-boiled Michigan iron-molder named James McGuire, called Deacon all through his baseball career.

The Deacon and the Lady teamed together on a semipro team in southern Michigan, a team that played only on Saturday and Sunday because the Deacon could not get off work except on weekends. And nobody else would play catch with Lady Baldwin, whose famous "snake ball" would have straightened out a rattlesnake. That was in 1882, when McGuire was eighteen years old. He played his last big league game in 1912, when he was almost fifty. In the intervening years he caught the offerings of eighty-eight different professional pitchers, not to mention an assortment of hairy-armed sandlotters and semipros.

The Deacon may have had the biggest hands in the professional leagues, and certainly, after several years of catching, he owned the ugliest—gnarled, twisted, bent out of shape, and swollen. When gloves were permitted, the Deacon used one, but it was no more protective than a wool mitten might have been. When he was catching for Toledo in the American Association in 1884, he had to accept the fiery pitches of sourpuss Hank O'Day (who had not yet graduated to umpire). McGuire would tuck a thick slice of beefsteak inside his skinny glove. When he took the glove off, it was not always easy to tell where McGuire's hand left off and the beefsteak began.

The Deacon started playing organized ball with Terre Haute when he was twenty and was sold next year to Detroit. There he was elected to play backstop for Wild Bill Donovan, who might have set distance records for wild pitches. One day McGuire signaled Donovan for a pitchout and Donovan almost pitched the ball out of the park. "It was one of the wildest pitches Bill ever made," McGuire said. But the Deacon made a grab for it with his bare hand. He got the ball on the tip of his middle finger and it stripped all the flesh off the finger, right to the bone. Bob Emslie, umpiring behind the plate, took one look at the mess and collapsed. But McGuire kept his feet and marched off to the clubhouse to have it mended. Less than a week later he was back behind the plate. "We were short of catchers," the Deacon explained.

In the big leagues (the National League and the American Association) McGuire played with Detroit, Philadelphia, Cleveland, Rochester (where he actually pitched four innings), Washington, Brooklyn, and the American League team in Detroit, too.

Most of McGuire's playing days were spent with Washington, where he set a permanent record by catching every inning in every single one of the 132 games that Washington played that season. Several times in his career McGuire served as playing manager—in Boston and Cleveland. He also, at different times, played in the infield and outfield. In Rochester he pitched those four innings of a game to no decision.

By 1912, having wound up his major league career as manager of Cleveland, he came back to Detroit to work as coach for Hughey Jennings's Tigers. The Deacon was on hand when Ty Cobb climbed into the stands one day in New York to punch out the crippled fan who had heckled him. And he was in Philadelphia when the Detroit team walked out on strike to protest Cobb's suspension.

To protect his franchise, Jennings had to recruit a collection of college players and local semipros to represent his Tigers against the Philadelphia Athletics. Aloysius Travers, pitcher for St. Joseph's College, took the mound for the temporary Tigers and managed to post the scary earned run average of 15.75, while allowing twenty-six hits in eight innings. As for the Deacon, he contributed one hit and one run to go along with his two errors. The Athletics won the game, 24–2. The next day the real Tigers came back and Deacon McGuire called it quits. But he stuck to the Tigers as coach (and later as scout) until he was sixty-three. Then he went back to Albion, Michigan, where he was raised (and where he owned real estate enough to keep him in comfort), to teach baseball to the boys at the local college. As for Aloysius Travers, he entered the priesthood, unrepentant.

McGuire left no notable records behind other than his longevity and the fact that he played for twelve different teams in three different major leagues, batting steadily at a career .278 average. He also played a minor role in one small tragedy—the loss by New York of the American League pennant on a wild pitch that gave the deciding game to Boston. Happy Jack Chesbro, the tough lad from North Adams, Massachusetts, had won forty-one games for the Highlanders and he had the deciding one practically in his hand when he let go the pitch that allowed the winning run to score. Long after the tragedy a few fans, including Happy Jack's widow, endeavored to "clear his name" (as of a gross misdeed) by offering testimony that it was all the fault of the rookie catcher, Red Kleinow. But Deacon McGuire, who was on the bench that day (until he pinch-hit for the dejected Chesbro in the eighth inning), never agreed.

"There wasn't a chance in the world to stop that spitter," he said. "It might just as well have gone over the top of the grandstand."

●

In the opening years of the twentieth century, the dominating ball players in the major leagues were, as usual, the pitchers. And unanimously named the best were Christy Mathewson of the New York Giants, Rube Waddell of the Philadelphia Athletics, Walter Johnson of the Washington Senators, and Denton T. "Cy" Young of the Boston Red Sox. Mathewson was the "Big Six" to the sportswriters and fans of the day, even though the significance of the title was never clear even to Christy himself. (He thought it might have meant "Big Six-Footer.") Actually, this had been a commonplace tag a few years earlier when New York City residents could still be stirred to a frenzy by the competition among the city's various volunteer fire companies. And it came to pass that the company that named itself Big Six was the acknowledged champion—in speed getting to a fire and in success putting fires out. There were, after that, in sports and out, many temporary "big sixes," so many that the term was not even capitalized. (Al Spink, in his own book, *The National Game*, designated the New York Metropolitans of 1884 "the big six of that section.")

Christy was described, in accordance with the era's traditions, as a thoroughly clean-living, abstemious, nongambling type— the ideal role model for all young male citizens. His book, *Pitching in a Pinch*, was a feature of the Boy Scout library. But Christy actually was a gregarious sort, perfectly willing to buy or accept a drink, given to occasional betting on cards or ball games, and not afraid from time to time to stay out late at night.

George Edward "Rube" Waddell (always "Eddie" to his boss,

Connie Mack) was presented by the press (and by those who knew him) as reckless, intemperate, and undisciplined. He was known to stay away from a ball game to engage in some pet shenanigan, like posing in a show window, playing a vacant-lot game with kids, or taking off to a favorite fishing hole. Yet he was unbeatable on his best days and always a favorite with fans, even if not with employers.

It is one of fate's ironies that when Rube Waddell died at the age of thirty-eight of tuberculosis, his early death was counted as a warning to the young to avoid a self-indulgent, dissipated life. Yet Christy Mathewson, the very image of the temperate, self-disciplined, and straight-living athlete, died at the age of forty-five of the same disease.

Perhaps there is further irony in the fact that Cy Young, who hardly let a day pass without a generous helping of his favorite restorative, red whiskey served in a brim-full tumbler, and who chewed tobacco as long as he owned teeth enough for the job, lived to be eighty-eight. His baseball career, too, was longer than any of the other Hall of Fame pitchers and no one will ever win as many games. When asked once how many games he *had* won in his career, he replied, "More than you'll ever see."

Walter Johnson, usually thought of as the fastest pitcher who ever lived, threw the ball sidearm and so succeeded in scaring the pants off many a right-handed batter who would see the fastball apparently coming right at him from the vicinity of third base. But Walter was actually afraid of hitting a batter because he knew his speed was likely to cripple a man for life. And Walter was not only a thorough gentleman, but a truly gentle man as well. Fate, alas, dealt big Walter to the sorry Washington Senators and he did not work in a World Series until his career was nearly over, in 1924 and 1925. (He lost two games in the 1924 Series, out of the three he pitched. And he won two games out of three in the next year's Series.) Walter, who was nicknamed Barney after Barney Oldfield, the fastest living auto racer, stands second to Cy Young in number of career wins. No one has matched him in the number of innings worked or in the number of shutouts. He stayed close to the game all of his life. One season he and George Weiss came within a breath or two of buying a baseball team together.

Yet despite the fame men like Ty Cobb and Honus Wagner earned throughout the baseball world, there were others who, for a season or two, shone far more brightly in the eyes of their hometown fans.

Brooklyn fans, in the pre–World War I days, knew they owned the finest pitcher in the world—an easy-going, soft-spoken southerner from Crabapple, Georgia, whom everyone called by his middle name, Napoleon, that being the title (instead of "King") generally awarded in those days to acknowledged top men in the game. But Nap Rucker had owned the name his entire life and he earned it all over again as soon as he began pitching for Brooklyn. Rucker, pitching for the bush league club in Atlanta, Georgia (where he had a teenage teammate named Ty Cobb), was "owned" by the Philadelphia Athletics. Had he joined them, Rucker would surely have made a greater name for himself, the Athletics in that era being permanent pennant contenders and four-time winners. But Connie Mack was wealthy with pitchers. Rube Waddell was his, along with Eddie Plank, Chief Bender, Jack Coombs, and Bullet Joe Bush. (Coombs won thirty-one games in 1910 and twenty-eight in 1911.)

During Nap Rucker's stay with the Dodgers, when his earned run average only once exceeded three runs per nine innings, he was encumbered with a team that was almost permanently out of the race. Nevertheless, he pitched a no-hit game against Boston in 1908, a year in which he worked in forty-two games, started thirty-five of them, completed thirty, and won seventeen. Rucker was especially beloved by the Brooklyn management because he was ready to go to the mound any time a left-hander was needed. And he was adored by the Brooklyn faithful because he always performed best against the despised New York Giants.

Charles Ebbets, the superthrifty Brooklyn owner, bought Rucker from Connie Mack for $500, and he might have thought that stingy bundle had been thrown away when young Rucker, in his first big league game, made two wild throws to first after fielding infield rollers, and added two wild pitches as the game progressed. Then poor Napoleon fielded a ground ball and stood dumbly holding the ball while a Boston runner stole home with the winning run.

After that, Rucker was about ready to buy a rail ticket back to Crabapple. But manager Patsy Donovan, impressed by Rucker's amazing curve, knew he had a winner and would not let him go. So Nap stayed on for ten seasons, during which he pitched 186 complete games—only two less than the great Jack Coombs pitched in fourteen seasons.

In the year 1916, when Brooklyn finally won a pennant, Nap Rucker was nearly crippled with bursitis. He appeared in only nine games and won two of them. His arm hurt him, he said, with every pitch and he had no speed left. Still, his manager, big-hearted Wilbert Robinson, contrived to stage a roaring farewell for the man who had been his strong left arm. In the fourth game of the World Series against the Red Sox, with Brooklyn hopelessly behind, Robby sent Rucker in to pitch the final two innings. Though his arm still tortured him, Nap managed to hold the Red Sox scoreless, while he struck out three. Whereupon the entire Brooklyn congregation stood up and sent their hero off with a spontaneous explosion of cheers such as not even Christy Mathewson had ever heard the equal.

In Chicago, the National League team was known for a while as the Spuds before they became the Cubs (they had also been known as the Orphans after their beloved "Pop," Cap Anson, had left them, and for a while they were the Colts). Of course, they had been, under Spalding and Anson, the White Stockings. But now the American League White Sox had borrowed the name and they were the enemy. Spuds or Cubs, they were still Chicago's heroes. And their mightiest pitcher was Ed Reulbach, who, in their hearts and minds, had no equal.

Reulbach was a Michigan boy, the son of a Detroit banker, who first earned glory as a pitcher for Notre Dame, a team that barnstormed every summer and that had once featured Louis

Sockalexis, the original Cleveland Indian. Reulbach, a big, strong boy, had previously pitched semipro ball in Sedalis, Missouri. The Chicago club discovered him when he was startling the natives with his power in the Vermont State League. In his first season with Chicago, 1905, when he had not yet turned twenty-three, Big Ed pitched two record-length ball games, one of eighteen innings and one of twenty-two. But heavy work was Big Ed's specialty. In his best year, 1908, he started thirty-five games, finished twenty-five of them, and won twenty-four. Perhaps Reulbach's greatest performance was the one-hitter he threw against the White Sox in the 1906 World Series. He and Mordecai "Three Finger" Brown turned out to be the only pitchers who could stifle the "hitless wonder" White Sox in that frantic Series before the wildest and largest crowds up to that time ever to fight their way into a baseball game. Despite biting weather and the apparent hopelessness of the White Sox cause, mobs gathered at the park gates in such crushing numbers that many a ticket-holder never got closer to his seat than the sidewalk across the road.

Reulbach won the second game, allowing the White Sox only one hit. Brown had lost the first 2–1, working against Nick Altrock (who had not yet begun his career as a clown). Both games were played in football weather before blanketed fans. Reulbach bore up best, perhaps because he was bigger. (Ed weighed nearly 200 pounds, against Brown's 175.) But when Ed tried again in the fourth game, his arm seemd to have frozen and he lasted only two innings. All the same, he led the league in winning percentage the next two seasons—winning seventeen games in 1907 and then twenty-four in 1908. Ed never had a losing season in his nine years with the Cubs and when, after being traded to Brooklyn, he sneaked away to play for more money with Newark in the Federal League, he won twenty-one games of the thirty he started. In his season with Brooklyn, a fifth-place club, Reulbach won eleven games out of forty-four in which he worked (he started twenty-nine).

The Chicago Spuds-Cubs never did grant that they were outclassed in that 1906 Series, even though Cubs president Charles Murphy, responding to the howling mob of White Sox fans, came out on a balcony and proclaimed that the White Sox were a "great team" and that his boys had been beaten by a "better team."

Better team, hell! the Cubs fans muttered. We were licked by the cops! The police, out in numbers to try to hold the crowds in check and keep the overflow from cutting too deeply on the field, did indeed have a hand in the final game when a long hit by George Davis of the White Sox fell into the overflow crowd for a ground-rule double. Wildfire Frank Schulte, who had been standing ready to catch the ball, was suddenly bumped aside. He turned at once and stuck his finger in the face of a cop. "You pushed me!" he screamed. The cop denied it and not even the umpires stood ready to overrule a Chicago cop. (Inasmuch as the White Sox, at the end of two innings, were leading 7–1, it is difficult to believe that a little self-restraint by the cop would have made that much difference.)

Big Ed Reulbach's exile with the Dodgers, lasting as it did only a season and a half, added little sparkle to his crown. But he did, in the opening game of the 1914 season, defeat the club that was destined to become the "Miracle Team" of the year— George Stallings's Boston Braves. While Ebbets, although it pained him, outbid the Federal League to hold on to all those he called his "good players," he apparently did not count Ed Reulbach among them. Or it may well have been that the Newark Feds set the price too high. So Ed, who had easier ways of making a living than wearing out his right arm throwing baseballs, moved down to Newark to set records there. After that, with the fading Boston Braves he at least broke even, winning seven and losing seven, leaving his major league record at 182 games won and 106 lost, with an earned run average of 2.28—better than Chief Bender's or Lefty Grove's or even Cy Young's. But those guys made it into the Hall of Fame and Ed did not.

Another man who never made the Hall of Fame, but should have, came along a decade and a half later and lasted in major league baseball longer than some people remember. That was Frank Crosetti, third baseman and shortstop with the championship New York Yankees and a third base coach for the Yanks until after he became a grandfather.

Frank Crosetti, when he was four years old, managed to contract measles, whooping cough, and pneumonia all at the same time. On the advice of their doctor, his devoted parents, once Frank was well, promptly moved their family from San Francisco to Los Gatos, where sickly Frankie could have a sunny yard to play in. And what Frankie liked to play was catch with his big brother, John. So John, as big brothers so often do, devoted many afternoon hours to throwing a ball of some sort to little Frankie, who would earnestly throw it back.

When Frankie was old enough to go to school and big enough to play real baseball, he made a place for himself on the grammar school team in Los Gatos and quickly became their star infielder.

After he reached high school age, the family returned to San Francisco. High school, however, held no charms for Frank. What he preferred, above study and learning, was the fun to be found at Funston Square. Here Frank and his mates could always find a ball game, or create one, to fill up the hours when they were supposed to be sitting at their desks. Before long the truant officer appeared at Frank's house to uncover the source of all those written excuses Frank would bring to school instead of his homework.

But scoldings proved of no avail. If Frank couldn't play ball, he could go watch it. So every day young Frank, schoolbooks under his arm, would take the trolley to one end of the line, then ride back again, so that he would arrive at the San Francisco Seals' ballpark just in time for the game. It was two weeks before his mother found out about this. Frank returned from "school" one day with his books tucked under his arm, and she let him finish his dinner in peace. Then, in full voice, she explained how she felt about his perfidy. Frank could think of no response other than that he didn't like school. What came of it finally was that Frank quit high school and took night classes to earn his diploma.

Daytimes he earned pocket money from time to time in a produce market and worked toward an advanced degree in baseball by playing different positions with semipro clubs throughout the city for three dollars a game. One of his fellow workers at the market, a youth named Joe Guerro, told Frank about a job he could get for Frank playing in an organized league for $200 a month. The team was in the copper league at Butte, Montana, and Frank, being only sixteen, would need his parents' permission to go there. For two hundred a month! That was grown-up wages in those days. And it looked like a wealth to Frank.

But not to his mother. She simply said, "No!" And while the discussion between Frank and his mother grew warmer, Frank's gentle father appeared in the doorway.

"Let him go," he said. Frank's mother began then to detail all the reasons why a sixteen-year-old child should not be exposed to the myriad dark temptations that might lurk in heathen Butte. But Papa Crosetti would not let her finish. "Let him go!" he suggested, pointing a calloused finger at Frank. And so Frank went, with his parents' semireluctant blessing, to set out on a professional baseball career that would not end until Frank had grown children of his own.

The Butte league, like so many industrial leagues of that day, was peopled mostly by men who held bogus jobs in the mines or copper mills. (Frank himself actually cut a few lengths of copper pipe to maintain his standing as an employee of one of the mills.) The players in the league were some pipe lengths farther up the scale than the young men who played for the sandlot teams in the city. The pitchers threw harder, the hitters drove the ball farther, and the fielders would interrupt the flight of fly balls and grounders with greater regularity. To the surprise of no one, then, young Frank, half frozen with anxiety, literally booted the first ground ball that came his way. (It bounced off the toe of his shoe.) Frank was promptly shifted from third base to first, where he did only slightly better.

Within a few weeks Frank had been tried at all infield positions and the outfield—wherever a hole in the roster needed to be filled. The team "manager" (more expert in mill work than base-ball) finally deemed Frank a lost cause. But Earle Bruckner, an ex–big leaguer who was catcher and real manager of the club, urged that Frank be kept. "The kid's got stuff," he said. "He'll improve." So Frank hung on and eventually began to earn cheers for the intensity of his play and his almost ferocious desire to snag a batted ball, or a throw, or to grab an unwatched base.

This was a hard-boiled league in every way. The diamonds were all baked hard as asphalt. The players were tough—tough in talk and tough in nature, many of them graduates of the organized leagues. The spectators, too, were hard-bitten, hard to please, and grimly bent on victory, each one with perhaps a full day's hard-earned pay riding on the outcome.

With the Butte Mines League season over, Frank found a place with the Young Men's Institute team in the San Francisco winter league, where he earned a steady following with a burst of base hits and some spectacular plays in the infield.

The South Side of San Francisco, where the Crosetti family had settled, was alive with boys who devoted all their spare time to baseball. But there was no Little League then where twelve batters in a row might receive a base on balls and where angry parents might vent their own frustrations (and ignorance) on their bewildered offspring, half of whom might have been wishing they could have stayed home to play hide-and-seek. Nor was there a Babe Ruth League where teenagers could play on well-barbered diamonds, where bats were supplied by the club, and baseballs could be lost unmourned.

In Frank's day, young ball players might have to do their own groundskeeping, find rocks or bits of plank for bases, bring their own bats to the game, and sometimes play with a badly used baseball wound several times with black friction tape to keep the insides from unraveling. Still, there were many boys like Frank, always ready to join any baseball game that was offered. All of them were devoted followers of the San Francisco Seals club in the Pacific Coast League, which was but a half step below the major leagues in the quality of its play. So it was a matter of almost universal excitement when Frank Crosetti, before he had even turned eighteen, was offered a contract with the Seals.

Thanks to his rough apprenticeship in the Butte Mines League, Frank's nervousness had almost worn off by the time he suited up to take over the third-base job for the Seals. Here Frank really started to perform up to his true talents, both at bat and on defense.

Although Frank today has a hard time remembering any specific heroic deeds he performed on the field, he vividly recalls some hairy moments off the field—the sort of things that may bring chuckles to recall but provided little joy to live through. One escapade that Frank can laugh at now was his experience with the hot nickels. On one road trip, because he had a choice outside room in the Portland (Oregon) Hotel, Frank yielded to the urging of some of his teammates who required access to the sidewalk below. The game was to heat nickels, by use of a burning candle and a pair of tweezers, to sizzling heat and then toss them out the window so they might enjoy the spectacle of passersby who joyously reached for these gifts from the sky, then yelped in dismay when they took hold of them. The boys—including innocent Frank—would laugh into each other's faces at the sight. But then a young lady in a wide-brimmed summer hat happened by and the red-hot nickel burned a hole in her hat brim. So she called the cops. Eventually the source of the nickels was identified and all the players involved had to chip in to pay not only the price of a new hat but the fee for the lawyer who ran down the culprits. Even Frank had to pay—just because it was his room.

Not more than a week later another disaster loomed. These were Prohibition times and, while alcoholic beverages of any kind were banned from all baseball locker rooms, no law could wipe out a thirst. So when the Seals were in Seattle, the whole team took off on an open day for Lake Washington, where Canadian beer, it was reported, could be had in limitless quantity. The proper quantity for some two dozen thirsty ball players and a few friends was several cases of beer, plus two full kegs. But before a bottle was opened or a keg tapped, word came that a convocation of G-men was moving lakeward. Quick as thought, cases and kegs were loaded into a skiff and dumped into thirty feet of water. And almost immediately afterward came word that it had been a false alarm. But false or not—what with their teammates all consulting over how to fetch the contraband from the deep—Frank and his young roommate decided that they did not need *another* news story connecting their names with any shame, so they hightailed it instantly for sober Seattle.

That rookie year, life was not all beer and skittles for the two young roommates. Frank and Jerry Brown lived in a villainous little sweatbox of a room in what Frank is certain must have been the most wretched hotel in the city. While the regulars were comfortably housed in the semiregal Monterey Hotel, Frank and Jerry sweated out each hot night in a screenless cell, and they had to roll out one night at two A.M. and, using clubs made of rolled-up newspapers, try to even the score with a dozen squadrons of impolitic mosquitoes (big as yellow jackets). Unfortunately there was no Virgil to remind them: *Forsan et haec olim meminisse juvabit.* (Someday we may enjoy recalling even things like these.) But, for a fact, they really did.

Frank's work with the Seals was free from jitters. He fiercely concentrated on the job at hand, and constantly exhorted his mates to do the same. His endless chatter (slogans and phrases that sometimes had no meaning to outsiders) would become his trademark throughout his career.

Frank hit hard with the Seals and played third base like a veteran. In his fourth year with the club he drew the attention of Bill Essick, West Coast scout for the Yankees, and Essick persuaded Ed Barrow that Crosetti belonged in the big leagues. Frank signed his first contract with the Yankees when he was twenty-one. He remained a Yankee as player and third-base coach for over thirty years.

Hardly a man (or woman) is now alive who remembers Frank "Cro" Crosetti as an active infielder with the Yankees, for he shared the diamond with names like Ruth, Gehrig, Dickey, and Coombs. To most fans today Cro is just the guy who directed third-base traffic for the Yankees for half a lifetime. Veteran Yankee fans will not forget the Cro, fidgeting there in the coaching box, hitching, patting, twitching, rubbing, clapping, waving, and calling out to advise batters and runners when to "take" a pitch (let it go by), when to bunt, when to start for second base on the pitch. Frank had no sign for "hit" because all Yankees went to bat "hitting" and needed only to be told when it was good strategy to "take."

Despite his countless contortions, Cro never had but three main signs: touching his cheek, brushing his shirt, and brushing his thigh, any one of which might have a different meaning in different games, and none of which counted unless it had been preceded by the agreed indication that a sign would be "on." There was also a signal to take a sign "off" and Cro sometimes would tease one of his veteran mates by putting on a sign and taking it off in rapid succession. Still, he was no man for fooling around when the ball was in play. He would growl about a first baseman who, when he missed a throw or a ground ball, would put on a show by pounding his fist on the bag instead of scrambling to recover the ball. Cro guarded the club's supply of baseballs as if he had been charged with watching them hatch. Showboats were his special despair and he had nothing but scorn for players who would curry favor with writers by spilling small secrets. To Cro, anything that happened in the clubhouse should *stay* in the clubhouse. This attitude naturally earned him no points with the media.

While it was occasionally suggested that Cro might become manager, that job was the very last one he ever desired. A few times, when a manager was banished or unable to work, Cro had to take over the job. But he confessed that the nervous strain was too much, and he usually, when the job was wished on him, hid deep in the dugout.

Still, there was probably not a coach, before or since, who taught so many young recruits their elementary grammar in baseball. ("They don't get enough schooling in the minors!" he would complain.) He enjoined rookie outfielders not to catch sacrifice flies standing still but to position themselves so they would be moving toward the diamond when making the catch. He criticised young pitchers who "pitched too soon"—that is, without reaching back far enough to get the full length of the arm and weight of the body into the pitch. He even undertook, without success, to explain to one umpire who had just signaled a ground-rule double that the blow, having glanced off a fielder's glove into the stands and out was a *home run*. Of course he was right. But he lost the argument.

It is odd that Cro, whose arguments with umpires were usually short and emphatically to the point, was actually fined $200 and suspended for a whole month for "abusing an umpire" in the 1942 World Series, when he played third base for a single game. What the "abuse" amounted to was a slight tap on the chest of umpire Summers when Cro was trying to call the ump's attention to Cro's right hand, streaming blood after being spiked by St. Louis outfielder Terry Moore. Cro probably forgot that the person of the umpire is sacred, never to be profaned by a common ball player's hand.

Chapter 8

LIFE IN THE BUSHES

While it must sometimes seem, to the modern reader, that major league baseball has persisted, at least through its more recent history, as a sort of pagan ritual involving the souls and intentions of the entire male (and much of the female) population, believe me, it isn't so.

Since soon after the Civil War, when baseball grew into an addiction throughout the major cities, there were indeed almost barbaric expressions of rivalry and, in celebration of victory over some favorite enemy, riotous parades and demonstrations that seemed to engage every sensate citizen in town. Nowadays, however, it has become fashionable, even for commentators with legitimate claims to literary attainment, to discover for us, in some of the more recondite aspects of major league baseball's score books, contests and achievements that do not merely involve our casual interest and our normal urge to identify with a winner but stir our deepest emotions and, for all I know, uplift and cleanse our very souls.

One justly famed observer has implied in print that Joe DiMaggio's effort to set a new record for consecutive games in which a batter has made a hit had the entire nation—or at least that part of it that could distinguish between third base and part of the human anatomy—had us all, as Walt Whitman might have phrased it, hanging breathless on his fate. Yet I am dead sure that during those electrifying days there were hundreds, even thousands, of men and women who, despite their own intense interest in the game, didn't give a damn whether Joe made it 56 in a row or 110. They were too intent on rooting the home team to victory, as were my own friends and relatives—who sometimes liked to chant: "Who's better than his brother Joe? Dominic Di-Mag-gi-o!"

The "consecutive game" record is an artificial contrivance anyway and, inasmuch as the difference between a "hit" and an "error" is a matter of one man's judgment (and that man not even an umpire), it has always seemed a certainty to me, and a few others, that somewhere along the stretch there was an error that suddenly became a hit and perhaps even a bit of connivance by a kindly opponent to give Joe an extra time at bat. Such things *have* happened, to my certain knowledge.

No matter, Joe's reputation would not have been dimmed by a single candlepower if he had never got beyond forty. He earned his fame and his following by his timely and solid hitting; by his grace, agility, and speed in the outfield; by his almost instinctive hawking of fly balls and his deadly accurate return throws to the diamond. All these talents engaged and excited his followers far more than his pursuit of an imaginary "record" that had little connection with the immediate standing of the team.

And somehow I am convinced that of all his notable accomplishments with bat, ball, and glove, this particular diadem is not the one, or even one of the first half dozen, that Joe most likes to pluck out of his memory and reexamine. Having spent or wasted too many hours of my life in the company of ball players—school, sandlot, semipro, bush, and major league—I have observed that most of them, when they speak or dream of the fun they have had in baseball, are wont to recall their very earliest memories (as I do). Mordecai Peter Centennial "Three Finger" Brown told a friend once that the days he would have liked to call back were not his many triumphs as a pitcher for the pennant-winning Chicago Cubs, but the days when he was playing third base on a sandlot team in Coxville, Indiana, made up entirely of coal miners. And he remembers best the game against Brazil, a "salaried" team, when he was forced to become a pitcher after Schultz, the regular pitcher, was hurt in a fall; he beat the Brazil team 9–3 and he was promptly offered a salaried job with the Brazil town team. Real money for playing ball!

"The game I pitched against the Giants in New York to decide the championship wasn't *in* it with that game in Brazil," he said. "Good old days, those! All the fun isn't in the big leagues."

It wasn't that there was *no* fun in the big leagues. It was simply that there was special fun in being young, being among your chosen friends, and seeing no end to the joys that filled every summer afternoon.

Waite Hoyt, who enjoyed many a difficult victory over assorted enemies when he was top man with the New York Yankees, still, in his later years, liked best to relive bush league days when he was still called Schoolboy and when everything tasted good. Farmed out by John McGraw to the bush league club in Lebanon, Pennsylvania, he got his first taste of fame, he told me once, when he played left field (as pitchers in the minor leagues often did) in a game against Reading. He did not remember how the game came out. But he recalled vividly what happened as he was leaving the park. There he found waiting for him the owner of the Reading club, with a pretty girl by his side.

"Hoyt!" the gentleman called. "My daughter has been waiting to meet you!" So Waite took her hand while she smiled worshipfully at him, and they walked out of the park side by side. That was all. No date. No romance. "But," said Waite, "it was my first taste of what it would be like to be *famous!*"

Actually after the bush league club folded up beneath him, Hoyt did spend a short stretch with the big club, the New York Giants, where he was consistently miserable, where his teammates openly resented his existence and told each other when Hoyt chanced to approach them, "Look what's here! Who let *that* in?" Being sent down to the Hartford club was a blessed relief, even if it was clearly a demotion. He wasn't even eighteen years old.

In Hartford, Hoyt met a man he would never forget, although Waite lived into his eighties. This was a roommate they gave him and with whom he spent most of the season sharing a front double room in a big house, an easy walk from the ballpark. The man was named Marty Neu (pronounced Nye) and forever afterward Hoyt pronounced Marty the gentlest man he had ever known. A typical country ball player, Hoyt said, with a long nose, a weather-reddened face, and arms that seemed to protude a foot past his sleeves. Without anyone's asking, Marty took full charge of young Hoyt the day he arrived at the Hartford grounds. He found the room, showed Waite the nearest laundry, and stayed by in the evenings to make sure Waite got to bed on time. The very first Sunday, with no games ever scheduled on the Lord's day in Hartford, Hoyt made ready to luxuriate in his big bed until noon. But Marty shook him awake at eight o'clock.

"Wake up!" he told Hoyt. "We'll be late!"

"Late for what?"

"For church! What do you think? It's Sunday!"

So Hoyt went to church. Not just that Sunday but every Sunday the team was in Hartford. But he pitched hardly any baseball, even on weekdays, for it rained and rained and rained that 1916 summer—a catastrophe caused, people said, by all that artillery cannonading in Europe. But Waite listened to a hundred baseball stories from Marty Neu, who was an inspired spinner of yarns. And while Hoyt forgot most of the stories, he never forgot that shining kindly face and that rasping farmer's voice—a warm relief from dull practice sessions in the locker room and games that began and never finished.

There was another man Hoyt never forgot, for he was featured in an episode that, until Waite could look back on it and laugh at his callow self, used to sear his memory. The man was one Hoyt sincerely admired—manager Lou Peiper of Lynn, where McGraw sent Hoyt after he had been summoned back from Hartford. Peiper, said Hoyt, was really a freakish-looking man, tall and skinny as a clothes pole, with a face like a movie comedian and always wearing a plaid cap set straight on his head and clothes that hung from his frame as if they were hanging from a hook. But he, too, was a gentleman, warm-hearted, soft-spoken, and friendly, in an easy, offhand manner. Except for the time Waite tried to correct him.

One day, when Hoyt had been a team member long enough to feel like one of the boys, with no need to put on a wise guy manner to keep anyone from guessing how uneasy he felt inside, he watched as Peiper put on the sign for the hit-and-run play. Suddenly Waite recalled a scene at the Polo Grounds: John McGraw, fungo bat in hand, snarling at the number of times the hit-and-run play had gone wrong, with the batter missing the ball and the runner left hopelessly adrift on the baseline. And Waite found himself almost hoping that Peiper's call would go wrong.

The play did go wrong. The batter failed to meet the ball with his bat and the runner was tagged out as if he were a little boy in a game of tag. Waite felt so much at ease with his boss now that he spoke right up.

"Mr. McGraw thinks that's a dumb play. It flops more often than it works. He plays it another way—the run-and-hit."

The dread silence that met his remark, and the sudden unbelieving stares of all his teammates, as if a nearby horse had spoken, told Waite instantly that he had just spilled his soup all over the table. He watched the red anger rise in Peiper's neck until it seemed to set his ears on fire.

Waite's own heart began to shrink.

"You . . . You . . ." Peiper spluttered. "If you . . . If I . . . Well, you goddamn well let me manage this ball club!"

These were the first (and the last) harsh words Peiper ever addressed to Hoyt—or to anyone else in Hoyt's hearing. And while they almost drove Waite to crawling under the bench at the time, they became a prized memory that Waite used to laugh at a half century later, just as John McGraw had laughed when Hoyt told him about it.

Hoyt also liked to recall the afternoons when the game in Lynn was over and he could change in the locker room, not into his street clothes but into his bathing suit (always made up in that day of trunks and top), and wander over the clipped green outfield to the wide white sandy beach and into the creaming surf. After that he would shower and dress and, with money in his pocket, buy candy or an ice-cream sundae at the drugstore and complete the evening at a five-cent movie.

There was a moment of real triumph, too, that also stayed with Hoyt all his long life. That was the time when, given a day off by the kindly Peiper, Waite traveled to Boston on the narrow-gauge (Boston, Revere Beach, and Lynn) railroad and took a trolley to Fenway Park to see the mighty Red Sox. He marched up to the press gate full of pride and confidence. "Professional ball player," he announced as he set out to push his way through the turnstile. But a sudden rude hand took him by the collar.

"Where the hell are *you* going?"

Hoyt looked up into the grim face of a special cop—in a light blue uniform instead of the dark blue of the *real* police. "Now beat it out of here." The cop flung Hoyt away from him as if he were a sack of meal.

"But I'm a professional . . ."

"Will you beat it? Or do I have to get rough?"

His face on fire but still undaunted, Waite walked down the street until he found a *regular* policeman, wearing the high "bobby"-type helmet the Boston police still affected in the pre–World War I days. The cop took time to listen to Hoyt's story, then led him back to the press gate. He spoke sternly to the "special."

"Send for the secretary."

It took not much more than a minute for the special to pass the word. Then a cheerful-looking man appeared to see what was to pay. Hoyt showed the man some identification.

"Why, sure," said the man. "You're McGraw's boy! Come with me." The kindly cop patted Waite's shoulder and Waite was led off to meet a half-dozen men sitting at desks, whose names Hoyt never remembered. But they all knew he was McGraw's darling, the schoolboy prodigy. And he was taken finally to a box seat on the field. This was the first time he had ever seen the great Red Sox in action, the "Giant-killers" who were on their way to still another championship. And, Hoyt recalled, they really didn't impress him much. Why, the great Harry Hooper stood spraddle-legged at the plate and let his bat droop over his shoulder like a banana stalk. Even Hoyt's coach at Erasmus Hall High School wouldn't have stood for that! As for the great left-hander, that kid Ruth, in his second season up from Providence, he actually did hit a home run, an unusual feat for a pitcher, but Hoyt thought Ruth seemed in too much of a hurry at the plate. Anyway, Ruth's homer was the only run the Red Sox made in the game and the St. Louis Browns beat them 3–1. American League? Why, the Lynn club could give *this* crowd a game. Waite returned to Lynn full of new confidence and made ready to celebrate his seventeenth birthday.

●

George Weiss was another man who, although he spent most of his baseball life in the majors, still would dwell most fondly on his days as leader of the "Colonials." As earlier related, the Colonials became amateur champions of New Haven—and when George took over the New Haven club in the Eastern League he made them champions, too. But his days with the Colonials (sometimes called the Collegians) seemed to stick longest in his memory. Those were the days when he used to fill out his roster with big leaguers—either on a Sunday when their clubs could not play or after the players had ended their careers in the leagues. Ty Cobb and Walter Johnson, then two of the most famous ball players in the land, became George's good friends and appeared often on Sundays on the Colonials' roster.

But George's most fulfilling moment, and the memory he cherished perhaps longest of all, was his success in scheduling a game for his Colonials in New York against the Yankees—a dream that his friends had warned him could never come true. But George was not a man to be persuaded that there was anything in the field of sports promotion that he couldn't accomplish. So he wrote to Harry Sparrow, secretary of the New York Yankees, and asked if he could bring his "All-College" team (they were mostly from Yale) to the Polo Grounds for a preseason game. To the surprise of everyone on the team except George, Sparrow replied that he did have one open date in April when he could accommodate them. George's whole team was nearly drunk with pride and delight. Never, since the memory of man ran not to the contrary, had a small-time semipro club been invited to meet a major league team in a big league park in a major city.

The day of the game dawned in gloom—cloudy, damp with the threat of imminent rain, and almost cold enough for skating. But the happy Colonials, every one of whom had been up and dressed at dawn, piled into the steamy railroad coach as if it were the parlor car to paradise. Not even the gaunt and empty Polo Grounds dismayed them. George remembered telling himself to fix this moment in his mind forever. Cold, damp, and gloomy? The young Colonials found that something to rejoice in. That would mean these old guys who faced them would be sure to feel stiffness in their aging joints before the youngsters would.

The stands were almost as empty as they were on that fabled day when the announcer, about to address the multitude as "Ladies and gentlemen," looked up at the stands and quickly changed it to "Kind sir . . . !" This time the Polo Grounds held, by exact count, thirty-four spectators, all paid. That worked out to $10.47 as the Colonials' share of the gate—just about enough to pay the round-trip fare from New Haven for George Weiss and the Colonials shortstop, a jolly lad named Joe Dugan.

George did, for a while, nurse a hope that his crew was actually going to beat the Yankees. The Colonials' spitball pitcher, Pie Way, with his cheek swollen by a cud of slippery elm, held the Yanks scoreless for four innings. The great "Home Run" Baker (whose job Joe Dugan would one day take) could manage only two feeble dribblers—one to third and one to first. And the spectators, favoring the college boys, offered frozen applause at the putouts.

But, alas, the chill, instead of stiffening the joints of the well-trained Yankees, began to tighten up the tendons of the Colonials, whose "spring training" had been workouts in the local gym or a few games of catch on a chilly playground. In the fifth inning the Yankee sluggers laid into poor Pie Way for long safe hits, and by the seventh inning they had scored five runs. Then they "called" the game because, the announcer declared, the visitors "had to catch a train"—as if trains to New Haven did not run every hour from Grand Central. Never mind. The Colonials *had* made five hits off Yankee pitching, and Pete Falsey and Joe Dugan and Denny Gilooly (an "ineligible" from Trinity College) had stolen four bases among them. The headlines in the New Haven newspapers the next day made it sound as if Weiss's crew had beaten the Yankees. And they did get their box scores in all the New York papers. Besides, George asked himself, was there any ball club in the area, including the Murlins, the local Eastern League team, that could actually give the Yankees a game in the Polo Grounds, as the Colonials had? Course not! (One of George Weiss's favorite phrases.)

Other vivid memories that George liked to revive involved Ty Cobb, who had practically become a regular with Weiss's semipros after Weiss had paid him, the first time, $100 more than the agreement called for and had tossed in rail fare and hotel charges as well. There was the time, for instance, when George had scheduled a Sunday game with the Putnam, Connecticut, semipros, who had hired for the occasion one of the best black pitchers in the country: Cannonball Dick Redding. Weiss made nothing special of this, for he had had a black teammate on his high school nine and had played other clubs who did not recognize any "color line." But when Ty Cobb, George's first baseman for the day, walked out on the field and saw lean and long-armed Dick firing his smoking fastballs to the Putnam catcher, Ty went into orbit.

"Get that nigger out of here!" he roared. "I don't play with a nigger on the field!"

George now was in a stew. If Ty Cobb did not play, the fans would demand their money back—and George *always* refunded the ticket money if advertised stars did not appear. But if Dick Redding were removed, the local fans would tear the fences down. So George and the Putnam manager sat down in private and worked out a compromise: Ty Cobb would play the first half of the game and Dick Redding would pitch only in the second half. Cobb growled about this arrangement, apparently feeling that his Confederate honor would be soiled if there were even a black ballplayer in the same park. But he agreed finally, and Dick Redding accepted the deal without a murmur.

The Putnam pitcher—Jim Hanley, who had had the traditional "cup of coffee" with the Yankees—held Cobb (and all the rest of the Colonials) hitless for five innings. But the Colonials star, another spitballer named Ray Keating, who had pitched for the Yankees much longer than his rival had, held Putnam scoreless for five full innings, too. Then Cobb withdrew, having contributed only an unassisted double play to the ceremonies. Dick Redding stalked out to the mound and made everybody's hair stand on end. Of the twelve batters he faced, Dick struck out eleven. Then he came to bat, blooped a two-base hit, and scored the run that won the game for Putnam. Recalling this game many years later, George Weiss allowed that Dick Redding, "if he were pitching today, would be on his way to the Hall of Fame."

"I'll always wonder," George said, "what Ty could have done with those screaming fastballs."

Even in his days in full charge of the New York Mets, George liked best to talk about his Colonials, and the days when he sat on the bench and felt as if he were taking part in all the action— against the Bloomer Girls, or the House of David, or the traveling Cubans—or when they moved to Waterbury to play the New York Giants. Realizing, as not every baseball executive did, that baseball was an entertainment rather than a gladiatorial contest, George used to brighten things up with sideshows. He brought in Nick Altrock—one-time star White Sox pitcher and ex-shoemaker—who specialized in an imitation boxing match in which he played both boxers, and he rented Germany Schaefer—the semiprofessional clown and professional infielder for six major league clubs—who liked to draw laughs by, among other stunts, running the bases backward when he hit a home run. (He hit only nine in his major league career.) Schaefer, known as the Prince all over the land, had dropped out of the major leagues when he found he could make more money just clowning it up with independent clubs like the Colonials. (The poor Prince didn't know it and neither did anyone else, but he had only two more years to live.)

Life in the Eastern League, after George Weiss had taken over the New Haven club and changed the name from Murlins to Professors, was not all strawberries and cream, or even hot dogs and popcorn, even though George (who had bought the franchise during the gloomy days of World War I for $5,000) found financing enough to rebuild the rundown baseball park and hire a big-name manager. The great Chief Meyers, mighty batsman of the New York Giants for seven seasons, took charge of the Professors. Bush league travel for one thing was still a trial. While the men in the majors might savor a little luxury in sleeping cars on their long trips to distant cities, minor league players still had to make do with the "Sullivan sleepers"—the day coaches, named after Ted Sullivan, organizer of the famous "Dubuques" from Iowa, where Charles Comiskey got his start. No one who ever lived through those days before air-conditioning will easily forget what it was like to sigmoid yourself on one of those scratchy day-coach seats, with one ear on the arm of the seat and one foot on the windowsill, trying to find a position to sleep in. George never forgot it. And he decided early in his career with the Professors to find a better way for the team to travel. So he bought two big touring cars to go with his own beloved new Packard, and would tour from city to city throughout the East in relative comfort. And the long nighttime rides of those far-off times lived forever after in George's memory. He used to talk almost dreamily of the near-empty roads and the long whispering tunnels of trees, with hardly a light showing anywhere outside the advancing glow of the headlights. There might be a home-going farm wagon, with a lantern hung from its rear axle, or a single lamp burning in a farmhouse, but no noise beyond the low steady roar of the motor, the endless purr of the tires, and the whish of the summer night air.

With the players in the seats behind them sleeping or sometimes breaking into sudden quiet song, George and his favorite friend, Sammy Hyman, a left-handed pitcher from Wethersfield who was the only one of the crew he would trust to drive his Packard, and the only one with whom he would share his most private thoughts and ambitions, sat together in front, and George would talk quietly of "far-off things and battles long ago." Often, George remembered, they talked not so much about ball games but about such matters as George's plans for phasing out the grocery business left him by his father, about helping his young brother and sister find their places in the world, Sammy's own chances of moving to the top, and what profession Sammy might follow when his left arm finally failed him.

The endless dark that opened steadily before their headlights to reveal more silent darkness, the fragrance of the unmowed hay fields, the slowly enveloping aroma, rendered almost sweet by distance, of a far-off cattle barn, the toneless beat of the rushing air, all lent a sort of solemn privacy to their passage that invited the most precious confidences. And George always felt that he and Sammy knew more about each other than even their families did.

There was never such quiet enjoyment in big league life as George found in the minors, and not so much plain fun either. George always relished being in the action, yelling encouragement and advice to his troops, shouting vilifications at the umpire, taking part in the general rejoicing over victories. He took special satisfaction in inventing new ways to involve the fans and widen the fame of the Professors. He created a "knothole gang" for kids who would pledge not to smoke before age twenty-one. He published a booklet to explain the game to women. He brought in costumed clowns to keep the fans entertained until the game began. He encouraged organized rooting, the waving of banners, the mounting of parades. And most of all he loved banquets, to which he often invited even big city sportswriters and celebrities from far away, financing their travel and picking up their hotel tabs. Almost all the sportswriters, he liked to recall, returned his "expense" checks because, they said, the party itself was more than worth the trip.

The happiest, best-attended, and wildest party George ever staged came after the Professors beat the Baltimore Orioles in the "Little World Series"—the Eastern League winners against the pennant winners of the International League. Hardly anyone who could understand a baseball game or read a newspaper gave the Professors a look-in for that triumph. The Orioles, by the standards of everyone who was supposed to know, were both literally and figuratively in a different league from the Professors. I don't believe even George really thought he could win either, but he always had hope. Odds in the New Haven cigar stores (the local betting shops) made the Orioles favorites by as much as 10 to 1.

But George had found a smart, aggressive, and stylish new manager for his club—Wild Bill Donovan, former manager of the Yanks and the Phillies—and Wild Bill had turned out a fleet-footed, scrappy, and crafty set of young ball players who never admitted *anyone* could beat them. They nearly drove the Orioles bughouse by the outrageous plays they contrived—even, at one time, scoring two men on a squeeze play, with number two, of course, coming on the dead run all the way from second base. In the second game, after the Orioles had won the first, Bill ordered a triple steal that practically won the game for the Professors.

The third game, the deciding game, was played in bitter cold—the fans all bundled up and still shivering—but there was not an empty seat in the stands. The Baltimore infield that day was the most famous (and the best) who ever wore the uniform: Styles, Bishop, Boley, and Maisel. Their top pitchers, both big-leaguers-to-be, were Jack Bentley and Jack Ogden. (They also had a young man from the mountains who gave his name as Robert Groves, who became Bob Grove when he reached the majors. But they were "saving" this left-hander to show him off to the big leagues.)

In the third game, the man on the mound for the Orioles was Rube Farnham, who never did make it to the majors, but who looked like a big leaguer that day to the Professors. In eight innings Farnham allowed them but three hits, and no runs. Meanwhile, with what George Weiss insisted was some help from his least favorite umpire, the Orioles scored five times and the Professors found themselves in the last of the ninth inning five runs behind. Some of the spectators had already given up. But not George. His heart lifted quickly when Marty Shay and Eddie Eayrs hit successive singles to put two men on base with only one out. Next man up was the man George thought was his secret weapon—Gus Gardella, a slugger drafted just for this game, from the Pittsfield team. But mighty Gus could do no more than trickle a ground ball to third base for an easy out, with no advance by the runners.

At this point, Fritz Maisel, acting manager for Baltimore in place of Jack Dunn, made a move that some old ball players might have warned him was certain to jinx his club: He ordered all the bats picked up from in front of the Baltimore bench and all the loose gear gathered into bags. Departing customers made a steady file through the stands. After all, there was no one left to swing a bat for the Professors but nineteen-year-old Johnny Cooney, a pitcher playing outfield today, but who hit more like a pitcher. Rube Farnham, assuming apparently, just as his manager had, that the game was as good as over, neglected to bear down, and walked Cooney on four pitches. Bases loaded and two out. A number of the departing spectators stopped and sat down again. George Weiss, according to his own account, "closed my eyes and prayed." He didn't recall what he prayed for, but it was surely not quite so nerve-straining as what he got.

The next New Haven batter was Pinky Hargrave, who had been flailing vainly at Farnham's curve all afternoon. Farnham's first offering to Pinky was his brutal fastball that whistled right under Pinky's chin. Pinky gave a little ground. Then came the nasty sidearm curve that Pinky had been reaching for all after-noon. The ball seemed to sweep in from around third base, then ducked down and away. Pinky reached for it like a man whose hat had fallen overboard. There was laughter somewhere in the stands. The next pitch was the fastball again, once more almost trimming Pinky's chin. Ball two, strike one. Everyone in the park could probably have told Pinky that the curve would come next, as indeed it did. And Pinky, exhibiting great disdain, let it go by. It nipped the plate and became strike two. Pinky braced for the fastball. But in came another curve. With a great deal more faith in the umpire than anyone else in the park would have dared harbor, Pinky just ignored this one. And damned if it didn't miss the strike zone and become ball three. Full count. Bases full. The runners all made ready to shift into high gear with the pitch. Farnham looked scornfully at each runner in turn. Then he started a full windup, giving every runner a flying start. The killer curve again! The scary sidearm! But Pinky, having seen it just one too many times, hauled off on it with perfect timing and laid the ugly part of the bat on it with the last ounce of his strength. The ringing "thwack" of bat meeting ball said "home run!" to George Weiss and he jumped to his feet to cry, "There it goes!" And just about everyone else in the park jumped up, too, screaming their joy. The ball fled for the fence—a fair ball by five feet, it cleared the fence by six, while Lawry, the Baltimore left fielder, wistfully watched it go. The entire congregation then seemed to go instantly mad, screaming, punching each other, waving hats and scorecards (every man in that day wore a hat). And George vowed that he was screaming as loudly as any three of the rest of them. Then came a sudden simmering down. There were still two out. And two more runs were needed. This time the real pitcher, Frank Woodward, was at bat.

The Oriole pitcher, however, seemed suddenly low on gas. Woodward drove a sharp single right over the shortstop's head. That put the tying run on a base. No one was hurrying out of the park now. Gene Martin, New Haven's left fielder, seemed to catch the spirit of the moment. Swinging with all the strength in back legs and arms, he sent a screaming line drive that might have put a hole in the first baseman's midsection if the man had been quick enough, and crazy enough, to get in front of it. It streaked to the green outfield, far out of the right fielder's reach. Frank Woodward, carrying that precious tying run and playing safe with it, stopped at third base, while Martin sped on to second.

The next batter for New Haven was Lew Malone, second baseman, who had already given the enemy one run through his errors. Perhaps he had taken a vow that, whatever came of this, he was damned if he was going to allow himself to be elected the goat. Without wasting a second, he laid into the very first pitch as if he meant to split the ball into several tiny pieces. He did not succeed in that. But he did manage to drive the goddamn ball ten times higher than the nearest steeple. The Baltimore right fielder had started in as the ball sped his way, then he suddenly realized the ball was still going up. Whooo! He skidded to a quick stop, turned, and sprinted for a distant area behind him. But the ball still outran him and fell to the ground several strides beyond his reach. White, soundless, beautiful, it hit the untrod turf and rolled swiftly on and on and on. Meanwhile, the base runners sped to the plate. And when Gene Martin came in with run number six—the winning run!—he was almost instantly lost in a mob of hysterical natives, George Weiss among them. The man who had hit the ball, Lew Malone, dutifully completed his jaunt, placing his foot plunk in the middle of second base, with not an umpire watching.

The fans now set about grabbing whatever New Haven players were running loose. They nailed Bill Donovan first and hoisted him quickly up on a throne consisting of half a dozen shoulders. They lifted a half-dozen other players, too, and began a screaming, aimless, weaving sort of snake dance that wound about the whole ballpark. Not even a Yale victory over Harvard had ever prompted a scene as wild as this.

The celebration (but not the snake dance) lasted all night, with knots of excited or even inebriated fans yelling their joy into each other's faces in every smoke shop, every lunchroom, every drugstore, every billiard parlor in town. Dozens of fans made instantly wealthy by the outlandish betting odds seemed intent on ridding their pockets this very night of all this unlooked-for bounty.

The lobby of the Hotel Taft, New Haven's Ritz, soon held a huge percentage of the city's population, minus a few college bookworms, some all-night conductors, and a dozen or so bed-ridden invalids. George Weiss's "press room" in the hotel was soon as crowded as a rush-hour subway car with every man in attendance trying to get close enough to George to slap his back, to shake his hand, or simply to grin wordlessly into his face.

Fans took up a collection that soon provided an extra $300 for Pinky Hargrave. A collection can set up in one cigar store eventually disgorged $1,000 to be divided among all the team members.

By the time set for the victory banquet the joy was still relatively unconfined and George Weiss seemed bent on keeping the town pumped up. Certainly the Taft had never at one time held so many of the sports world's high-priced bylines. Babe Ruth was there, to guarantee he would hit seventy-five home runs in the coming season (he hit forty-one); Judge Landis was slated to toss a bomb into the multitude by delivering a demand for an open player draft—right in front of many major and minor league nabobs who had already declared war on each other over this issue. The guest of honor naturally would be the most illustrious man of the moment: Wild Bill Donovan. And there to do him honor would be practically every sportswriter with any claim to renown: Hugh Fullerton, the man who broke the Black Sox story; Fred Lieb, the baseball historian; Sid Mercer; John Kieran. Bozeman Bulger was the only invited one who failed to make the scene.

These were still Prohibition days, so the illicit drink was set out in bottles labeled "table sauce," which every guest immediately undertook to apply to his thirsty face. Joe Dugan, now the Run-Home Joe of the Yankees, had a dozen brand-new jokes to share. Babe Ruth and Bill Donovan could not agree on how many games Ruth had won as a pitcher for Providence when Donovan was managing there. George Weiss, called on to speak, turned scarlet to his scalp, choked out one or two words, and was promptly rescued by the toastmaster with a few leftover jokes. Then the mighty judge—all five feet six inches of him—arose to call for the unlimited draft. Only, instead, to the silent dismay of this room of deeply addicted two-dollar bettors, most of whom had just made a mild killing on the game, the righteous judge laid into the sin of gambling—any kind of gambling, for any size bet at all. Thanks to the "table sauce," there was even unanimous—but restrained—applause when Landis finally sat down. Unanimous, that is, except for Run-Home Joe Dugan, who had already run home to his father's fireside.

Telling this tale always brought to George's mind the frightful tragedy that abruptly ended Wild Bill's life, and nearly finished Weiss's as well. Both men, after the 1923 season (in which New Haven came in second), set out to attend the major league meetings in Chicago—it being George's main preoccupation these days to keep his club in the black by selling ball players to the majors. The two of them, along with several wagonloads of other baseball folk, sat up late in the Gold Star Blue Ribbon Pullman Extra-Fare train to Chicago, the Twentieth Century Limited. When all the yarns had been spun at last, George and Bill returned to their compartment, where they began a friendly dispute over which man would take the choice lower berth and which would "sleep in the attic." Bill allowed that it was *always* the rule that the boss took the lower. George said no, the lower berth *always* went to the senior citizen and Bill was certainly older. The argument went no further, for the conductor put his head in at that point to invite Bill to come have a smoke. So Bill went out and George promptly climbed into the upper berth. He never saw Bill alive again.

Just a few miles out of Erie, in a steady, blinding rain and mist, the third section of the Twentieth Century plowed into the second section, where Bill and George had been ticketed, and sliced several sleeping cars right in two. Bill Donovan was killed instantly and George awoke with a gaping wound in his back that brought him right to the doorstep of death and kept him in the hospital for weeks. He came to, he said, in time to "enjoy my own funeral," for his room was laden with flowers and fruit enough to fill a church.

●

No such disaster ever darkened Mickey Mantle's memories of his days in the minor leagues. They gave him, he thought, some of the happiest moments of his early youth, while his first trip to join the Yankees was a time of tears and homesickness. Mickey even likes to laugh about the game in which, assigned to play shortstop for Independence, Kansas, in a class D league, he misplayed five ground balls and threw one of them clean out of everybody's reach. And he relished recalling the bus rides, which were supposed to be a drag, but which were just merry excursions to the teenage contingent, when everybody carried a water gun and each boy delighted to souse anyone he could get a clear shot at. Anyone, that is, except the manager, Harry Craft, and he was usually too happy with the way his kids were wiping out the rest of the league to begrudge them a little roughhouse.

Shenanigans of this sort would be decidedly "bush" in the eyes of major leaguers. (Yogi Berra, when managing the Yanks, practically took legal action against one of his men who played a harmonica while traveling home after a defeat.) And Mickey himself undoubtedly found less innocent ways of making life merry when he attained big league status. But for now it was a choice way of loosing your high spirits on the world. An even rougher caper, that provided far more excitement, and thus more deeply savored fun, was melon-fighting, which was the sport of choice when the team was housed in some small-town "modestly priced hotel," where the whole team might share a single floor but would make the entire hotel and its corridors and staircases their battleground. The war might begin in one room, where a store of melons, many of them partly eaten, had been cut into handy missile-sized sections. But when the pasting began, and some chosen victim escaped into the hallway, the campaign would find new sectors, to the loud alarm of the grown-up guests, any one of whom might find himself the accidental target of a volley of chunks of overripe fruit.

Occasionally the boys' natural adolescent urge toward aimless rebellion would prompt them to play that old-fashioned game of dropping paper bags filled with water from upstairs windows on whatever target of opportunity offered itself down below. Or, driven by a wilder impulse, they might take to filling the fire pails with water, then hiding behind some corner on the staircase, to empty the pail into the face of the next victim who chanced along—be it guest, teammate, man or woman—with the only clue to the perpetrator's identity being the hysterical laughter trailing him as he fled.

Of course, Harry Craft, were he present, would visit condign punishment on the transgressors. But Harry often took himself off on day-long errands, leaving the animal spirits uncaged, and he learned of the deeds only when the anguished proprietor of the hotel, or a delegation of outraged guests, brought him the word. Then the entire payroll might find themselves squatting on the outfield grass while Harry, in quiet but riveting tones, scorched their young ears with his appraisal of their pranks and the possible consequences—usually a price that guilty and innocent alike had to chip into.

(Lest anyone conclude that such capers were always bush-league in origin, it might be recalled that, in a more distant day, major league ball players were equally disinclined to grow up. McGraw's New York Giants, while in training in Marlin, Texas, used air rifles to extinguish all the light globes that marked the entry drive to their hotel and once unleashed the second-floor fire hose to create a pleasant waterfall on the front stairs. McGraw was not pleased.)

Mickey recalled one time when his habit of sulking over his own errors received instant reprisal—sudden and sharp—and he laughed at the memory as if he were glad it happened. Playing shortstop for Joplin, Missouri, in the Yankee chain, he had made his usual quota of misplays at shortstop and was still simmering with self-disgust when, after a putout, the ball was fired around the infield from position to position in the traditional celebration of success. But when the ball came to Mickey, he was still growling at himself for his failure to contribute and he simply slapped at the ball with his glove. In immediate retribution, the ball kept coming and took him right on the mouth, providing him with an enormous fat lip that almost closed off his nostrils. He did make one more error but decided to take it in stride, having already paid the price.

But perhaps the happiest part of Mickey's initiation into professional baseball was the time he traveled with the Yankees although he was not yet a Yankee—just a husky, healthy teenager on his way to success, traveling the big league circuit with no need to earn his keep and no real worry except that his money might not last from one payday to the next. To ensure his happiness he had been awarded a roomie from Chicago, Bill Skowron, a rugged, equally self-contained young man who had been nicknamed Moose because his father thought, when Bill was a child, that he looked like Mussolini. Bill and Mickey, free every evening after working out with the big boys and riding the bench through a game in St. Louis, Chicago, Detroit, or Cleveland, eagerly sought the bright lights. At least once every day they made it to a movie. Unable to pay hotel prices for their meals, they subsisted on hamburgers, milkshakes, and french fries and occasionally a bag of penny candy. And every new city, where they could wander as they pleased and size up the movies and the girls, was a new excitement. But, Mickey recalled, one of the biggest thrills came at the end of the trip when Frank Scott, traveling secretary of the Yankees, asked them to supply him with a list of their meal expenditures so he could pay them off. "My God!" Mickey whispered. "Does the club pay for my meals?" The club did indeed and the trip wound up with Mickey showing a profit on his expenses. They had paid him ten dollars a day! And he had spent barely five! "Well," Scott told him, "Mr. Weiss said I should be good to you." Mickey savored this new delight all the way back to his family in Commerce, Oklahoma. So this is what it was like to be a Yankee!

So much for the upper expanses of our communion of saints. Most plain baseball fans, it must be understood, treasure memories not of the thirty or forty big league games they have attended but live over again instead the games they played in. And most of us attained no greater glory than that we may have earned on a grubby schoolyard or a vacant lot or a borrowed diamond on a semipro circuit. Yet such memories are dearer still and persist even beyond the recollection of Willie Mays's losing his hat as he returned the ball to the diamond after one of the most sensational catches one fan ever told another about.

In a far-off and forgotten league known to the few who played in it as the Border League because it included ball clubs from both North Dakota and Manitoba, there were marvels, or at least oddities, to treasure as long as men lived who had played there. The league included boys who had starred for local high schools, a few men who had actually attained temporary roles in the minor leagues, and a large quota of seasoned semipros. There were eight clubs in the league, each representing a mill town in North Dakota or Manitoba. The league had been organized by a husky who worked as a brakeman on a branch of the Great Northern Railway that ran from Devil's Lake, North Dakota, to Brandon, Manitoba, and the league included most sizable hamlets in between. Most of their citizens had originally been lured there from the East by a young French Canadian priest who sold them on the wonders of the Turtle Mountains—a squat row of hills that straddled the border.

The star for Devil's Lake was a large Native American named Joe Day, the only member of the club who had once been in what passed for the big time—the Columbus club with the American Association. Joe was a man completely conscious of the importance of his stature, as his club learned one day when his dignity was threatened. After a putout, the ball was passed around the infield, then rolled gently toward the pitcher's mound. Joe stood there and watched it roll. The ball stopped some three long strides away. Joe took one step toward it and then held his ground.

"Let's have the ball, Joe," the catcher urged him. Joe did not move. All his teammates then joined in gentle verbal nudging. "The ball, Joe! Let's go, Joe!" And the fans were less polite. "Let's play some ball, Joe." "For God's sake, pick up the ball!" "Pick up the ball, you dumb Siwash!" Joe, who had been standing with the ball almost at his feet, then turned in a military about-face and marched to the mound, where he folded his arms over his chest, assuming a statuesque posture. In a voice that reached to the edges of the field, he declared, "Um da *pitcha!*" Thereupon the third baseman meekly trotted over to retrieve the ball and place it in big Joe's hand while all the fans howled derision.

All the North Dakota players in this league liked best to play in Canada. These were Prohibition times in the United States, but in Canada good beer could be had in every town for pocket change. It became routine for the U.S. teams to schedule a beer bash following every game in Canada regardless of the game's outcome. And sometimes one or two of the participants would carry a throbbing head to the ballpark the next day. Whether that was Mitchie Garceau's trouble on the day he pulled his famous rock, no one will ever know. But most everyone who attended the game that day was ready to agree that there was *something* askew in Mitchie's head.

Mitchie, in a game at Killarney, Manitoba, started off with a nice clean single out of the shortstop's reach. Once on base, he took a dangerously long lead. Yet no one seemed to notice. Gene Coghlan, next at bat, lifted a mighty fly to deep center field. Mitchie took two steps toward second base, and froze in his tracks. Contrary advice assailed him from every quarter. "Tag up!" "Run!" "Get Back!" "Run!" Coghlan pulled into first base and came to a dead stop. There was Mitchie blocking the base path ahead of him! "For Christ's sake, run!" Gene suggested. And Mitchie ran—but he ran toward first! Gene held up his hands in dismay and the fans and the coaches all bellowed advice. Mitchie, utterly bewildered now, turned and sped toward second.

He rounded the bag, looked right and left and behind him, gaped at the screaming fans, then broke into a dead run straight for home via the pitcher's box! Now the shouting fans suddenly seemed reft of their senses as they screamed advice, imprecations, and disbelief. But Mitchie, having lost his hat, continued, wild-eyed, for the plate. Then one foghorn voice from the stands bellowed, "Slide!" And Mitchie, about twenty feet from the plate, went into a desperate slide that ended some ten feet short. It didn't matter. By this time both boys were out.

And through an act of God, the game ended there, with a sudden roll of thunder and a drenching burst of rain. Whether Mitchie ever understood what he had done wrong, no tongue will tell. But the few who lived to recall the deed will never forget it.

●

Life in the bush leagues was generally tranquil, even if not especially remunerative. But it had its hairy moments. In Lynch, Kentucky, in 1925, Shufflin' Phil Douglas, barred from the major leagues because he wrote a drunken letter offering to desert the Giants, was pitching for Coxton against Lynch. When he started to warm up, he observed to his horror that the home plate umpire wore a pistol on either hip. The umpire, catching Phil's eye, pointed to the pistols.

"I don't want any trouble out of you today," the umpire observed.

"I don't want no trouble either," said Phil. "I just want you to call them like you see them."

The umpire did. And Phil pitched a no-hit, no-run game. And not a shot was fired.

In other bush league contests umpires were not so circumspect. In Bryan, Texas, of the Lone Star League, the Bryan club was fined $250 after a game in which an unidentified fan assaulted an umpire and laid him up for three days. In New Orleans, in the relatively peaceful days after World War II, fans set a record of sorts by showering several crates full of empty pop bottles (all returnable) in the direction of the plate umpire when he called one of the local team's base runners out at home. And soon after the wreckage had been cleared from the playing field, Manager Hugh Luby of New Orleans was ejected for continuing the argument beyond the umpire's patience. Whereupon a new cascade of empty bottles flew from the stands along with the loaded pocketbook of one superexcited lady. Only one of the missiles came close to the mark, scoring a near hit by nicking umpire Victor Delmore on the wrist. Delmore remained in the fray, however. But he *did* issue thirteen free walks to New Orleans batters. And they *still* lost the game to the Nashville Volunteers. The lady's husband hastily retrieved her handbag and, one trusts, lectured her severely on the folly of substituting pocketbooks for pop bottles.

Life among the barnstorming clubs, in the sandlots, and on the semipro diamonds was not always light and merry, even when your club was winning. With the traveling House of David—the homeless club that made a halfhearted and altogether hopeless effort to look like a group of religious brothers by all wearing beards—it could be heavy on the soul. Riding the team bus from one town to the next, with a game or even two every day, was cramped, sleepless, itchy, and smothering. The "Sullivan sleepers" that the minor leaguers bitched about would have been like Pullmans to the bearded brethren. And the small-town fans they catered to always featured four or five imitation wise guys who might yank at a player's beard to see if it was real. It always was and the yank could bring tears to their eyes. Beards in that day usually appeared only on doctors, circus ladies, and Santa Claus.

Don Hendrickson, who became a regular pitcher for the Boston Braves, started his professional baseball life as a catcher with the House of David and he remembered working three games on the same day and sometimes five in two days—with a few impolite yanks on the beard that had taken him a full year to cultivate. The "season" meant playing seven days a week, with two games on Saturday and three on a holiday, with not more than an hour or two of sleep fitted in.

Here was a week that Don recalled vividly: a game in Chicago on Sunday; a game in Columbus, Missouri, on Monday; Tuesday, a game in Amarillo, Texas; a scheduled game in Phoenix, Arizona, on Wednesday that turned out to be a softball game, so they had to pile, sleepless, back into the bus and hasten on to Bernardino, California, to play a game on Thursday. On Friday they were on the ocean—headed for a game in Hawaii.

Don finally started pitching only when the team ran out of pitchers. And he kept on pitching on the same sort of schedule until the Yankee scout Bill Essick saw him and turned him into a Yankee farmhand. After a spell in the minors, Don arrived first in Milwaukee and then landed in Boston. Pitching both ends of a doubleheader there? Why that was like a day off to Hendrickson. He even got to bed on time. And he had time to shave every morning.

It would probably be wrong to rate the Pasquel brothers' Mexican League a bush league. But how else to characterize a league where the fans threw firecrackers at the players, stood up and cheered for a sacrifice bunt, and made bets openly from inning to inning, and where the price of knocking an umpire cold during a game was a two-week suspension for the club manager who knocked him out? But while it lasted, the Pasquel Mexican League, unlike the *real* league of today, seemed like a ball player's paradise—three games a week, enormous advances in salary and bonuses for signing, and five-year contracts. Indeed, more than one or two players who "jumped" the majors to sign with the Pasquel brothers simply pocketed their "year in advance" and went back home. Jorge Pasquel—co-owner of this temporary Mexican League—observing that men who had violated their big league contracts to sign with Mexico were barred from American baseball for five years, suggested that the same medicine be prescribed for the ones who simply took the money and ran. Baseball (the major leagues' name for themselves) did not respond. The Pasquel experiment, however, did not last. And the jumpers, or most of them, were finally reinstated.

There were institutional teams of a sort that could not be

properly classified as bush league because they did not actually comprise a league at all, even though they were peopled by players who had "tried out" and been selected and sometimes actually recruited from school and sandlot. The New York City Police Department and the Department of Sanitation each fielded baseball teams of near-professional quality. Perhaps it was not surprising that so many first-rate ball players should choose to be policemen. But the Department of Sanitation—assigned the work of keeping the city clean and disposing of its garbage—hardly seemed a proper haven for young men of transcendent physical skills. Yet the Sanitation team was a worthy rival of the cops and was surely the equal of many a minor league professional club. Their recruitment, however, was a sight more brazen than that of the police, who really had no sure method of attracting ball players of any special skill. The Department of Sanitation, hampered by a rule that applicants be assessed on a first-come, first-served basis, sought out some interesting inventions to assure that the ball players came in first. The doors of the department headquarters were generally opened at some reasonable hour, before nine. But there was a back door that opened at four A.M. And it was to this door that pitchers, catchers, and fielders were privately directed. As a result, they were given appointments for the required "physical," and promptly granted a job if they passed. (It is not recorded that *any* of these backdoor applicants ever rode a garbage truck.)

One man I know of did advance from the Sanitation Department to the police by a petty subterfuge of his own. Once he had received an opportunity to take the police exam, he suddenly developed a "strained back" that required he take a day off from his Sanitation duties. He used the day off to make application for a cop's job and, to verify his aching back, he made an appointment with a chiropractor. Once he had received the ministrations of the chiropractor (who managed to "cure" the pain that wasn't there) he took the physical examination for the police and passed it with a score of 100 percent. The eager chiropractor, when he heard the news, joyfully announced to all who listened to or read his announcements that *one* treatment had returned this ailing patient to perfect health. And there was no voice to say him nay.

The patient himself performed ably for the police both on patrol and on the diamond. (He brought me the news one day that to the center fielder in Yankee Stadium home plate was invisible—hidden by the pitcher's mound.) In his full-time assignment he advanced to detective in record time.

Softball, which developed from what was known in the early years of the century as "indoor baseball" (played mostly by girls), never attained the national stature or even so much as an inkling of the mystic quality assigned to our national game—partly, of course, because it never became more than mildly professionalized and largely because it demanded no such superlative physical skills or attainments—no ninety-mile-an-hour pitches, no four-hundred-foot home runs. But despite Little League and Babe Ruth League that helped herd so many of the nation's young (not all of them willingly) onto baseball diamonds, softball has become our true sandlot version of the game. Because it can be adapted to smaller fields and more informal equipment and can be engaged in with equal fervor by old and young, it can be played almost anywhere by men or women of almost any age, with no uniforms more specialized than a suitably marked cap, a T-shirt with a team emblem, an old pair of pants, and a set of sneakers.

Actually, softball resembles original baseball more closely than the official game does. The ball is nearly the same size, the pitcher really "pitches" the ball—i.e., delivers it underhand—and often there is a real shortstop, or short-fielder, to roam the near outfield close to the baseline.

The same spirit usually informs the game, with rivalries muted by friendship and neighborliness, and with umpires un-uniformed and unprofessional. Often a softball game is a standard preliminary to a major beer party, with both teams equally involved in the after-game festivities. So while there are no minstrels to sing the glories of the game, or philosophers to elucidate its mysteries, and certainly no historians to magnify its heroes, it does feed rich satisfaction into the veins of plain folk throughout the land.

Softball is even played in many places without the use of a glove by anyone other than the catcher. The ball may bruise but breaks no bones nor threatens any deadly injury. (Come to think of it, I did stand by once—even, in a sense, participate in—a softball killing. A pitch I delivered to a sturdy young batter one prewar afternoon was driven back almost directly over my head with three times the speed with which it had been delivered. Well above me, and just a little to the side, it met a hapless sparrow in midflight. There was a sharp "smack" and both ball and sparrow fell dead nearly at my feet. And I am afraid I was too concerned with the sparrow and with the marvel of the event to field the ball in time to nail the runner.)

As softball spread throughout the land it became a more demanding game, with pitches delivered at near-hardball speeds, with stealing permitted, and with catcher accoutred in mask, protector, and glove. But then there came a tamer version, returning to a form even more closely resembling the ancient New York Game. This was "slow-pitch" softball, in which the pitcher was returned almost to his original role of server, the catcher often gloveless, and not a spiked shoe to be seen.

Women, it turned out, could hold their own against men in a softball game, and there was even a woman pitcher who struck out male batters by the dozen. In the fast-pitch game there were all-girl teams that played regular schedules and frequently held male teams even. Alas, there was seldom a professional sportswriter at hand to immortalize any of these doings, so heroines as well as heroes of the game have gone unsung. But at least we have been spared the glut of statistics that sometimes seem to make up the real game of big-time baseball, rather than the record of wins and losses. And the celebrations after softball victories are usually enjoyed, by players and spectators alike, in each other's company. Softball heroes and heroines are all too obviously fashioned from the common clay.

Chapter 9

FALSE GODS

The only authentic divinity organized baseball ever acknowledged was an undersized and relatively under-
educated federal judge who had dropped out of high
school and studied law at the YMCA. Named for a famous Civil
War battle in which his father had seen action, Kenesaw Mountain Landis tried to live up to his name by playing the part of a
firm dispenser of rock-solid justice. Unfortunately, both in his
courtroom and during his term as commissioner of baseball, he
sometimes seemed more bent on the playing than the dispensing.

Landis was possessed of a breathtaking egotism and an almost
pathological urge to flaunt his power. He earned early public
notice by freeing, on the ground that he had been sorely tempted
through his employer's failure to pay him enough, a young man
who admitted making off with $750,000 in government bonds.
But he visited inordinately harsh sentences on IWW organizers
because he deemed them Bolsheviks, anti-Americans, and pro-
Germans—at a time when the American press and most of the
public were aflame with an urge to hang the German Kaiser and
all his minions, put all pro-Germans and Bolsheviks to the fire
and sword, and clobber any "Red" they could lay their hands on.
Landis even expressed openly his own earnest desire to lay hold

of the Kaiser and all his court and order them to be lined up and shot. No need for a fair trial in *his* court for any of those bastards! Pro-Germans, Bolsheviks, Socialists, union organizers—let them all burn in hell!

These aspects of the good gray judge's true nature are fully and fairly explored in J. G. Taylor Spink's *Judge Landis and Twenty-five Years of Baseball* (New York, 1947)—a remarkably even-handed treatment, considering Landis's openly expressed disdain for Spink.

As Spink's narrative makes clear, Landis was not, as some folk seem to remember, named to his lordly post in a desperate effort to wipe organized baseball clean of the stain left on its shield by the notorious Black Sox scandal. He had been seriously consid-ered first in the aftermath of the Carl Mays ruckus, which very nearly split baseball in two, but baseball executives had earlier made note of him when he heard the Federal League case. Carl Mays, who pitched underhand, had won forty-three games for the Boston Red Sox in 1917–18 (and later became notorious when one of his pitches killed Cleveland shortstop Ray Chap-man). He walked away from the Red Sox in 1919, fed up, he said, with the sloppy fielding behind him.

"I'm through with this club," he declared. "I'll never pitch another game for the Red Sox."

And he never did. He returned immediately to Boston, paid no heed to an appeal by Red Sox owner Harry Frazee to talk things over, and went fishing.

Almost at once several big league clubs, including the New York Yankees, began to extend queries to Frazee about a possible deal for Mays. But Ban Johnson, president of the American League, promptly informed all the club owners in the league that there would be no deal until Mays had returned to the club that owned him. Colonel Huston, co-owner of the New York Yankees, assured Johnson that he would call off negotiations. But within a week, Ban Johnson picked up his morning paper to read: "Carl Mays Traded to New York." Johnson's short fuse promptly began to sputter. He immediately ordered Mays suspended and instructed the American League umpires not to permit Mays to appear in Yankee uniform in a league game. But the Yankees responded with a temporary injunction restraining Johnson from enforcing his order. Mays then pitched and won a game for the Yankees.

The American League instantly split into two factions, with five clubs taking Johnson's side and the three remaining—New York, Chicago, and Boston—making ready to secede and join the National League to form a new twelve-club circuit. (A new club in Detroit was to become the twelfth member.)

Both sides gathered up lawyers by the wagonload and finally a permanent restraining order was issued to keep Johnson from using league money to advance his cause in the Mays case. Johnson's answer to that was to issue an order of his own to halt payment of the third-place purse won that season by the Yankees. Whereupon the Yankees, not to be stymied, filed a half-million-dollar lawsuit against Johnson and the three clubs that had taken his side.

That was just too much for everyone. The rebellious five had no more money to throw away. And the Detroit owner, though loyal to Johnson, was made jittery at the prospect of a rival major league club in Detroit. So all twelve sat down together and agreed on an armistice. The Yanks were granted their third-place money and Mays's contract with the Yanks was honored. It had become obvious to all by this time that baseball's National Commission had been stripped of its authority and Garry Herrmann, who had been commission chairman, was left without a chair to sit on. In early 1920, therefore, Herrmann raised the idea before the club owners of having a neutral, nonbaseball "commissioner" to rule over the game. And he suggested Kenesaw Mountain Landis, U.S. district court judge for the Northern District of Illinois. Everyone seemed to approve of this, except Ban Johnson.

On January 15, 1920, the *Sporting News* published a picture of Judge Landis, wearing his soon-to-be-famous sulky expression and a beat-up felt hat atop his unruly stack of hair. The caption was: "Called Man of the Hour." Most executives favored

Landis, not because of his sound judgment in ruling on the Federal League case—the Federal League was trying to invalidate baseball's reserve rule—but because the crafty judge (who may very well have known that the rule was in violation of the antitrust law) simply stalled and stalled until the Fed began to run out of money and had to cave in. But in the course of the trial Landis had made one ringing statement that "baseball is a national institution!" That had an especially sweet sound to the league executives, who made that point again and again in their protracted struggle to maintain their right to keep a ball player under contract for life.

Baseball fans in general knew of Judge Landis, too, because he had earned headlines all over the nation by slapping a fine of $29,400,000 on the Standard Oil Company for forcing rebates from railroads. And of course many could recall his bold stand against the Kaiser in the wartime days when teaching German in school, or even owning German pottery, was deemed a form of treason. For besides wishing aloud that he could condemn the Kaiser and all of his kind to the firing squad, he had labeled all Socialists and all labor agitators "scum," "filth," and "slimy rats."

Newspapermen, however, were not unanimous in their worship of the judge. Taylor Spink quotes at length in his book a statement by Jack Lait, who was a newspaper reporter in Chicago when Landis sat on the federal bench: "Landis was an irascible, tyrannical despot," Lait wrote, in a sort of obituary notice at the time of the judge's death in 1944. "He regarded the courtroom as his private preserve and even extended his autocracy to the corridor beyond."

Lait told of a day when Landis returned from lunch to find the reporters lounging in the courthouse hall. He ordered them to disperse. All did, except Lait, who was finishing a sandwich. He allowed he would stay put, as this was public property, outside the judge's jurisdiction. For that lèse-majesté Landis called Lait's boss and demanded that the reporter be fired. The boss also refused to follow orders.

It was typical of Landis, Lait wrote, to send a federal marshal to bring in the wife, children, and even the minister of one witness so he could line them up and harangue them "off the record." It would have been illegal for him to subpoena them, so he just "sent for them." Another time, according to Lait, Landis ordered a federal marshal to hold a reluctant witness "in my chambers while he thinks it over." No order of arrest. No charges. No commitment. Just illegal confinement.

Landis also, Lait asserted, would abuse lawyers and threaten them with being held in contempt, just because they insisted on putting on the record prejudicial remarks Landis uttered from the bench.

Landis, lawyers complained, by Lait's account, often indicated to the jury with grimaces and gestures his contempt for a witness or for the accused. His sudden bursts of mercy were often as unpredictable and improper as his frequent expressing of a private prejudice, as when he acquitted the young admitted thief.

While Landis's courtroom antics delighted many reporters, they led to the nearly constant overturning of his eccentric verdicts by a higher court. Even the famous $29,400,000 fine that put his name in newspapers throughout the land was overturned on appeal. But very few readers made note of that. His nondecision in the Federal League case made no headlines, nor did his outrage during that trial at the use of the word "labor" to describe a ball player's condition. The good judge described himself as "shocked" by that term. "Labor" seemed to be a dirty word in his lexicon. The baseball magnates preferred to recall his labeling of the game as a "national institution" and they gladly paid out the cash needed to buy their "laborers" back from the dying Federal League—something well over two million dollars. And the club owners of both leagues from then on looked on the crafty and silent judge as their savior.

There had been some earlier instances of agitation for a neutral arbitrator or even a czar of some worth to settle disagreements that seemed to throw the National Commission into a tizzy. But nobody had mentioned Landis until the Mays case came so close to wrecking the American League. Earlier, young George Sisler was awarded to St. Louis by the National Commission despite the fact that (at age seventeen) George had signed with a minor league club that sold his contract to Pittsburgh. Barney Dreyfuss of Pittsburgh let out a howl of outrage at this decision and declared that the game needed a one-man director, who wore no league's collar. But he didn't say "Landis." He hollered even more loudly when, in what he thought was a parallel case, the American League, in the person of Connie Mack's Athletics, refused to abide by a National Commission decision that awarded Athletics pitcher Scott Perry to the Boston Braves because of an earlier contract. Connie Mack and his bosses, the Shibe brothers, took that one to court and got an injunction that blocked the transfer. "No fair!' Barney cried. "First the commission takes my boy away and you don't make a peep. Then the *American* League loses out on a deal and you go to court about it! I said it before! We need a *neutral* commissioner!" Even National League president John Tener sided with Barney on this. That bloody American League wants everything its own way! Tener immediately ordered all the clubs in his league to cease all contact with those American League bastards. "Call off the World Series!" he demanded. But the club owners weren't going to spite themselves that way, for God's sake. The Series meant thousands! So Tener, who had risen from Chicago White Sox pitcher to governor of Pennsylvania before ascending to league president, resigned from baseball, and John Heydler, secretary-treasurer of the league, moved into the job.

Barney Dreyfuss, however, continued his private campaign for a one-man commissioner with no ties to either league or any club. And when the aborted "World Series strike" of 1918 threw a scare into the club owners, Barney won a handful of converts, even though the strike never really developed and the Series was played in peace—as war went on in Europe.

The strike was decided on by Red Sox and Chicago Cubs ball players when the lords of the game decided the gate receipts would not enable them to spread the meager rewards of the Series over the first four clubs. "No go!" the players insisted. "We want fifteen hundred dollars each!"

"Fifteen hundred guilders?" the owners cried. "Come, take half!" Or perhaps it was "dollars." Whatever it was, the players announced that it would be no pay, no play. The word of impending strike spread everywhere except through the insufficiently crowded stands. The players, when summoned out to play, remained in the locker rooms. And, because "strike" in that day brought visions of bombs and Bolsheviks, mounted police, summoned by the Red Sox management, rode into the park and patrolled the sidelines, ready to attack at the first sign of armed rebellion. Meanwhile, in the umpires' dressing room a maudlin scene developed. Ban Johnson, who had taken aboard an overdose of illegal whiskey during pregame ceremonials at the Copley Plaza Hotel, reeled into the room with a friend at either side to keep him erect. He flung one arm over the shoulder of good old Harry Hooper and called on old Harry, as spokesman for the disgruntled players, to knock this foolishness off out of respect for the wounded soldier boys (there may have been two) in the stands, and their grieving families and gallant comrades, and to let his followers go out and play their hearts out for Old Glory. Harry and Les Mann, spokesman for the Cubs, saw talking further sense was hopeless and they gave up the struggle. (Taylor Spink, in reporting this, had harsh words to say about the "mercenary-minded players." He said nothing about Ban Johnson's condition. Red Smith told me that part.)

The club owners in general, after this messy performance, decided that there had to be some better way to settle these disagreements, and they were almost unanimous in their desire to find an impartial director. Even John Heydler, freshman president of the National League, agreed that this was the only solution. He promptly offered to toss a coin with Ban Johnson to decide which one of them would name the new one-man commission. But Ban Johnson, fully aware that if Heydler won he would name Landis, refused to take part. For the next two seasons, then, they had to settle all interleague controversies between themselves.

Judge Landis by this time was clearly "available" (although he was coy as a new bride toward all overtures) and when the Black

Sox scandal spilled over, he was again the "Man of the Hour."

There had been whispers of dark doings all through the 1919 World Series, but most of these were damned as mere whinings of sore losers. Still, Charles Comiskey (whose suspicions were first aroused when a newsman, Hugh Fullerton, told him he suspected the White Sox might have lost the first two games on purpose), was troubled enough to go to Heydler, president of the opposite league, and tell him that Kid Gleason, manager of Comiskey's White Sox, had told him of "something lousy going on." Comiskey at this time was not even on speaking terms with Ban Johnson, so he counted on Heydler to take up the matter with Ban. And Johnson, roused from sleep at four A.M., listened to the tale and simply growled, "That's the yelp of a beaten cur!" But Johnson, too, while he would not admit it in Comiskey's hearing, thought there *were* a few odd things that needed explaining, and he started what turned out to be an intense, deep-delving, and fruitful investigation. And Comiskey himself, troubled further by Chicago catcher Ray Schalk's statement (later denied) that pitcher Ed Cicotte had "crossed him up" several times in the first game, offered a $10,000 reward, once the games were over, for anyone who could come up with proof of any crooked work in the eight-game series.

Spink confesses that the *Sporting News* editor, Earl Obenshain, published a statement, clearly anti-Semitic (although Spink does not notice this) in its tenor, with its use of the commonplace caricature of the Jewish countenance, to describe what he felt were the real "peddlers" of these scandalous lies: "Because a lot of dirty, long-nosed, thick-lipped, and strong-smelling gamblers butted into the World Series—an *American* event by the way— and some of said gamblers got crossed, stories were peddled that something was wrong . . ."

The trouble with this bold defense of Real Americanism is that a number of very real Americans soon confessed that they had indeed taken bribes for helping to throw games to the Cincinnati Reds. And Taylor Spink asserts that it was Ban Johnson's investigation that finally brought the scandal to light. But it took almost a year, and the 1920 baseball season was nearly finished, before facts were laid out and the confessions revealed.

Because the Chicago White Sox were still in the pennant race, some "practical" soul suggested that the story be withheld until the World Series was over. But Ban Johnson, afire now with righteous indignation, said he would be damned if he allowed any guilty players to take part in another World Series. So his discoveries were laid before a Chicago grand jury—originally convened to look into an apparently fixed game pitched by Claude Hendrix of the Phillies in the current (1920) season. And John Heydler, still National League president, offered accusations not only against Hal Chase but also against Heinie Zimmerman, then with the New York Giants, and Lee Magee of the Reds. Other names came out in the testimony, too. Benny Kauff, the man who owned more than a hundred dress-up suits (and the supposed National League version of Ty Cobb) was named, too, as a possible tool of the gamblers, plus Bill Burns, a noted gambler, along with Abe Attell, former featherweight champion; another former boxer, Bill Maharg; and Arnold Rothstein, perhaps the most notorious gambler in the land.

In August 1920, the grand jury sent up indictments against thirteen people, including all eight accused White Sox players and a few gamblers, including Abe Attell and Bill Burns. Arnold Rothstein, although he was the man Abe Attell had assured all his "clients" was behind the deal, was exonerated by the jury. (Rothstein, who always insisted that he had turned Attell down when he was asked to finance the arrangement, had flaunted his innocence earlier by betting $9,000 on the White Sox.)

But nobody went to jail, because all the papers from the grand jury investigation mysteriously disappeared before the trial. "Rothstein stole them!" Ban Johnson declared.

"I'll sue Johnson for a hundred thousand dollars!" Rothstein thundered.

But he never did. And Johnson pushed for a criminal trial, confessions or no.

Landis had already been named Lord High Executioner of Baseball and Johnson expected him to act. But Landis simply sat tight for weeks while Ban Johnson, largely at his own expense, scurried about after witnesses. He finally came up with just one, Bill Burns, with only two weeks to act before the period elapsed within which, according to law, a trial on the indictments had to begin. But Johnson, with the earnest aid of the district attorney and his assistant, submitted evidence enough to enable the grand jury to reindict the lot, along with five other gamblers from the general area.

However, Abe Attell, the man who seemed to have been in the middle of the negotiations between gamblers and ball players, had fled to Canada and the prosecution was left without a scrap of paper to prove anything. The jury named everyone "not guilty." Chick Gandil, reputed the toughest character in the group, promptly delivered a statement to all attendant reporters: "I guess that will learn Ban Johnson that he can't frame an honest bunch of players!" Upon that happy note, jury and accused all gathered at an Italian restaurant and rejoiced together until past midnight at the triumph of Justice.

Judge Charles McDonald, however, expressed open disapproval of the verdict and hoped aloud that the trial would at least help "purge baseball for a generation to come."

It was at this point that Landis assumed the role of avenging angel and decreed that none of the accused would "ever play professional baseball again." (A few of them did find work under distant skies with "outlaw" teams—beyond the reach of Landis.) Chicago fans organized a major move to seek reinstatement of Buck Weaver, whose work in the Series had been flawless, and who, while he admitted having been at the meeting when the dumping of games had been discussed, had taken no money and had always played to win. But Landis declared that Weaver's very presence at the meeting tainted him sufficiently to establish his guilt.

Perhaps it would not have been amiss to wonder why the good judge, so quick to temper judgment with mercy in the case of the youth who "was not being paid enough" when he was stealing hundreds of dollars from the mails, could not have observed that a number of the ball players, too, had been working for miserable salaries and had been rudely rejected when they sought any increase. But Landis's heart had turned to stone. He even expressed outrage when the *Sporting News*, more than twenty years later, ran a story about poor old Joe Jackson, one of the Black Sox, but now a toothless aging man running a liquor store. Running such an article, said Landis, was "deplorable."

But the Black Sox scandal was still fresh in everyone's mind— and surely in the judge's—when Landis suffered again, without warning, from a sudden softness of the heart. This was the case of Rube Benton, Giants pitcher, who accused Buck Herzog, third baseman with the Chicago Cubs, of offering him cash to throw games. He could come up with no witnesses and Herzog retaliated by reporting that Benton had known of the frame-up in the 1919 World Series and had, on the basis of a tip by one of the gamblers involved, made a killing by betting on Cincinnati. Herzog had two ball players to support his charge. As a result the National League, in the person of president Heydler, found Benton an undesirable player and released him to the minor league club in St. Paul, where, one supposed, his undesirability would not prove a handicap. But Benton, by posting a brilliant record in St. Paul, regained his desirability, at least in the eyes of Garry Herrmann, boss of the Cincinnati Reds, who had owned Benton once before. Heydler blocked the deal; Benton, he said, was not only undesirable but irresponsible and the National League would have none of him. The matter was put up to the National League club owners at their annual meeting and they voted to pass the buck to Landis.

The buck stopped right there. In the face of contrary decisions in nearly identical cases and sworn affidavits from two reputable ball players, Landis decreed that Benton was free of sin—apparently because the charges had been brought two years late. After all, said the suddenly mellow judge, inasmuch as Benton had been pitching for a year and a half without corrupting a soul, he should not "be deprived of his livelihood." But some people growled that Benny Kauff and Buck Weaver and others had lived blameless lives for the same period, yet were still deemed too stained with wickedness to return to the leagues.

Heydler, actually, for the first time in his life, rebelled against one of Landis's decisions. Whatever the commissioner said, Heydler vowed, Benton was still not welcome in the *National* League, which had decided years before to make all decisions as to who should or should not play in *their* yard. A long, secret session with Landis, however, resulted in a 180-degree shift in Heydler's mind. As far as *he* was concerned, he now declared, Landis's decison was final and Benton could go pitch for Cincinnati or any other club that he might be switched to.

●

There was another "gamblers in the pantry" scare in 1923, when a magazine called *Collyer's Eye*, which dealt largely in horse racing and so was perhaps the "gamblers' bible," as the *Sporting News* had been named the baseball bible, printed a story about two ball players who had been approached by gamblers. According to the magazine, Pat Duncan and Sam Bohne, left fielder and second baseman, respectively, of the Cincinnati club, had been offered $15,000 each to help throw a series to the New York Giants.

Heydler girded himself immediately for the chase (meanwhile tipping Landis off that he was on the scent) and heard the two players affirm, under oath, that the story was pure malarkey. Thereupon, at Heydler's urging, the two players filed suit against *Collyer's Eye*—a suit that was eventually settled for $100 and court costs.

The publisher of *Collyer's Eye*, Bert Collyer, who apparently had both eyes open, sent a long telegram to Landis asserting that the gambling fellowship was still active in baseball and offering to provide details. Landis never answered the telegram. Among the judge's talents, apparently, was a shrewd understanding of how large a chunk he could chew.

In 1924, however, a new bribery case fell into the judge's lap and he made short (and, in my opinion, shameful) work of it.

The case began when Heinie Sand, shortstop for the Phillies, told his manager, Arthur Fletcher, that Jimmy O'Connell, the Giants' rookie outfielder, had approached him before the game and murmured, "It'd be worth five hundred bucks to you if you didn't bear down too hard on us today."

"You must be nuts," Sand said he told him. "Get away from me!"

Fletcher, after the next day's game (won by the Giants, 5–1), telephoned John Heydler at home that night and repeated what Sand had said. The next day Heydler came to meet both Sand and Fletcher, and Sand told his tale again. Heydler then telephoned Landis and Landis hastened to New York. ("Hastening" in those preairplane days meant taking an overnight train.)

The judge heard Sand's story and immediately directed John McGraw and Horace Stoneham (the Giants' owner) to appear before him. McGraw protested that *he* should have been told first about this business. But Landis reminded John that *he* was "da pitcha"—that is, the man who threw the ball, even if he didn't pick it up. He summoned O'Connell to his room at once.

O'Connell, fresh to New York, newly married, was the picture of innocence when he appeared. And he admitted that he had indeed made that offer to Sand. Cozy Dolan, the Giants' coach, a man of rather limited learning, had told him to carry that message, O'Connell said. But there was more to it than that: After getting Sand's refusal he said he had gone back to the batting cage, where George Kelly, the Giants' first baseman, had asked him what Sand had said. Ross Youngs (whose square moniker was Royce Youngs) and Frank Frisch had also asked him the same question.

Landis, after assuring O'Connell that his confession rendered him ineligible for life, summoned Dolan, Frisch, Youngs, and Kelly to his presence.

Cozy Dolan, who had apparently been reading too many courtroom stories, steadfastly replied "I don't remember" to every question the judge posed. Dolan didn't remember speaking to O'Connell. He didn't remember even being at the game. Well, did he recall whom O'Connell had accused?

"I don't quite get your view there, Judge. I just can't follow you."

The judge explained and explained and Dolan always remained just an arm's length from understanding. Then the judge demanded hotly, "Do you want to answer my questions?"

At this point Dolan probably did recall what he had vowed to his teammates he would say to the judge. He suddenly turned belligerent.

"You know damned well I didn't have anything to do with this! I don't want you to force this on me and I won't stand for it!"

The judge responded with an icy stare. "If you are in that frame of mind," he said, "you can cut out right here."

Poor Cozy's courage trickled suddenly away.

"I am not in that frame of mind," he said meekly.

"You are telling me in that belligerent manner what you want to stand for." The judge had not even raised his voice. "Maybe you could get me in physical combat. You are a younger man than I am."

"Judge, I don't want you to think that I am that kind of a man."

Still, the judge went on. "But maybe I could put up some sort of defense, if you want to try it."

With that Cozy melted completely and drew back a little from the total loss of memory that had been his refuge from the start. He began to recall a few things "now that you read them off to me." But he had never had any such talk with O'Connell "in all my life, so help me, God!"

"What I meant when I said I don't remember," Dolan went on, wretchedly, "was I didn't know anything about it. That was my way of answering, Judge. I am not the best-educated fellow in the world."

Then, the judge, instead of questioning Dolan, as it seems logical he should have, about who or what prompted him to send O'Connell to ask that incriminating question, began to quiz him about certain tales of "Broadway gamblers" and "withheld facts" that had appeared in the newspapers. Had a man named Prim from the *World* come to see Dolan? A short fellow?

"Well, there had been a fellow up yesterday."

"Was he six foot six, or five feet?"

"Three or four fellows were up."

"All from the *World?*"

"No, named Johnson."

With Dolan thus reduced to incoherence, the judge pulled his dignity about him and Cozy Dolan fled from the presence, never to return to organized baseball. But the sportswriters were not content. The upcoming World Series (which seemed to have been Landis's true concern) was safely scheduled, but the newspapers kept flooding the judge with new questions. To disprove all suggestions that he had held anything back or had not dug into the matter all the way, Landis finally released a stenographic copy of the interview.

But very obvious questions still remained. The judge had examined Frisch, Kelly, and Youngs. But he had failed to follow up on one obvious line of inquiry. All three men had flatly denied ever talking to O'Connell about offering a bribe. But Frisch had commented, "I think Dolan may have been kidding." And then when asked later if he had heard any talk at all about bribery, Frisch replied, "The only thing you hear is a lot of kidding around. That is all I hear. You always hear a lot of stuff like that. A lot of kidding."

Youngs, too, had heard some kidding. "You hear fellows talking around," said he, "and that boys are offering money. Dolan might have been talking or something like that."

One especially shrewd sportswriter, Bill McGeehan, asked the question in his column that the judge might well have asked: "What were the boys giggling about?"

Bribery was a joke? There was something funny about putting

a naive young man up to offering a bribe? And offering it, for God's sake, to one of the hapless Phillies, whom the Giants could lick in the middle of the night?

But, of course, the kindly judge was not about to wash all of baseball's dirty linen when the World's Series was impending. It was enough just to wash the game's face without hurting anyone but a foolish rookie, who was surely in awe of his mighty team-mates, and an almost inarticulate and not particularly valuable coach, who was also suspended for life. For if Landis were really the avenging angel, the incorruptible guardian of baseball's mor-als, he would have pressed to find out exactly who "on the bench" had found "offering" something to laugh about.

And had he been less concerned with his public image, less devoted to his role as the Lord High Executioner who smote bad guys hip and thigh, he might very easily have seen that the whole business could be reduced to a stupid practical joke that worked too well. And he would not have completely ruined the athletic future of Jimmy O'Connell, who, barred from baseball and even from professional basketball after his disgrace, would end up work-ing on the San Francisco docks. If he had forgiven O'Connell, the judge bleated much later, why, he would have had every blacklisted ball player whining on his doorstep for reinstatement!

Meanwhile, the World Series—Washington against the New York Giants—grew closer. And Ban Johnson and Barney Drey-fuss were calling for a federal investigation—something that would have knocked the guts out of the New York Giants' lineup or, better still from Barney Dreyfuss's angle, have made his Pitts-burgh Pirates the champions rather than the Giants. Congress-man Sol Bloom of New York even promised to introduce a bill that would "regulate interstate baseball." Well, this was one thing that scared the bad stuff out of Landis and the club owners more than outright anarchy. Government regulation? Jesus!

Fortunately no such horrid consummation ensued. But the O'Connell case lived on in the newspapers even after the end of the World Series, which Taylor Spink described as one of the most thrilling ever played. Before the Series had even begun,

Barney Dreyfuss had set out to talk Landis into poking more deeply into the mess. Landis had come to Washington to see the Series and was stopping at the Willard Hotel, where Dreyfuss, as Taylor Spink tells the story in his book, set out to face him. He had, he declared, "additional evidence" in the O'Connell case. But Landis, denned up in his hotel room, sent out word that he was "not in." Dreyfuss, then, accompanied by the Pittsburgh manager, Bill McKechnie, undertook to waylay Landis in the hotel elevator. But when he caught up with Landis there and asked when he might present his case, the judge snarled, "I will not be in!"

"Why not?" said McKechnie, red in the neck from this treatment.

This time the judge blew his white stack. "Who are you?" he demanded. (He knew damn well who McKechnie was.) "I have nothing to do with you!" And that was the extent of the discussion, for Landis fled from the elevator the moment it reached the lobby. And Dreyfuss's tale was never told. Or at least Taylor Spink never heard it.

Cozy Dolan, however, made a sudden spectacular reappearance. According to Taylor Spink's story of the case, Dolan hired William Fallon, perhaps the most famed criminal lawyer in the land, and talked of suing the judge for defamation of character. Cozy's own version of his interview with Landis, as reported by Spink, was a good deal more grammatical than the one in the press, although it made no more sense. In it, Cozy had asked the judge for another interview and immediately told the judge to his face, "You know damn well I am not guilty!" With that, Dolan reported, "the judge rushed at me, almost poked his finger in my eye, and yelled: 'Dolan, you *are* guilty!' Then we exchanged a lot of ugly words and the judge finally cried: 'I am an old man, Dolan, but I can still take care of myself!' To this I replied 'I didn't come here to fight but to clear my name. You are taking the bread and butter out of my mouth.' At that, he ordered me from his room."

According to Taylor Spink's report—and most of Taylor's stories are painstakingly accurate—Fallon revealed to a newsman that John McGraw was paying the bill for the defamation suit. The papers were drawn up, but Dolan suddenly chickened out, explaining that he had heard Landis was going to reinstate him. But Landis never did. And Cozy, instead of going to court, returned to his home in Oshkosh, Wisconsin, a somewhat sadder, but probably not one whit a wiser, man.

And despite all this poking and prying, this ferreting out of gamblers and harrying them into the abyss, all these threats and suspensions and purgings and talk of criminal indictments, gambling and baseball have continued to bed down together decade after decade. I know that, in my youth, a whole section of the Fenway Park grandstand was taken over by gamblers, who, like spectators at a cockfight, shouted and signaled to each other, to make bets on every pitch. Of course, they have been routed long since and have learned to keep their voices down, wherever they sit. But more than one knowledgeable bookmaker has told me that, in the season, there is more "action" on baseball than on any other sport in the nation. Whether there is corruption of ball players, too, I certainly doubt, now that salaries have delivered most of them from temptation. But I do know that one famous umpire did allow privately, speaking of what he had seen in the 1960s, that he "did not like" some of the performances he had observed in games worked by one of the game's noted catchers. And the implication was plain.

Ban Johnson, according to Spink, conducted his own investigation of gambling in the Pacific Coast League during Landis's reign and he found gamblers were thriving there, while Los Angeles gamblers handled millions of dollars in wagers on that Washington-Pittsburgh World Series.

Judge Landis's pettiness, his vindictiveness, and his bristling egotism were never better exemplified than in his relationship with Taylor Spink. Yet Spink's book about him is a model of fairness and restraint. While he omits no detail of the small-minded manner in which Landis treated him and the petty revenge and sarcasm he visited upon poor Taylor, Spink's book is in the end an almost worshipful view of baseball's only tyrant.

Landis never had any real quarrel with Spink, nor any basis for his spiteful treatment of the man. He chose to dislike Spink simply because a fervid sportswriter named Stanley Frank (one of his colleagues liked to refer to him as "Frankly Stank") wrote a long worshipful piece about Spink in which he labeled him Mr. Baseball, and referred to his publication as "the Baseball Bible." And Landis's dislike was magnified when Spink's paper, the *Sporting News*, published an admiring review of the article by Dan Daniel that described Spink and the commissioner as "pals."

In revenge for this, the commissioner stalled for weeks over the usually routine decision to allow the *Sporting News* to publish the annual baseball *Guide*. Then, after admitting Spink to his office to discuss the matter, Landis spent the whole time systematically humiliating Taylor, urging others in the room to watch their steps because "Mr. Baseball" was present. Insisting that Spink had somehow inspired the worshipful review of Frank's article, Landis referred to him in the presence of a visitor as "the conscience of baseball" and the "watchdog" of the game—titles appended in the Daniel review. And when Spink finally had a chance to broach the real purpose of the meeting—the question of whether he was to publish the *Guide*—Landis snapped "No!" and suggested that Spink's publication of the book would just brighten Spink's own image as "Mr. Baseball." With that, Landis grabbed his coat and fled without a good-bye, leaving Spink red-faced and open-mouthed. Spink then made the mistake of plopping himself into a bench outside the judge's office to tell Phil Piton, one of the judge's handymen, who had always been most friendly to Spink, just how angry and miserable he felt. Piton, apparently, retained most of what he heard and hurried to put it down in shorthand.

The next day Spink learned that Landis "wanted to see him." This time it was an angry cross-examination, based on Piton's report. There was a stenographer to take down Spink's replies to questions about his remarks to Piton. At the end, Spink asked if he might be sent a copy of the stenographer's record and Landis assured him one would be sent. But it never was. And as Taylor left, he asked Landis, "Are we still friends?"

"I have no friends!" Landis snapped.

Then, to underline his displeasure, Landis, in one of his silliest moves, had the commissioner's office take over the publication of the annual *Guide*. It did not come out, however, until the season was two-thirds over, long after the men who most used the *Guide* had need for it. And it was a disaster. Red Smith, sports columnist at that time for the *Philadelphia Record* (and always the number-one sportswriter in my private ratings), greeted the Landis publication with the line: "Landis Batting .125 as Pinch-Hitter for Spink." And he added: "Judge Kenesaw Landis is a fool. And if that be treason, go ahead and fine *me* $29,000,000."

Landis didn't fine anybody anything. But he had already, to my mind, made an utter fool of himself. The next year, the club owners would not release any figures at all to Landis's *Guide*. And soon thereafter Spink was again publishing the annual "bible."

●

Two of the other divinities of baseball in Landis's day were Ty Cobb and Tris Speaker. Cobb by this time was player-manager of the Detroit Tigers, and Speaker manager of the Cleveland Indians, and both became members of baseball's Hall of Fame. And both were beneficiaries of Landis's unwillingness to dig much more deeply than a finger's length into any major baseball scandal.

This scandal never earned the sort of headlines that the Black Sox scandal had. But it is one that, had Landis not put a lid on it, might have shivered timbers throughout both major leagues. For, while it did not attain public notice until the Black Sox scandal was seven years old and largely forgotten, it actually took place in the same year. And it would have, or should have, put the Black Sox in the shade. For what fan could sit quiet on hearing that Cobb and Speaker had been themselves engaged in a fix? Yet, if Landis had not brushed the evidence aside, a ten-year-old boy could have seen that both men were clearly guilty at least of conniving to win bets on a game in which both their teams were involved.

The accusation was first made by one Hubert "Dutch" Leonard, who had pitched for the Red Sox and Detroit and who had been a friend of both Speaker and Cobb.

(Leonard clearly carried a grudge against both men after he had been relegated to the Pacific Coast League by Cobb, and Speaker had failed to claim him on waivers.)

In between the games of September 24 and 25, 1919, Leonard charged, he and Joe Wood, Cleveland outfielder, had met under the stands with Cobb and Speaker (the opposing managers) to "talk baseball." According to Leonard, he and Cobb had expressed their strong desire for the Detroit club to finish third—there being no fourth-place money at that time. And a victory over Cleveland—which had already clinched second place—would insure their finishing in the money. Tris Speaker, according to Leonard, then assured Cobb he "needn't worry about tomorrow's game" because "you'll win tomorrow." Thereupon they all agreed that, inasmuch as the outcome of the game was certain, they might as well get some money down. Then Cobb, according to Leonard, sent a man named Fred West, a sort of grown-up errand boy, to pick up the money and place the bets. "I put up fifteen hundred dollars," said Leonard, "Cobb, Wood, and Speaker put up a thousand dollars each."

Part of the evidence Leonard presented was a letter from Joe Wood that Taylor Spink reprints in his book and part of which reads as follows:

"Enclosed please find certified check for sixteen hundred and thirty dollars.

"Dear friend 'Dutch':

"The only bet West could get up was $600 against $420 (10 to 7). Cobb did not get up a cent. . . ."

Spink also reprints (it was published in newspapers at the time) a letter from Ty Cobb to Leonard—a letter that Cobb admitted

he wrote. In it he said: "Wood and myself are considerably dis-
appointed in our business proposition, as we had $2,000 to put
into it and the other side quoted $1,400, and when we finally
secured that much money, it was about 2 o'clock and they refused
to deal with us. . . ."

When Landis questioned Cobb (Spink reports the interroga-
tion), Cobb explained that when Leonard asked about making
a bet on the ball game he had simply pointed out West as a man
who could get the money down for him, and he insisted he had
no knowledge of any fix. Speaker simply pointed out that he was
not mentioned in the letter. And two of the men actually engaged
in the game did not, after seven years, "remember anything
wrong."

But Ban Johnson, who had made his own investigation, declared that neither Cobb nor Speaker was any longer fit to play
in the American League. Both men were let go by their clubs.
The Pittsburgh club in the National League tried to engage
Speaker as coach but was urged by "someone high in baseball"
not to sign him. Landis took no action against either man. He
invited Leonard to come make his accusation in person and
Leonard refused, so Landis traveled to California to question him.
The questioning was private and Landis kept it that way. But it
did not result in any action by Landis. Ban Johnson "went public"
on his own. He revealed that the dropping of Cobb and Speaker
had been decided on at a secret meeting of the American League
directors, who had also voted at that time to turn all the evidence
over to Landis. Not to pass the buck, Johnson declared, but
simply to make clear to him why they had declared the two players
ineligible.

"We saw no reason for bringing disgrace upon their families.
We wanted to be decent about it" was Johnson's explanation
(according to Spink). And Landis was the one, Johnson insisted,
who had released the Leonard charge, which, according to Johnson, "he had no right to do." To Johnson, it was strictly a business
matter: Two league employees had been let go because of
misconduct.

The outcome of this Johnson-Landis spat was that the American League club owners, at their next meeting, facing a threat by Landis to dump Johnson out of baseball, voted that Johnson should "take a much-needed rest." Meanwhile, Cobb and Speaker, although dropped by the clubs they had been managing, returned to organized baseball—Cobb with Connie Mack's Philadelphia Athletics and Speaker with Clark Griffith's Washington Senators.

But Johnson's much-needed rest was short indeed. He returned the next season and took back the reins. One of his first deeds was to suspend Ty Cobb, along with a half-dozen others, for being involved in a row during a White Sox–Athletics game. This earned Johnson a few fresh enemies and at a meeting held in New York on July 8, 1927, Johnson took a reading of his stars and handed in his resignation.

Cobb and Speaker remained in baseball one more season. Landis took no action against them and they were described as "cleared." But that imaginary ten-year-old boy I invoked earlier still believes, on the basis of the written evidence, that Ty Cobb and Joe Wood were clearly guilty of discussing a bet on a ball game in which they were involved, and that, at least, Dutch Leonard's charges had not been disproved. And innocent-minded as he is, the boy might want to know how much more serious were the charges against Pete Rose. Was there an eyewitness to declare *he* had agreed to *throw* a game?

There have been other "fixes" in the professional game that never drew special oversight, or even scolding. Mickey Mantle, as already noted, invited a pitcher to groove a pitch that would enable him to attain a home-run record he was seeking, and the pitcher obliged. And Waite Hoyt, great Yankee pitcher, liked to tell of the way Harry Heilmann helped him win the game he thought he needed to earn a $2,500 bonus. Hoyt seemed on the verge of disaster, for the previous evening the whole Yankees club, having already nailed the 1928 pennant by beating Detroit, had given over to imbibing illicit (these were Prohibition times) beverages beyond measure. In the second inning Hoyt had observed, to his dismay, that Benny Bengough, his stumpy catcher, had put his pants on backward. Hoyt, in his second at bat, contrived to scratch out a single and he moaned in despair as he reached first base. "What a game!" he muttered. "And this game is worth twenty-five hundred bucks to me."

"Well, why the hell didn't you say so before?" growled Heilmann, who was playing first that day.

So when Harry came to bat the next inning, Hoyt felt sure he could count him as an out. But Harry sent the first pitch for a screaming single that nearly removed Hoyt's ear. "A fine friend you are," Hoyt told himself. He set to work on the next batter, and as he completed his motion he saw that Harry had taken off for second base. Trying to *steal* second, for God's sake? Why, the guy couldn't outrun a duck! So Hoyt sent a high pitch in to Bengough and Benny snapped a quick throw to second that beat Heilmann by a boat-length. And *that* threat was put away. Thank you, Harry! (Soon afterward Babe Ruth, to whom a hangover was less disabling than a severe attack of dandruff, hit a three-run homer that made all else extraneous.)

●

One of the lesser and latter-day divinities of baseball—and most other professional sports—was a man who never played any professional sport in his life. He was a big man, grossly overweight, in fact, yet not just a fat man; Toots Shor was stronger and taller than most people he dealt with, built and mannered like a bouncer. This is just what he had been for several years— a bouncer at Billy LaHiff's speakeasy, the West Side saloon favored by politicians, gangsters, and stars of show business. Toots Shor, when the repeal of Prohibition abolished Billy LaHiff's by turning it into a joint even common people might patronize, opened a restaurant of his own, which he, with make-believe self-belittlement, liked to insist was "just a saloon."

Toots Shor's almost immediately became the chosen after-hours club of ball players, sportswriters, radio announcers, gossip columnists, and big shots of the theatrical world. In a way, it rivaled the Stork Club—a one-time speakeasy that had become the snobs' retreat, where nobodies were turned from the door or offered the most undesirable tables, and where favored figures, like Walter Winchell—failed-vaudeville-actor-turned-gossip-columnist—"owned" special tables where worshipers might view them from a proper distance.

There seems no doubt that Toots Shor, although he would scornfully deny that he even harbored such notions, did set out to imitate the Stork Club by shunting nobodies to least-favored tables (upstairs usually) and by courting the famous—even the notorious—with an almost pathetic earnestness.

He managed to make it a signal of election to the inner circle when he hailed a man a "crumb-bum." That uninspired sobriquet passed as the choicest wit among those who felt somehow knighted by it. Members of this amorphous brotherhood all felt privileged to insult the great man in return. But no one ever used the descriptive that would have fitted him most aptly—"slob."

Toots counted among his friends almost every member of the New York Yankees, all the major and minor radio and TV personalities, newspaper columnists Earl Wilson and Leonard Lyons, professional football players by the dozen, and a number of criminals, including the unspeakable Frank Costello (who had his own special table in a corner). The most acknowledged "big shots" were awarded front-row tables that were always promptly adorned with a sumptuous bouquet of celery and olives as a sort of symbol of their standing.

Toots's adoration for Joe DiMaggio, even above others of comparable fame, was almost comic. When Joe walked in of an evening, Toots had neither eyes nor ears for any other human in the room. His slightly bloated and often rather sulky face glowing like a suddenly lighted lamp, Toots would hasten up to lay an exclusive claim to the attention of the Great One—who was actually a shy and somewhat inarticulate man, not given to extravagant gestures of any sort. But whatever few words Joe might offer in response to the warmth of Toots's greeting were caught up and treasured by Toots, to be repeated perhaps in different company, always preceded by an emphatic "Joe said . . . ! Joe said . . . !"

Dropping names in this manner—the practice of so many insecure folk—was endemic at Toots Shor's. But Toots was also afflicted by an almost pathological terror of association with no-bodies—a goodly number of whom, naturally, flocked into Toots Shor's in the hope of somehow picking up a little rubbed-off glamour.

One evening a middle-aged, decently dressed couple sat at Toors Shor's bar with drinks in front of them, when Toots himself in his flat-footed manner waddled by. The man quickly turned and introduced himself to Toots and explained that, because he himself owned a bar and restaurant in Syracuse, he had come here especially to meet the man he had "heard so much about." Toots looked down at the stranger, his lips curling, and wrinkled his nose as if someone had just passed a brimful slop jar under his chin.

"Sorry!" Toots declared, in the resonant whine he seemed to reserve for strangers. "I don't know ya!"

The man was left open-mouthed, but the lady reacted with amazing celerity. In one quick swipe she emptied the contents of her highball glass in Toots's glowering face. The great man spluttered, wiped his face with one hand, and roared, "These people are going out!" With that, he snatched up the unpaid check that lay in front of the couple and regally tore it in two. The couple moved off their stools at once. "Damn right we're going out," the man muttered.

The bartender, on the other side of the circular bar now, leaned close to me and muttered, "Too bad it wasn't a Bloody Mary."

This "I-don't-know-ya" bit had been performed uncounted times, I was told. But this was the only instance of its paying off so handsomely. There was at least one time, however, when Toots found himself, to his almost emasculating dismay, on the lower end of the seesaw. That was when one of the objects of Toots's most fervent admiration, Frank Sinatra—an authentic big shot by almost anyone's reckoning—took serious offense at one of Toots's insulting "jokes" and abruptly left the premises. Whereupon Toots, utterly undone, took after him like an abandoned puppy dog. "I didn't mean it!" he was screaming. "Wait! Wait! Frankie! I didn't mean it!" But Frankie chose to believe he *did* mean it. If Toots actually broke into tears, no one recalls. Perhaps he cried himself to sleep that night.

Toots Shor's, in spite of Toots, or maybe partly because of him, was a really pleasant retreat for postmidnight visitors when the boss was away, as he often was. The bartenders were well-paid, cheerful, and decidedly sophisticated men who did not take the boss or the self-important guests too seriously. One bartender, when Toots was tenderly shepherding Joe DiMaggio to a preferred spot at the bar, leaned over and sang sotto voce in my ear, "Sweetheart, sweetheart, sweetheart"—lyrics of the popular song in that day.

But I know that Toots paid his bartenders well, unfailingly sent several large pitchers of beer to the kitchen crew, and probably favored the waiters in some small way, too, for I never met a disgruntled employee there. One imagines, then, that, had Toots not been so driven to separate himself from his origins, he might have been fit company even for confirmed nobodies, like me and my kind.

In the late, late hours, one was usually sure of finding at Toots Shor's a number of raffish characters who, while never having attained the status of a big shot—or having once attained it had lost it—were invariably well-met and given to merriment of a decidedly eccentric sort, as were the bartenders themselves at that hour. One of the bartenders, with the collusion of a rootless character named Healy (who, according to legend, had once been a top gangster's chauffeur), conferred a fake identity on me one night in response to the request of some post-theater out-of-towners. Wide-eyed and diffident, the young couple had asked if there were any "celebrities" present, as they had heard tell at home.

"Why there's one right over there," said the bartender, with complete solemnity. And he identified me immediately as a famous baseball player to whom, by God's design, I did bear a slight resemblance. And as the couple gazed at me worshipfully, Healy, instantly accepting a part in the plot, whispered earnestly in my ear, "Play along with us, Red!" and the bartender, as if he had just recalled that I had ordered a drink, dutifully filled a glass for me with more of the stimulant of which I had already consumed my fill. So I played along, without knowing what the hell was the object of the game, nor in my current state of rapture, really giving a damn. I offered proper yeses and noes when the young people questioned me timidly about the home run I had hit to win the All-Star game and I even invented a birthplace that, afterward, I dumbly hoped was close to the proper one. (It was hundreds of miles in the wrong direction.) So they offered to finance a drink for me, which I graciously (I think) refused. And because, as those two villainous conspirators well knew, I did have more than the ordinary store of baseball trivia in my head, I was able to conduct a brief discussion about past pennant races— interrupted by sudden seizures of involuntary laughter that brought quick dismay to the faces of Healy and the bartender, who would instantly break in with offers of drink or with irrelevant comments of their own. The young people, after shaking my hand and calling me with smiling courtesy by my make-believe name, took their leave. Just what had been the point of the masquerade, I never will know. But Healy and Lennie (the bartender) pounded the bar in glee when the victims had gone. Perhaps they were thinking of what the young people would brag about to their friends back in East Whatever.

One spin-off from this silly affair was that a waiter, who had overheard only part of the exchange, was himself convinced of my false identity and twice, when I chanced to pass by as he was going to work, addressed me most heartily by my phony name. Ultimately, I realized that he had not been in on the joke and I set him straight—to his very visible disappointment.

Not all my personal recollections of life among the Toots-Shorians are merry ones, however. Fixed in my mind forever is the vision of one gone-by big shot who stood by the checkroom, silently facing the front door, motionless and glum, like a statue of Grief. I forget his name, but he had been, the bartender told me, a New York hero a decade before—a stalwart of the Fordham football team that had earned national fame, somewhat before my time. And without doubt he had lost count of the nights when his very entrance into these quarters had brought him hails of joyous welcome, along with offers of free drinks from admiring company. And here he stood now, arrayed in his show-window-new cheap overcoat with its collar of imitation fur, waiting, I suppose, for *someone* to appear who would recognize and bear him company. But no one ever did. Ultimately, not simply unknown but ignored, he would vanish into the night, without ever checking his coat or buying a drink.

Another spook of long ago, more notorious than famous, and still recognized and greeted with adequate but restrained delight, was a figure from the Black Sox scandal, an undersized, somewhat frail looking ancient who would hand out to anyone who looked at him twice a card that read: "Abe Attell. For 25 Years Former Featherweight Champion." (Whether he meant he had been champion for twenty-five years or *former* champion for that period he never explained.) Abe seemed to show up there whenever chance brought me by, so I imagine he must have come in every night. The night that remains in my memory, however, is when he appeared with his gray hairs dyed jet black, from crown to temples.

"Looks likes a fuckin' Indian," one of the bartenders allowed.

Then there was the somewhat reluctant visit I paid there in company with a famous playwright who had just taken me to dinner to discuss the possibility of turning one of my novels into a play. After dinner (at a Second Avenue restaurant) he suggested we wind up the evening with a visit to Toots Shor's. Because it was still at the height of the drinking hours, I was a good deal less than eager to go (but not stupid enough to refuse).

When we reached Toots's place it was crowded almost full, with barely room enough to keep the front door clear. My host bade me wait just inside, while he sized up the crowd, packed tight as a subway jam around the bar. Then, twisting, squirming, begging passage, like a conductor collecting fares in a crowded trolley, he struggled the whole circuit of the bar and returned to me, shaking his head.

"There's nobody here!" he reported.

Toots Shor would have worded it differently: "There's *nobodies* here!"

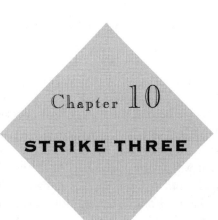

Chapter 10

STRIKE THREE

/● *When this story began,* Babe Ruth was still a pitcher with the Boston Red Sox and the eight Black Sox had not yet been committed to infamy. Yet before long, Babe Ruth (sometimes confused, by old men who paid no mind to baseball, with President Cleveland's new little daughter, who was known throughout the nation in the 1890s as Baby Ruth) had turned the minds of baseball fans from all fret over Black Sox wickedness. This was a new day in baseball! The era of the home run and the lively ball!

But the postwar years actually were hard times for plain people and, Babe Ruth or no, most of them were dealing every day with problems far more distracting than ferreting out bad guys from our national game or driving thrown balls over distant fences. When young people gathered at the living room piano, they were likely to sing, rather than the patriotic ballads that urged all to "Keep the Home Fires Burning," ditties that carried more than a hint of rue.

One popular song of the time implored whatever power had such matters in its keeping to "Bring Back Those Wonderful Days" when there was "milk without the water" and "the bread that wheat once was in," and deplored the daily ration of "victory cakes," for sugar, despite the war's end, was still impossibly dear and in tight supply. Meats, particularly bacon, which had been theoretically scarce because most of it was being reserved for "the soldier boys," were beyond the reach of most pocketbooks. And the song "Ain't We Got Fun" helped working people celebrate the fact that "hard times were made for people like us."

Of course, it was against God's law, in the minds of the men and women who ordered our affairs, to upset the natural order of things by taking any official action (other than poorhouses and private charity) to lift plain folk out of poverty. Instead, we were all urged to "Smile!" as the one sure way to better our sorry lot. Professional Pollyannas, who knew that people would be better off if they would just *cheer up*, changed that line in "Ain't We Got Fun" to "but *smiles* were made for people like us." Bad enough to go moping around about what a tough life you led without ruining the day for everyone else!

My mother may well have shared that feeling, or was convinced by hearing it so often that good cheer was a cure-all, for she hardly let a day pass without assuring us, "Someday we'll all be rich!" I'm sorry, Nora, but you were wrong, unless you meant that someday we would all be reasonably sure where our next meal was coming from.

At least we were never disheartened about organized baseball. I'm sure my older brother and his friends must have learned about the Black Sox, but it never dampened our devotion to the Boston Red Sox. And we did have, like most of our fellows, other more dire woes to fret us. It was a cold winter and my brother and I for a time had to take turns wearing the shoes (while the other pair was at the cobbler's). And a picture lives in my mind of my mother standing almost breathless as she watches the grocer—moved by God knows what access of kindness—measuring her out a pound of sugar. Grocers in that day bought sugar by the barrel, so he held the bag right over the open barrel, filling it with firm application, lest a grain should fall on the floor. Once he had the bag filled, he caressed it all about, either to make doubly sure no spare grains went to waste or just because he mourned its departure so deeply. And Nora seemed to hold her breath, not convinced until she had the bag in her hands that the grocer was *really* going through with the deal.

I do not mean to say that we were in exceptional straits. Most of the people we knew—and of course thousands we never knew—shared our condition. And, every last male—child or grown-up—we ever met was addicted to baseball and sought news daily of the fate of the Red Sox and the doings of Babe Ruth. But when the ball clubs were active, few held such doings first in their minds when there was need to discover where the next dollar was coming from.

There were other distractions, too, even for those who had time to waste on "sport" in which they were mere spectators. The hero, or one of the heroes, of my early years was Jack Dempsey, who entered my consciousness when he defeated Jess Willard. I personally would not have known either one from the old-clothes man. But I do recall most vividly when my brother showed me five pennies he had won on a bet. He had chosen Dempsey to beat Willard, so I realized then that Dempsey was a person of substance. I also heard, in the next few seasons, as I grew more aware of the world beyond me, that Dempsey had been rated a "slacker" because he had, like many an athlete in other wars, found "defense" work to keep himself out of the hostilities. But his defeat of a man so much larger and heavier than himself apparently turned him back into a hero.

By the time Dempsey fought Luis Firpo, the Wild Bull of the Pampas, I was as committed as my brother to Dempsey's cause. I do recall that people who knew more about such matters than I did felt that Dempsey had slipped downhill as evidenced by the fact that a boxer named Tommy Gibbons had stayed on his feet all the way through fifteen rounds with Dempsey (he got no pay for it, either).

Of course, neither my brother nor I saw the Firpo fight, for even if it had been staged next door we could not have found the price. There were radios by that time but few "loudspeakers" and we could not have afforded even a little crystal set, such as many boys owned. So all we got of the fight was the news that Dempsey, after having been knocked clean out of the ring by Firpo, had crawled back in and belted the big man unconscious. Of course, we read afterward that Dempsey had been, in crude violation of the rules, helped back into the ring by one of the officials. But we didn't believe a word of it.

There was a "perfect game" in that era too, pitched by Charles Robertson, a muscular young man from Texas, working for the Chicago White Sox against the Detroit Tigers. This was the first "perfect game" (no hit, no run, no reach—only twenty-seven batters) in fourteen years—since Addie Joss of Cleveland pitched one against the White Sox on October 2, 1908—when neither my brother nor I was around to hear about it. (Cy Young had pitched one for Boston in 1904 and our father *did* tell us about that.)

This game that Robertson pitched was a dull one, except for the continual bitching by Tiger fans and players, who just *knew* that Robby must be using some illegal stuff to make his pitches so unhittable. Harry Heilmann, Detroit's mighty slugger, captured one ball that he had missed and tried to convince the umpire that there was some trace of improper gunk still left on it. The umpire did not agree. Ty Cobb, manager of the Tigers, hustled out to first base at one point, convinced that the Chicago first baseman had concealed the contraband in his glove. But he, too, came up empty.

The Detroit crowd booed Robby heartily, inning after inning, accusing him of doctoring the ball. But Robby kept on putting the Tigers down. He struck out six and only six balls were driven into the outfield. Then, when he had sent the final batter to the bench, the Detroit fans, or most of them, rushed excitedly down to the field and carried Robby off in triumph. Enemy or no, he had made history! Why, he would be enshrined now along with Addie Joss and Cy Young—one of the greatest! Actually, Robby never had a winning season with the White Sox, and ended his career nearly forgotten, having never enjoyed a winning record in his eight big-league seasons.

This, however, meant nothing to us. We had never heard of Robertson! The great pitchers of our era were Christy Mathewson, whose book *Pitching in a Pinch* we had read until it was dogeared; Walter Johnson, who, everyone knows, had the fastest fastball in the world; plus the entire pitching staff of the Red Sox—Bullet Joe Bush, iron man Sam Jones (he pitched and won a doubleheader), Waite Hoyt, who was not much older than *we* were, and Herb Pennock, who had been pitching forever.

Time came, of course, when, like every other boy we knew who had any sense at all, we hungrily sought the news each day about the home run race between Babe Ruth (who would always be a Bostonian in our hearts, even if he had been sold to the Yankees) and Lou Gherig, who was no friend of ours if he was going to compete with the Babe.

The Red Sox in that day had been wrung dry by Harry Frazee, the traitor who sold most of our heroes to the Yankees, so it was only on rare evenings that we could hear the sudden newsboy on the corner shouting, "Yay! Red Sox win!"

Just the same, that's where our private heroes played. We adored Stuffy McInnis, the first baseman who never made an error, and second baseman Del Pratt, who specialized in two-base hits, and Everett Scott, who never missed a game. We never knew that the great Stuffy, who eventually became a coach at Harvard, also led the league (as noted earlier) in "trading hits."

Of course, most of these doughty fellows were also shipped, like Ruth and Mays and the rest, down to the New York Yankees, to provide cash to bolster Harry Frazee's bank balance—made wobbly by some of his theatrical experiments. But despite the descent of the Red Sox to almost permanent hold on last place in the league, we found new idols to magnify. If they were Red Sox, they were ours. We still had Joe Dugan, playing briefly on our side, before he, too, was peddled to the Yankees, and Muddy Ruel, strong-armed catcher. And when they were gone, at least Harry Frazee went with them, with no mourning by anyone we knew of. (Ban Johnson's farewell was to lift a glass in everyone's favorite back-of-the-hand toast: "Here's to Frazee, he's a good old soul. Yes, he is, in a pig's asshole!")

A new (reluctant) owner, Bob Quinn, who eventually could not find capital enough to fight off the evils of the coming Depression, still found champions of a sort we could lend our hearts to. There was Bob Ehmke (whose real first name was Howard), the only Boston pitcher who posted a winning season in 1924 (he also lost as many games as any pitcher in the league that season). And we had ancient, forty-year-old, John Picus (he played under the name of John Picus Quinn), who nearly managed to break even. Our personal favorite was the new shortstop, Dudley Lee, who hit mostly singles but hit a lot of them, and who, we heard, was not above giving out an autograph to a boy.

We saw no ball games at Fenway Park in those difficult days, but then very few other people did, some because they could not afford to and many because they had to work all day, every day—and Boston still did not permit baseball games on Sunday. Actually, the Twilight League, where college players could temporarily shed their amateur standing by taking care not to accept checks or to permit their real names to be published, seemed to take the place of big league ball in the lives of many working stiffs who did at least have the evenings off. And the play at Fenway Park, should anyone, as we used to say, ride up in a hack and ask you about it, was really not at a much higher level.

Dozens of forgotten men sought transient fame on the Red Sox roster, and a few castoffs completed their playing careers there. And two or three players of great promise contributed nothing much more than promise to the Sox and made it all good somewhere else. Charles "Red" Ruffing came to Boston, where, in a sort of warm-up for his all-star career with the Yankees, he lost more baseball games in one season than any other pitcher who dared to draw a big league salary. Danny MacFayden, a four-eyed lad who, when he moved up from semipro to the Red Sox, looked just like what he had been when we first saw him—a winning pitcher for a favorite enemy of ours, Somerville High School—at least lost fewer games than Ruffing did.

Many people who can recall these years remember them as the days of Hoover prosperity, for everyone seemed to be growing rich—everyone, that is, except the farmers and the people on a weekly wage. While the Hoover shills were freely passing out brass coins wearing the legend "Good for Four More Years of Prosperity," the farmers were trying to persuade the electorate that, inasmuch as their farms were feeding the whole bloody nation, they deserved some protection against collapsing prices. And working people, "requested" to work extra hours (or not work at all), were glumly accepting fifty cents "supper money" as overtime pay.

Shoe factories and textile mills upon which New England "prosperity" had been built had already begun to slip away to the southland, where the abolition of slavery had, for generations, taught men and women to learn to live on slave wages.

Nevertheless, a few people were making a success of the baseball business. In Baltimore, whither George Weiss had been lured to take over the orphaned Orioles, cheap baseball and winning ball clubs provided, if not a gold mine, at least a thriving secondhand shop. (When the Depression *did* strike there, men and women who sought welfare, or "relief" as it was named, had to apply at the police station. It seemed perfectly clear to the all-rightniks then, as even now, that welfare was a type of con game that needed police oversight.)

Throughout the twenties our family was scattered some, seeking free schooling and steady jobs. For a time my brother and I helped our mother pay the rent by working five hours an evening in a nearby bowling alley, where most of the men talked baseball or boxing. And even when we had to move miles away, our hearts remained with the Red Sox, no matter that they were now, as the saying went, almost "on the town." We had steady access to radios then and while we had little occasion to rejoice, we lived constantly in hope. Better indeed than living in despair.

We were even able to select one hero from among the many Boston hirelings who were fated to make good in other pastures. That was third baseman Billy Werber, who had been bumped

from the Yankees by Frank Crosetti. Billy, according to a few
soreheads we listened to, was an arrogant young man, with an
inflated opinion of his worth. But no matter how inflated that
opinion may have been, we shared it. In our thinking, when
Werber made it to first, by any means, he was the same as on
second, for he would indeed take off at any moment to help
himself to one more base. We were never there to watch him,
though, for by now even if we could afford a bleacher ticket,
other needs pressed upon us. But we needed only the radio and
the newspapers to keep track of Billy. Why, for God's sake, the
man one day actually took *two* bases on balls! Realizing, of course,
that when a runner gets a base on balls, everyone relaxes while
the man trots down to first, Werber didn't trot down. He knew
the ball was in play, walk or no walk, so when he reached first
base at top speed he just kept on going. And no one had sense
enough to try to stop him, until it was too late.

That was the kind of stuff to feed the troops of incurable fans
like us!

But Werber was by no means all that happened to the Red
Sox to relight our flagging spirits. Millionaire Tom Yawkey, having publicly vowed to make Boston a winner again, had rebuilt
not only the team but the whole bloody ballpark. The wooden
bleachers having burned down once, they burned down again
after Yawkey took over. So Tom said the hell with wooden stands
and built a whole new park of steel and concrete—even flattening
"Duffy's Cliff," the outrageous little hill that drove visiting left
fielders to using bad words out loud but which Duffy Lewis could
scramble up like a squirrel.

Besides Werber, who stayed around long enough to lead the
league twice in stolen bases, my brother and I most relished the
reports of what the Ferrell brothers were up to—Wesley, the
pitcher, and Rick, the catcher. Not so spectacular a pair as the
Dean brothers, who earned most of the headlines, but always up
to *something* to make us yell. Wes Ferrell was as good a hitter as
he was a pitcher—and he was a damn good pitcher still! He
served as a pinch hitter time and time again. He even hit *seven*

home runs one season, the same year (1935) when he led the league's pitchers with twenty-five wins. And brother Rick that year hit .301.

Before Tom Yawkey came to the rescue, however, our afternoons were often brightened by the antics of Boston's new heavyweights, Smead Jolley and Bob Fothergill, who, had they both climbed on the scale at the same time, would likely have broken the bloody springs. One thing you could say for Jolley, whose efforts in the outfield to make connections with a fly ball would make even the umpire laugh, he was a worse catcher than he was a fielder, and he tried both jobs. Fothergill, who was shorter and fatter, was really over the hill when he came to Boston and he apparently was winded by the climb. He was trusted in the outfield only four times. The rest of the time he pinch-hit—but never for Jolley, who could really hammer the ball. Dale Alexander, who came along about the same time, was the first authentic slugger Red Sox fans had seen since the glory days. He led the American League in batting in his only season in Boston. But at first base he was about as deft a fielder as Smead Jolley, who probably escaped getting hit on the head with a fly ball only because he seldom got that close. And Alexander may possibly have held onto his season batting championship because he missed a few times at bat from having been left too long under the sunlamp while the trainer watched the game. It took him weeks to recover from the cooking.

Connie Mack, owner-manager of the Philadelphia Athletics, trying to recover some of what he had lost when the great panic hit Wall Street, began to sell his stars at the very time Yawkey showed up with his millions. Picking over Mack's bargain counter, Yawkey chose Bob "Lefty" Grove, the dour mountaineer, and Rube Walberg, a left-hander who had just had his first losing season in eight years. (He contributed three more losing seasons to the Red Sox.) Yawkey bought Ferrell then, for about the price of a scorecard—because Wesley was on the outs with the Cleveland manager and had refused to report. Then he found another left-hander in Rochester, Fritz Ostermueller, a steady worker, much easier to get along with than Ferrell, and a man who kept his nature on a steady keel, he told me once, by never reading the newspapers after he had lost a game. With all these, plus the return of Herb Pennock, who had been our hero fifteen years before, the Red Sox turned into winners, or at least into breakers-even, a position they had not attained before in sixteen years.

It is true that we, so long resigned to seeing "promise" turn to dismay, were not really undone when Lefty Grove, for instance, developed a sore arm (he already, many who met him agreed, owned a twenty-four-karat sore head). Connie Mack actually offered Yawkey his money back when Grove's arm went bad. But Yawkey said no. Nothing was offered, however, when Walberg won only six games all year, and Max Bishop, an authentic big name, was beat out for the second-base job by one Bill Cissell who had been a "who he?" most of his baseball life.

Of course, the whole nation had been singing "Happy Days Are Here Again" ever since Herbert Hoover, who had seen "the whole nation in danger" when the Bonus Army marched almost up to his door, had been eased out by the new Roosevelt. And the song rose in fresh volume when news broke in Boston that Clark Griffith had sold his very own son-in-law, Joe Cronin, peerless shortstop, and authoritative slugger (he hit triples by the dozen), to Tom Yawkey for a quarter million dollars. Joe was no has-been. He hit three hundred or better in Boston most of the time and he became a hardfisted (and hardheaded) manager for the Sox. With Cronin's leadership, or his goading, the Red Sox all came to life at once—nearly everyone, anyway. Babe Dahlgren, the new first baseman, never quite suited Joe, although the fans thought his fielding near magic—compared at least to what they had borne from Jolley and Alexander. But Cronin allowed that, for one thing, Babe's "arms were too short" (he did not unbend his arm properly).

With Cronin to goad (or jolly) him, Lefty Grove found there were other ways than fastballs to get batters out. And touchy Wes Ferrell cooled down enough to win twenty-five games. (He did bust a little furniture in the clubhouse.) And Cronin added a fancy touch of his own one September afternoon when one of his sizzling line drives took the Cleveland third baseman square on the skull and bounced off into the hands of the shortstop, for one out. Then, the bases being full at the time, the shortstop tossed to second to catch Werber, and the second baseman made it a triple play by forwarding the ball to first to put the Red Sox out altogether.

Cronin, too, at a much later date, when we were all grown up and gone away, made a solid contribution to the supremacy of the race (and the glory of the Confederacy), as pointed out earlier, when, after joining in a pretense of "looking over" three black players, including Jackie Robinson, he told them all he'd "let them know" and then went sniggering back to the clubhouse to join in a hearty laugh at the very idea of their *ever* taking on a "nigger." (The Sox were the last to hire a black man.)

Of course, all through this depression and NRA period, when the five-day week, once thought a sin against God's will, became standard even for lowlifes like ourselves, the big names were Babe Ruth and Dizzy Dean. What more could possibly be said about either one? Well, perhaps it might not be wholly out of order to recall that Babe was not really the "drunken brawler," as some who never even set eyes on him will charge today. Nor was he, as one dainty publisher who could not even bear to read a book about Babe did exclaim, "a horror." A man of his time and place and haphazard upbringing Babe surely was. He was a rowdy child who began to smoke at age eight and to drink beer not much later. As a small boy, he was unruly. His playroom was his father's bar. His playgrounds were the streets close by. When he needed money for candy, he found he could sneak it out of his father's till. When he got beat for that, he would go steal it again and share his wealth with all the kids on the street. For this, he was removed from his family and put in a Catholic home for naughty boys, where he learned to play baseball. He was a catcher on the baseball team and because he was left-handed he had to wear the glove on the wrong hand. All the same, he became the best baseball player in the school. And when he left school to become a real baseball player, he entered a world where good manners were never of any special account.

Grown to manhood, a famous athlete, a wealthy man, he was still better attuned to the locker room than he was to polite company. But there was never a mean or selfish or cruel motive in his nature. Still, as a friend of mine (and of his) once told me, "He would shame you."

Typical of his crudities was his behavior one afternoon when he sat in the company of friends, teammates, and their wives, and suddenly stood up to announce, with no special emphasis, "I've got to take a piss." Whereupon he left the room, with a scandalized teammate quickly following.

"My God, Jidge!" the man muttered to him. "You don't use a word like that when there's *women* around."

"What word?"

"Piss, for Christ's sake. If you have to say that, say 'urinate.' "

In due time, suitably schooled, Babe returned, penitent, and declared, "Jeez, I'm sorry! I oughtn't to of said that. I ought to of said urinate!"

There were no such apologies, however, when Babe was in his own home. One evening Waite Hoyt brought his new bride to visit the great man and they were greeted at the door by Mrs. Ruth, highball in hand. Babe, she explained, was closeted with his accountant but would join them promptly. Within twenty minutes, the Babe did appear, to greet Hoyt with his standard "Hiya, stud!" as he showed the accountant to the door. Then he turned, before ever being introduced to the new Mrs. Hoyt, and spotted his wife with the highball.

"For Christ's sake!" he inquired politely, "Are you going to get pissy-assed again tonight?"

That time, *everybody* was embarrassed—except Babe. Yes, he *would* shame you!

Yet there was another side to Babe that not too many seem to remember. He was a notorious soft touch. Just as in his youngest days, when he shared his stolen dollars with the kids on the street, he was always ready to slip a five or a ten or a fifty to the teammate who needed it. Once, when he was himself afflicted with the disease that would kill him, he was asked to visit an old man who had lost his eyesight but who still held on to his dearest wish, to meet Babe Ruth. So Babe went, and he took the man's hand and answered his questions, and set the man to weeping with joy. "I've looked forward to this all my life," the man whispered. Then Babe left him and Babe's eyes, too, were wet. "That poor old guy!" he said. "What a hell of a note!" Yet someone might have said the same about Babe.

Near the very end of Babe's life, when his voice was only a rasping whisper and his body had shrunk to a caricature of his active self, Waite Hoyt and Waite's wife, Ellen, came to visit him again. They sat with him only the few minutes that seemed about all Babe could stand. But as they started to leave he begged them to wait. Then he shuffled out to the kitchen and took from the refrigertor a single orchid in a tiny vase. He handed this to Ellen and whispered, "Now don't forget the old Babe." Ellen wept. And Waite, recalling the incident told me earnestly, "He was really *nice!*"

I am sure Dizzy Dean was nice, too, in his own way. He was a generous man, certainly, and full of fun. He also owned a devotion to his brother Paul that revealed the essential kindness of his nature. And Paul returned that devotion twofold. One story told of the brothers seemed to illustrate, in a small way, the degree to which they identified with each other. When both boys were playing for the St. Louis Cardinals, one of Dizzy's teammates, after a loud verbal scuffle with Dizzy during which a few wild punches were exchanged, returned to the bench and, it being almost his time at bat, selected a bat from the collection. Whereupon Paul leapt to his feet to restrain him. "Don't hit him with no bat!" he shouted. "Fists is all right. But don't hit him with no bat!"

The private hero of most poor folks in 1931 was a true child of the Depression, the center fielder for the St. Louis Cardinals who had earlier bummed his way to his first Florida training camp,

riding part of the journey on the brake rods of a freight car—
and jailed overnight as a vagrant along the way. He reported for
work in khaki pants and a dirty hunting jacket, with grease on
his face and his hair and clothing soiled with cinders, and wearing
a full week's beard.

While Pepper Martin made a more civilized appearance in
1931, he still showed up from time to time wearing grease and
oil left over from working on his midget racing car. He had got
his full-time job on the Cardinals by demanding it. After being
shifted back and forth to the minors and kept on the utility role
with the major club, he walked into Branch Rickey's office and
told the boss he was tired of riding the bench. "Play me or trade
me!" he insisted. So Rickey made him the regular center fielder.

A good thing, too, because in the 1931 World Series against
the favored Philadelphia Athletics, who had won 107 games in
the regular season, Martin played like a madman. Facing the
Athletics' Lefty Grove, who had led the American League that
year with thirty-one wins and only four losses, Pepper Martin,
in the first game, drove out a double and two singles—not enough
to win the game, but a good foretaste of what was coming. The
next day, the Cardinals won the game, while Pepper made two
hits, stole second base both times, and contributed two runs. In
the third game, played in Philadelphia, Pepper faced Grove and
again made two hits as the Cardinals won. The next day they
lost. But that was not Pepper's fault. The Cardinals made but
two hits and Martin had both of them—a double and a single
followed by another stolen base. Then, with the Series tied at
two, Martin, having at last been moved up to fourth in the batting
order, really broke loose, batting in four of the Cardinals' five
runs with a home run and two singles.

For the remainder of the Series, Pepper was quiet. But he had
already set a record with twelve hits, for a Series avearge of .500.
And he had stolen five bases and driven in five runs. In the final
game, with the Athletics having put the tying runs on base,
Pepper took off after a solid line drive by Max Bishop and, with
a spectacular grab, turned it into the final out.

Pepper, who still had not got used to being a hero, although crowds had been yelling his name at every train stop between Philadelphia and St. Louis, was able to retain his equilibrium even when the very czar of baseball, mighty Judge Landis, told him, "Martin, I wish I could change places with you today."

"That would be all right with me, Judge," said Pepper, "if I could swap my forty-five-hundred-dollar salary for yours." (The judge was drawing about ten times as much.)

Like most vaudeville "heroes" of that day (meaning people who had got their names in the papers in connection with some mighty victory or major disaster), Pepper was promptly signed up for a national series of "appearances" at $1,500 a shot. Pepper bore up under this for a full month. Then, having completed his "appearance" in Louisville, Kentucky, he abruptly called it off.

"I ain't no actor!" Pepper declared. And he passed up the final $7,500. "I'm just cheating the public," he explained. Obviously he had had a far different upbringing from the Wall Street folks who had, in the preceding decades, counted the public fair game.

It was not until well after Pepper Martin's startling display of unlooked-for skill, speed, and power that anyone took note of the fact that he wore, as one of his middle names, the prophetic name of Roosevelt.

Of course, Roosevelt, at that time, was the name of a dead president, although there *was* a Roosevelt who had been elected governor of New York (and had been opposed by the *New York Post* on the grounds that he was a cripple, obviously unable to fill such a demanding post).

The last time I can recall having been so deeply involved in baseball that I neglected my regularly assigned duties as a grown-up errand boy was when I shared my companion's delight two years earlier at Connie Mack's apparently muddle-headed decision to start the 1929 World Series by sending to the pitcher's mound our one-time hero, superannuated Howard Ehmke, who by our reckoning was not much younger than my own father. And of course, Connie Mack, all sportswriters agreed, had to be nuts to send this ancient to pitch a crucial ball game. He was thirty-five, for God's sake—about halfway to the grave! Why, if this old bird lasts even three innings . . . But Ehmke lasted all nine innings. And along the way he struck out thirteen Chicago batters, setting a new record for strikeouts in a World Series game. It was, indeed, the last major league game he ever won. But who, as the once-popular song phrased it, could ask for anything more? Nobody I knew, certainly.

The Wall Street crash followed shortly after. But the Depression did not immediately begin. Wall Street soothsayers solemnly diagnosed the stock market as fundamentally sound and, with the aid of a steadfastly loyal administration, urged all the lesser folk that *now* was the time to buy these suddenly deflated stocks. (Meanwhile, they busily divested themselves of the very holdings they were hawking so earnestly.)

The only time after that that I can recall having the urge and the time to dwell on matters other than stretching a two-dollar bill across a full day's fare was the moment when I found myself in Herald Square or some such place, along with a few hundred additional idlers, watching with intermittent interest an outdoor scoreboard that recorded the progress of the first game in the 1932 World Series between the Yankees and the Chicago Cubs. One of my former Red Sox heroes, Red Ruffing of the Yankees, faced Guy Bush of the Cubs in the Series' first game, and that is all that was notable to me. I don't recall who won nor were there any memorable moments for me. I do remember the man who stood beside me, an older man than I but equally shabby and equally indifferent to the game. He was a smaller man than I and obviously happy to accept whatever brief companionship I could offer. He clearly believed that I shared his own lot and he did not boggle at allowing he, too, was "unemployed"—a condition that, in that bleak day, was accepted as a sort of chronic disease. He did not realize that I happened that day to have some six or eight bucks in my pocket. And when I abruptly asked him if he could use a cup of coffee, he eagerly agreed. Leaving the game to sort itself out with no encouragement from us, we repaired to a nearby one-armed lunchroom where, it turned out, he could also "use" a poached egg on toast. We sat side by side as he tried to ingest his food without quite wolfing it. And he told me, between bites, of the job he had held for ten years. Doing what I will never recall. What I do recall, almost painfully, is the wistful pride with which he reported, "I had four men under me." Four men under him. Now there were hundreds of thousands all evenly situated with him. And that lovely day, he seemed to be acknowledging, would never return. Never.

My own horizon brightened notably soon afterward, when I found work running errands for a small concern employed by the Democratic National Committee. Pay was small but steady, and the atmosphere was one of unremitting cheer. For everyone knew, except those random, overfed Republicans we ran into from time to time, that we were *winning,* and old Canvas-Shoes Hoover was just whistling in the dark, or moaning in the gloom, as he expressed confidence that no one could possibly cast a vote for a man who would take us off the gold standard—whatever the hell that was.

Although by this time my brother and I were firmly anchored in New York, the Red Sox were still our champions. And we perhaps loved them all the more for their sharing our own lot—mired just north of an abbreviated slide into the cellar. Of course, these were still the Smead Jolley days for the Red Sox. But by the time Roosevelt had worked the magic of repairing the economy by putting money in the hands of the hard up, the Red Sox were beginning to break even again and we had bade good-bye to Babe Ruth and all the other Red Sox graduates except Red Ruffing.

Sunday afternoons were usually spent close to the radio, where he would listen to a man named Hoy—no kin to Dummy Hoy, famous outfielder of the previous century—as he soothingly recited everything of good or ill that befell the Red Sox at Fenway Park. We had not discovered softball yet, there being no open space near us. But in our narrow yard we did manage, with two neighbors, to work in a lot of infield play, skipping a ball across the sod to be fielded and returned. And I managed to live again,

in a semifantasy, the days when I was grabbing up sizzling grounders from a gravelly infield with my own Brookline Beacons.

In this era, when night baseball had been played in certain
bush league and sandlot groupings for a season or two (and was
a fairly dismal spectacle, with fly balls often soaring far above
the lights to remain out of sight for a second or two), there was
serious talk of turning our national pastime into a night-time
attraction in the majors. Men who felt they knew the most about
such matters allowed it would be "a different game" and "not
real baseball" and would hardly be worth watching. I have to
admit that the game I attended one night in Long Island City
was hardly worth watching, or even hearing about, and like most
people I knew, I accepted the dictum of my betters that the thing
was just a foolish fancy.

Shows how much I knew. For, of course, when massive lighting
was supplied, the game, while it may have been different to the
players and the writers who had to work nights, seemed a much
more vivid spectacle and a damn sight easier to fit into a working
person's schedule. It must also, to some degree, have eased the
burden of the truant officers.

The Red Sox in this era, with Jimmy Foxx suddenly promoted
from Philadelphia to add explosives to the Boston batting order,
actually became contenders—something they had not been for
some twenty years—and the struggle between the Yankees and
the Red Sox, not for fourth place but for the pennant, again
stirred our souls. (Jimmy Foxx, although he probably never knew
it, put a sudden end to the baseball career of a young man I knew
who had earned a try-out with the Sox. Pitching batting practice
one afternoon in spring training, my friend spun a fat pitch down
to big Jimmy. Jimmy laid into the ball with all the incredible
strength of those blacksmith arms and drove it straight at the
pitcher. My friend took the ball right in the center of his forehead
and fell instantly to the turf. He was revived quickly, examined
at once, and found to have suffered nothing more than the con-
cussion and monstrous swelling just over his eyes. He immediately
left the park, the town, and his big league ambitions behind him
forever.)

There was another knockout in this prewar era that saddened our own circle even more deeply. Joe Louis, the invincible "Brown Bomber," who had been laying victims low with thrilling regularity, was badly whipped by the Nazi hero, Max Schmeling, valiant warrior who flattened a process server who tried to hand him a summons in a hotel lobby. To our way of thinking, Schmeling was no invincible superman. He had already been knocked around more than a little by a lad named Steve Hamas, who had been conned into going to Germany to fight Schmeling, even though one of Steve's arms was injured and nearly useless. And Steve himself, who had followed through on the deal against his own judgment because his manager insisted, mourned his lost championship for many seasons. So did Joe Louis, who had not yet held the championship, but eventually got his revenge—after he learned not to drop his left hand when he crossed his right. And Joe, who was not given to hating his opponents, once did grant that he "never liked that Smelling." (In their second encounter, Louis beat Schmeling until he yelled in pain and dismay.)

While boxing had been the only sport in which I was ever more than a mediocre performer, it was by no means a passion of mine and I did not follow it with the avidity with which I had for many seasons followed baseball. And when softball suddenly came into my life, it was like a rebirth, for I, having moved to a neighborhood that gave me access to a park and playground, soon discovered that this game was baseball all over again—only modified enough to suit part-time performers with a little rust beginning to gather in their joints. Of course, young people played it, too, for it was a true neighborhood game, requiring not nearly so much room as baseball and no expensive equipment. Rivalries were never bitter. As in my boyhood, one day's teammate might be the next day's enemy. There were no titles to pursue, no averages to compile, no standings to keep track of.

By some forgotten quirk of chance—perhaps by default—I found myself pitcher for a team of younger men (boys, some of them) who called themselves the Mustangs, and who sometimes took on rivals from nearby neighborhoods with whom it was fun to exchange good-natured taunts. Occasionally there would be a group of much older men, some of them actually former paid athletes. To see some of those ancients (in their forties and fifties) dashing down the baselines with their scant hair flying could dim a fellow's fears about his own future. Sometimes a girl would take part. There was one young lady in the neighborhood who could throw a softball from the plate to the fence, and I recall most vividly the day a stray ball rolled near her and a lad from some other neighborhood ran toward her, with his cupped hands held out, as if inviting a toss from a baby. But Josie had long ago learned from her brothers to get her elbow behind her shoulder when she threw. And she uncorked a pitch that broke through the guy's hands and struck him on the ribs with a wallop that might have laid him low had he come a little closer. After that, on the occasions when we called on Josie to fill out the nine for us, this lad regarded her with ultimate circumspection.

We always had trouble with umpires in these contests, for we often had to recruit a man from the opposition to stand behind the pitcher and call the strikes. Often the clown's obvious bias would result in his being disowned by both sides, as occurred one day when the ump had stayed overtime at the local pub before taking up his duties. After a succession of doubtful calls, there came a squibbling grounder to the third baseman that instantly was picked up and delivered to the first baseman a full stride ahead of the runner. Whether the umpire was even watching the play—who knows? But he did let out a hearty "Safe!" and spread his arms as if he were about to take flight. Everyone, and I mean *everyone*, including the runner, turned to stare at him. The runner, knowing he was out, had already started to the bench. And the opposing captain, who had accepted a number of sour plate calls with not much more than a smirk, found this one too raw to swallow, so the umpire by unanimous consent was escorted to a seat among the spectators.

Another time, a towering pop-up, just over the pitcher's mound with runners on first and second, an obvious infield fly on which the batter, by baseball rules, was automatically out,

was never called by the umpire. Whereupon the second baseman
let the ball drop and helped himself to an easy double play—the
runners having confidently held their ground. Our captain, a
rugged and voluble young man who was a New York City cop in
his working hours, let out a scream of disbelief and outrage. With
both arms raised as if he were ready to dismember poor Tom,
the umpire, he rushed out and bellowed into Tom's face, "Infield
fly! For Christ's sake! Infield fly! The batter is *out!* You goddamn
dummy! Don't you even know the *rules,* for Christ's sake!"

Tom, backing off from the apparent atack, held out his hands
in appeasement.

"Wait a minute! Wait a minute!" he piped. "If there had just
been a little breeze come up. Just a little breeze!" He swept one
hand to indicate the force of that mighty breeze. "Why, it would
have pushed the ball out into the outfield. Just a little breeze!"

Aghast, as most of us were, at the sheer idiocy of this plea,
Pete the cop dropped his hands and broke into laughter. "Oh,
go on home!" he cried. "And let's get somebody who knows the
rules. Go on home, Tom, and read the rule book."

Tom did not go home—at least not immediately. But he was
never invited again to screw up our play.

These little eccentricities, however, actually added merriment
to our contests, which were never allowed to descend into mortal
combat. Who won or lost the bloody game was not a point to
brood on—or for that matter even remember. A week after the
season ended, I couldn't recall the outcome of more than one or
two of the games. And two months later I had forgotten them
all.

One lovely moment I do remember, though, was a game I
pitched against some group of outlanders—from twenty blocks
away perhaps—in which I set out to stifle a sudden enemy out-
burst by striking out their mightiest batsman with two runners
on base. I managed to put two strikes on the man, by fouls or
called strikes—I'll never know which. For the third strike I set
out with a full motion to whiz my alleged "fastball" past him.
Then, just before releasing the ball, I stopped my forward swing

abruptly and let the ball go. It floated gently up toward the batter like a bubble on a quiet stream. And he hauled off with all his strength, obviously timing his swing to my fastball, and missed the ball completely, nearly falling to his knees as he did so.

He stood up at once and faced the crowd.

"He *fooled* me!" he cried. And broke into laughter.

To me that will always represent the spirit that originally informed the game of baseball in those ancient afternoons. It was not a religious experience. Not a sacred rite. Not a tournament of knights-errant.

It was fun.

INDEX

Alexander, Dale, 251
Alexander, Grover Cleveland, 140
Allison, Doug, 63, 64, 66
Almond, Edward M., 138
Altrock, Nick, 175, 193
American Association (AA), 82, 95
Anson, Cap, 24, 77–79, 86, 87, 88, 119, 134, 136, 159, 174
Attell, Abe, 221, 222, 241

Babe Ruth's All-Stars, 149
Baker, Frank "Home Run," 146, 191
Baldwin, Kid, 83
Baldwin, Lady, 91–92, 168
Baltimore Black Sox, 149
Baltimore Orioles (AA), 123
Baltimore Orioles (AL), 249
Baltimore Orioles (IL), 196–201
Baltimore Orioles (NL), 40, 51, 52, 158
Baltimore Stars, 144
Baltimore Sun, 122–23
Bancroft, Frank, 154
Barnes, Ross, 69
Barrow, Ed, 7, 181
Baseball Guide, 231–32
Baseball Magazine, 76
Beckley, Jake, 50
Bedient, Hugh, 16
Bender, Chief, 173, 176

Bengough, Benny, 236
Bennett, Charlie, 92
Bentley, Jack, 196
Benton, Rube, 223, 224
Berra, Yogi, 202
Billings, James, 73
Birmingham Black Barons, 149
Bishop, Max, 252, 256
Black Sox scandal, 44, 167, 200, 214, 219–24, 232, 241, 243, 244
Bloom, Sol, 228
Bohne, Sam, 224
Boston Americans, 10, 16
Boston Beaneaters, 11, 48, 49–50, 93, 128–29
Boston Braves, 10, 176, 208, 218
Boston Globe, 76
Boston Herald, 25
Boston Puritans, 10, 46
Boston Reds, 67–70, 71–72, 76, 125
Boston Red Sox, 7–9, 10, 15, 17, 37, 150, 152, 171, 174, 189, 190, 214, 218–19, 233, 243–253, 258–61
Boston Traveler, 10
Boyle, Jack, 93
Bradley (umpire), 25
Brainard, Asa, 63, 65, 66
Breitenstein, Ted, 95, 103

Brickley, Charley, 43
Brooklyn Atlantics, 67, 119
Brooklyn Bridegrooms, 93, 115
Brooklyn Dodgers, 109, 151, 173, 175, 176
Brooklyn Royal Giants, 144
Brooklyn Superbas, 53
Brotherhood of Professional Baseball Players, strike by, 23, 75–77, 95, 96, 111, 113, 114, 124, 155
Brown, Jerry, 181
Brown, Mordecai "Three Finger," 175, 185–86
Browning, Pete, 110–16
Bruckner, Earle, 179
Brush, John T., 153, 158
Buckley, Dick, 155
Buffalo Bisons, 128
Buffalo Buffeds, 165
Buffalo Express, 45
Bulger, Bozeman, 200
Burkett, Jesse, 102
Burns, Bill, 22, 221
Bush, Bullet Joe, 9, 173, 247
Bush, Guy, 258
Bushong, Doc, 93
Byrnes, Jack, 100

Cantillon, Joe, 49
Cantwell, Robert, 46
Carter, Kid, 139
Cartwright, Alexander, 56, 83
Caruthers, Bob, 93, 94
catapult ball, 12, 125
Caylor, Oliver Hazard Perry, 76–77, 82
Chadwick, Henry, 46
Chalmers, George, 140
Chamberlain, Ice-Box, 94
Chance, Frank, 161, 164
Chandler, Happy, 147, 151
Chapman, Ray, 54, 214
Chase, Hal, 144–45, 160–68, 221
Chattanooga Lookouts, 149
Chesbro, Happy Jack, 170
"Chicago" (shutout), 64
Chicago American Giants, 139
Chicago Browns, 128
Chicago Colts, 105
Chicago Cubs, 49, 146, 174–76, 186, 218–19, 223, 258
Chicago Eckfords, 82–83

Chicago Excelsiors, 68
Chicago Maroons, 154
Chicago Tribune, 25
Chicago White Sox, 46, 164–65, 174, 175, 176, 220–23, 235, 246
Chicago White Stockings (NL), 23, 24, 45, 75, 76, 85–89, 91, 93, 99, 119, 128, 132, 134, 159, 174
Childs, Cupid, 40
Cicotte, Ed, 220
Cincinnati Buckeyes, 118–19
Cincinnati Enquirer, 25
Cincinnati Reds, 13, 82, 114, 158, 162, 165, 220–23, 224
Cincinnati Red Stockings, 10, 58, 60–68, 122
Cissell, Bill, 252
cities, rivalries between, 40–44
Clarkson, John, 52, 93
classification rule, 75, 76, 77
Clemente, Roberto, 152
Clements, John, 96
Cleveland Blues, 123, 128, 130, 131–32
Cleveland Indians, 150, 232
Cleveland Infants, 111, 114
Cleveland Naps, 246
Cleveland Spiders, 40, 51–52, 102–104, 154, 155
Cobb, Ty, 44, 53, 145–46, 155, 170, 173, 190, 192, 193, 221, 232–35, 246
Coghlan, Gene, 206
Collins, Eddie, 42
Collins, Jimmy, 16
Collyer, Bert, 224
Collyer's Eye, 224
Columbus Buckeyes, 205
Comiskey, Charles, 76, 77, 84–86, 88, 93–96, 194, 220
Conant, William, 73
Conlan, Jocko, 50–51
Connolly (umpire), 25
Cooley, Duff, 49–50
Coombs, Jack, 173, 174
Cooney, Johnny, 197
Costello, Frank, 237
Coveleski, Harry, 41
Craft, Harry, 202, 203
Criger, Lou, 16

Croker, Boss, 156
Cronin, Joe, 252–53
Crosetti, Frank, 177–83, 250
Crosetti, John, 177
Cross, Lave, 104, 132
Cuban Giants, 135–36, 139
Cuthbert, Eddie, 57, 84

Dahlen, Bill, 105
Dahlgren, Babe, 252
Daily, Hugh, 126–29
Daniel, Dan, 231
Davis, George, 107, 176
Day, Joe, 205–6
Dean, Dizzy, 148, 253, 255
Dean, Paul, 255
Deasley, Tom, 129
Delahanty, Big Ed, 105–9
Delmore, Victor, 208
Dempsey, Jack, 245–46
Detroit (NL), 91–92, 131, 136
Detroit Tigers, 53, 170, 232, 233, 235–36, 246
Detroit Wolverines, 48
Devery, Bill, 164
Devlin, Art, 53
Devlin, Jim, 94
Diddlebock, Joe, 96
DiMaggio, Joe, 184–85, 237–38, 239
Dinneen, Bill, 16
Doby, Larry, 150
Dolan, Cozy, 225–27, 229–30
Donovan, Patsy, 174
Donovan, Wild Bill, 169, 196, 199, 200, 201–2
Douglas, Shufflin' Phil, 207
Down, Tommy, 96
Dreyfuss, Barney, 16, 47, 218, 228, 229
Dubuque Rabbits, 84
Dugan, Joe, 191, 200, 201, 247
Duncan, Frank, 146
Duncan, Pat, 224
Dunlap, "Sure-Shot" Fred, 73, 94–95, 129–32
Dunn, Jack, 197

Eayrs, Eddie, 197
Ebbets, Charles, 53, 173
Eggler, Dave, 63, 64–65, 66, 67
Ehmke, Howard, 248, 257–58

Eibel, Hank, 141
Elberfeld, Kid, 163, 164
Ellick (umpire), 48
Ely, Bones, 50
Emslie, Bob, 25, 47, 169
Essick, Bill, 181, 209
Evers, Johnny, 161

Fallon, William, 229–30
Falsey, Pete, 192
Farnham, Rube, 197, 198
Farrell, Frank, 164
Federal League, 165, 214–15, 216
Ferrell, Rick, 250–51
Ferrell, Wes, 250–51, 252–53
Firpo, Luis, 245–46
Fisk, Jim, 60–61
Fitzsimmons, Bob, 101–2
"fixes," 8, 24, 224–30, 232–36, 247
    see also Black Sox scandal; gambling
Fletcher, Arthur, 225
Flint, Silver "The Only," 84, 120
Fogel, Horace, 159
Forbes, Frank, 140
Foster, Rube, 139, 143
Fothergill, Bob, 251
Foutz, Dave, 93, 94
Fowler, Bud, 79, 135
Foxx, Jimmy, 260
Frank, Stanley, 231
Frazee, Harry, 214, 247
Freedman, Andrew, 156–60
Frick, Ford, 151
Frisch, Frank, 225, 227
Fruin, Jerry, 83
Fullerton, Hugh, 200, 220
fungo, 125

Galvin, Pud, 128
gambling, 16, 24, 27, 44–47, 60, 88, 163–64, 165–67, 201
    see also Black Sox scandal; "fixes"
Gandil, Chick, 222
Garceau, Mitchie, 206–7
Gardella, Gus, 197
Gardner, Larry, 9
Gehrig, Lou, 42, 144–45, 247
Gibbons, Tommy, 245
Gibson, Josh, 145, 150
Gilooly, Denny, 192

Glasscock, Pebbly Jack, 94, 131, 132, 153, 154
Gleason, Bill "Kid," 93, 220
Gough, John G., 70
Gould, Charlie, 63
Grand Avenue Never Sweats, 153
Grant, Frank, 79, 135
Grant, Ulysses S., 60, 61
Green, Pumpsie, 152
Greenlee, Gus, 150
Griffith, Clark, 162, 164, 235, 252
Groh, Heinie, 13
Grove, Lefty, 176, 196, 251, 252, 256

Hall, Bloney, 141
Hamas, Steve, 261
Hanley, Jim, 193
Hanlon, Ned, 51
Hargrave, Pinky, 197–98, 200
Harrington, Jerry, 114
Hartford Dark Blues, 45, 70, 117
Harvey, Charles, 143
Harvey, Lefty, 144
Heilmann, Harry, 235, 246
Hendrickson, Don, 208–9
Hendrix, Claude, 221
Herman, Babe, 149
Herr, Ed, 94
Herrmann, Garry, 166, 215, 223
Herzog, Buck, 165, 223
Heydler, John, 21, 166–67, 218, 220, 223, 224, 225
Higgins, Jack, 35
Higham, Richard, 24
high school baseball, 42–43
Hill, Johnny, 139
Hill, Pete, 146
Hill, Still Bill, 103
Hillerich and Bradsby, 113
Homestead Grays, 144–45
Hooper, Harry, 7, 190, 219
"Hop Bitters" club, 119
Hornsby, Rogers, 152
House of David, 193, 208–9
Howard, Arlene, 151
Howard, Elston, 150–51, 152
Hoyt, Ellen, 255
Hoyt, Waite, 9, 37–39, 54, 186–90, 235, 247, 254, 255
Hudson, Nat, 93

Humphrey Athletic Club, 43
Hunt, Dick, 66
Hurst, Tim, 49
Huston, Colonel, 214–15
Hyman, Sammy, 195

Indianapolis Admirals, 124
Indianapolis Hoosiers, 119, 122, 154–55

Jackson, Joe, 223
Jennings, Hughey, 170
Johnson, Ban, 106, 214–15, 219, 220–23, 228, 230, 234, 235, 247–48
Johnson, Charles "Home Run," 146
Johnson, Walter, 138, 155, 171, 172, 190, 247
Johnstone (umpire), 24
Jolley, Smead, 251, 259
Jones, Charlie, 74–75
Jones, Frank, 68
Jones, Sam, 247
Jones, Tom, 162
Joss, Addie, 246
Judge, Joe, 140, 141
Judge Landis and Twenty-Five Years in Baseball (Spink), 214

Kauff, Benny, 221, 224
Keating, Ray, 193
Keefe, Tim, 90, 156
Kelly, Charles, 79, 135
Kelly, George, 50, 225
Kelly, Mike, 23, 76, 84, 86, 87, 88, 93, 104–5, 115, 117–19, 125, 130
Kerin, Jack, 46, 52
Kerins, Jack, 121, 122
Keystones, 117–18
Kieran, John, 200
Killelea, Hank, 16
King, Silver, 90, 93
Kleinow, Red, 171
Klem, Bill, 48
Kling, Johnny, 146
Knickerbockers, 58
Koenecke, Len, 109–10
Krieg, John, 128–29

Labelle, Magloire, 26–27
LaHiff, Billy, 236

Lait, Jack, 216–17
Lajoie, Nap, 162
Landis, Kenesaw Mountain, 45, 48, 75, 147, 167, 168, 200, 213–235, 257
Lange, Bill, 49, 50, 105–6
Langford, Ad, 140
Lansingburgh Haymakers, 60
Latham, Walter Arlington, 86–88, 96, 160
Lee, Dudley, 248
Leland Giants, 139, 143
Leonard, Andy, 65–66
Leonard, Buck, 144
Leonard, Dutch, 233, 234, 235
Lewis, Duffy, 250
Lieb, Fred, 200
Lincoln Giants, 140–42, 143, 145
Lincoln Giants–Philadelphia Phillies doubleheader (1915), 140–41
Lipman, David, 149
"Little World Series," 196–201
Lloyd, John Henry, 145–46
Loftus, Tom, 107, 109, 114
Lord Baltimores, 70, 127
Louis, Joe, 261
Louisville Colonels (AA), 94, 110, 111, 122
Louisville Colonels (NL), 103, 114
Louisville Grays, 45, 99
Luby, Hugh, 208
Lucas, Henry, 94, 128
Luderus, Fred, 140
Lynn Live Oaks, 58
Lyons, Leonard, 237

McAleer, Jimmy, 51
MacArthur, Douglas, 138
McBride, Dick, 99
McCarthy, Tommy, 94
McCormick, Jim, 88, 118
McDonald, Charles, 222
MacFayden, Danny, 248
McGeehan, Bill, 227
McGraw, John, 16, 24, 25, 28, 38, 47, 106, 107, 109, 146–47, 159, 160, 165, 166, 167, 186, 188, 189, 203, 225, 230
McGreevey, Nuf Ced, 16, 80, 152
McGuire, Deacon, 168–69
McInnis, Stuffy, 7, 8, 10, 247

Mack, Connie, 42, 44, 50, 77, 148, 172, 173, 218, 235, 251, 252, 257
McKean, Big Ed, 51
McKechnie, Bill, 229
McMahon, Ed, 143
McMahon, Jack, 64, 65
McMahon, Jesse, 143
McVey, Cal, 68–69, 70, 119
Magee, Lee, 221
Magerkurth, George, 46–47
Maharg, Bill, 221
Maisel, Fritz, 197
Malone, Lew, 199
Mann, Les, 219
Mantle, Mickey, 11, 12, 19, 39, 202–5, 235
Maris, Roger, 152
Martin, Gene, 198–99
Martin, Pepper, 255–57
Massachusetts game, 56
Mathewson, Christy, 45, 140, 165, 171, 172, 247
Mays, Carl, 53–54, 214, 217
Mays, Willie, 152, 205
Mercer, Sid, 166, 200
Mexican League, 209
Meyers, Chief, 194
Milligan, Jocko, 94
Mills, Charlie, 63, 66
Mills, Ed, 66
Mirror of American Sports, 85
Missouri Republican, 90
Mobile Bears, 149
Moore, Terry, 183
Morley, James, 160–61
Morrissey, John, 60
Morse, Jacob, 76
"muffin," 28
Muldoon, Mike, 131
Murnane, Tim, 76
Murphy, Charles, 176
Mutrie, Jim, 51, 127, 128, 156, 159
Myers, George, 154

Nashville Volunteers, 208
National Association of Professional Base-ball Players, 70, 72
National Game, The (Spink), 171
Negro Leagues, 46, 135–36, 138, 139, 149

Neu, Marty, 187
Newark Peppers, 175, 176
New Haven Colonials, 43–44, 190–194
New Haven Professors, 194–201
New York City Department of Sanitation team, 210–11
New York City Police Department team, 210–11
New York Game, 27, 47, 56–60, 71, 116–17, 212
New York Giants, 7, 13, 38, 43, 47, 50, 51, 53, 54, 79, 102, 106, 143, 155–60, 165–67, 171, 173, 186, 193, 194, 203, 221, 223, 224, 225, 228–30
New York Highlanders, 160, 163–164, 170–71
New York Ironsides, 143
New York Metropolitans, 89–91, 127, 129, 171
New York Mets, 193
New York Mutuals, 58, 60–67, 69–70
New York Post, 257
New York World, 90, 227
New York Yankees, 150–51, 152, 161, 177, 181–83, 186, 190–192, 200, 202, 204–5, 209, 214–15, 235–36, 237, 247, 248, 250, 258, 260
Niehoff, Bert, 140–41
Nolan, Ed "The Only," 84, 118, 119–20

Obenshain, Earl, 220
O'Brien, Dick, 72
O'Connell, Jimmy, 225, 228
O'Connell, Pat, 123
O'Day, Hank, 169
Ogden, Jack, 196
One-Hole Cat, 10, 12
Ormsby (umpire), 48
O'Rourke, Jim, 69, 72–73, 74, 128
O'Rourke (umpire), 25
Ostermueller, Fritz, 251–52

Page Fence Giants, 136
Paige, Satchel, 145, 147–51
Parker, Dan, 134–35
Parnell, Charles, 61

Pasquel, Jorge, 209
Payne, Jap, 146
Pearce, Dickey, 63, 65, 84
Peiper, Lou, 187
Peitz, Heinie, 95, 103
Pennock, Herb, 247, 252
Perritt, Will "Poll," 166
Perry, Scott, 218
Pete, Uncle, 17–20
Pettit, W. B., 119, 120
Petway, Buddy, 146
Philadelphia Acmes, 130
Philadelphia Athletics (AL), 42, 44, 146, 170, 171, 173, 218, 235, 251, 256
Philadelphia Athletics (AA), 98
Philadelphia game, 56
Philadelphia Giants, 139
Philadelphia Keystones, 57
Philadelphia Phillies, 48, 93, 105, 140–41, 221, 225, 228
Philadelphia Record, 232
Phillips, Big Bill, 131
Picus, John, 248
Pike, Lip, 80, 84
Pitching in a Pinch (Mathewson), 171, 247
Piton, Phil, 231
Pittsburgh Alleghenies, 120, 122
Pittsburgh Crawfords, 150
Pittsburgh Pirates, 16, 47, 114, 218, 228, 234
Plank, Eddie, 173
Players' League, 76, 111, 113
Powell, Jack, 104
Power, Vic, 151
Powers, Jack, 51–52
Powers, Phil, 48
Pratt, Del, 247
Providence Grays, 74, 116

Quaker Giants, 139
Quigley, Earnest, 25
Quinn, Bob, 248
Quinn, Joe, 96
Quirk, Smiley, 29–31

race, baseball and, 78–80, 133–52, 253
Radbourn, Charles "Old Hoss," 116
Ramsey, Thomas "Toad," 121–25

Raridan, Bill, 166
Redding, Cannonball Dick, 143–44, 192
Regan, Mike, 166
reserve rule, 75, 77, 106–7, 216
Reulbach, Ed, 174–76
Rhines, Billy, 114
Rickey, Branch, 147, 256
Ring, Jimmy, 166
rivalries, inter-city, 40–44
Robertson, Charles, 246–47
Robinson, Jackie, 133, 134, 135, 145, 147, 151, 152, 253
Robinson, Wilbert, 52, 174
Rockford Forest Citys, 68, 69
Rose, Pete, 235
Rothstein, Arnold, 221
rounders, 11
"Royal Rooters," 15, 80
Rucker, Nap, 173–74
Ruel, Muddy, 247
Ruffing, Charles "Red," 248, 258, 259
Rusie, Amos, 102, 153–60
Ruth, Babe, 7–9, 68, 148, 190, 200, 201, 236, 243, 245, 247, 253–255, 259
Ryan, Nolan, 155

St. Louis Browns (AA), 44, 81–97, 98, 122, 124, 131
St. Louis Browns (AL), 145, 190
St. Louis Browns (NL), 24, 104
St. Louis Cardinals, 115, 151, 162, 218, 255
St. Louis–Chicago "Championship of the World," 85
St. Louis Maroons (NL), 45
St. Louis Maroons (UA), 94–95, 131
San Antonio Black Broncos, 142
Sand, Heinie, 225
San Francisco Seals, 177, 179–81
Schaefer, Germany, 193
Schalk, Ray, 220
Schang, Wally, 7
Schmeling, Max, 261
Schulte, Frank, 176
Schulz, Hal, 163
Scott, Everett, 7, 247
Scott, Frank, 204–5

scrub, 10, 11–12, 13
Shay, Marty, 197
Shor, Toots, 236–42
Sinatra, Frank, 238–39
Sisler, George, 217–18
Skowron, Bill, 204
Smart, Joe, 16
Smith, George, 159
Smith, Red, 219, 232
Snodgrass, Fred, 16–17
Sockalexis, Louis, 102–4, 116, 175
Soden, Arthur, 73–75, 76
softball, 211–12, 261–64
Spalding, A. G., 23, 52–53, 56, 68, 75, 76, 85–86, 87, 88, 93, 99, 125–26, 158, 159, 174
Sparrow, Harry, 191
Speaker, Tris, 44, 232–35
Spink, Al, 44, 81, 84–85, 89–90, 97, 171
Spink, J. G. Taylor, 214, 216, 219, 220, 228, 229–32, 233, 234
Spirit of the Times, 45
Sporting News, 44, 81, 215, 220, 223, 224, 231
Stage (umpire), 25
Stahl, Jake "The Giant Killer," 16
Stallings, George, 10, 176
Start, Joe, 117, 125
Stengel, Casey, 38
Stewart, A. T., 62
Stewart, Bob, 46
St. Louis–Detroit "World Series," 91–92
Stoneham, Horace, 225
Stovey, George, 79, 135
Strang, Sammy, 24, 80
Streaker, John "Cub," 51
"strike" of 1918, 218–19
Sullivan, Ted, 84, 194
Sweazy, Charles, 62, 66
Sweeney, Charles, 94, 95
"syndicate" issue, 157–58
Syracuse Stars, 84

Tebeau, Patsy, 51, 52, 102, 103–4
Temple Cup, 40, 158
Tener, John K., 77, 218
ten man teams, 70
Tenney, Fred, 11
Terry, Adonis Bill, 105–6

Thomas, Augustus, 90
Thomas, Julius, 141
Thompson, Frank, 135–36
Toledo Blue Stockings, 133, 169
town ball, 56, 116–17
"trading hits," 8, 247
Travers, Aloysius, 170
Troy, John J. "Dasher," 155
Truman, Margaret, 68
Trusty, Shep, 136
Tweed, Boss, 58, 60, 61
Twilight League, 41–42, 248

umpires, 15, 16, 19–20, 22–23, 24–
    27, 28, 46–47, 48–49, 50–53,
    54–55, 59, 78, 115, 183, 207–
    208, 262–63
Unions of Morrisania, 62

Veeck, Bill, 145, 150
Virtue, Jake, 51
von der Ahe, Chris, 81–97, 121

Waddell, Rube, 72, 171–72, 173
Wagner, Honus, 16, 145–46, 173
Walberg, Rube, 251, 252
Walker, Charlie, 65
Walker, Moses Fleetwood, 79, 116,
    133, 135
Walker, Welday Wilberforce, 79,
    116, 133
Ward, John Montgomery "Monte,"
    75, 77, 79, 102
Washington Nationals, 68, 127
Washington Senators (AL), 106,
    107, 140, 171, 172, 228–30,
    235
Washington Senators (NL), 52, 169
Waterman, Fred, 63, 64, 65
Way, Pie, 191, 192
Weaver, Buck, 222, 224
Weiss, George, 43, 54–55, 173,
    190–202, 249
Welch, Curt, 87, 93, 94, 95, 129
Welch, Mickey, 90
Werber, Billy, 249–50
West, Fred, 233

Whens, 121–22
White, Bill, 94
White, Sol, 136, 139
Wickware, "The Red Ant," 138
"wides," 71
Wiley, Doc, 141–42
Willard, Jess, 245
Williams, Clarence, 139
Williams, Cyclone Joe, 140–44,
    145, 146
Williams, Joe, 134, 135
Williams, String Bean, 144
Williams, Ted, 152
Wilmington Quicksteps, 120
Wilson, Earl, 237
Wilson, Hack, 149
Wilson, Woodrow, 138
Wiltse, George, 143
Winchell, Walter, 237
Wolters, Rinie, 65, 66
Wolverton, Harry, 164
Wood, Joe, 233, 235
Woodward, Frank, 198, 199
World Series:
    of 1903, 16
    of 1906, 175, 176
    of 1911, 146
    of 1912, 7, 16
    of 1916, 174
    of 1918, 218–19
    of 1919, 220
    of 1924, 172, 183, 227, 228–30
    of 1925, 172
    of 1929, 257–58
    of 1931, 256
    of 1932, 258
    of 1933, 48
Wright, George, 62, 64, 70, 74
Wright, Harry, 62, 66, 68, 71–72

"Yale Ineligibles," 43
Yawkey, Tom, 250, 251
Young, Cy, 171, 172, 176, 246
Young, Nick, 48, 115, 158
Youngs, Ross, 225, 227

Zimmerman, Heinie, 221